IN THE
SERVICE OF GOD

IN THE
SERVICE OF GOD

Conversations with Teachers of
Torah in Jerusalem

Shalom Freedman

JASON ARONSON INC.
Northvale, New Jersey
London

This book was set in 12 pt. Berkeley Oldstyle by AeroType, Inc., Amherst, NH.

Library of Congress Cataloging-in-Publication Data

Freedman, Shalom.
    In the service of God : conversations with teachers of Torah in Jerusalem / Shalom Freedman.
      p. cm.
    ISBN 1-56821-455-3
    1. Rabbis—Jerusalem—Interviews. 2. Jewish scholars—Jerusalem—
Interviews. 3. Old Testament scholars—Jerusalem—Interviews.
4. Judaism—Study and teaching—Jerusalem. 5. Judaism—20th century.
6. God (Judaism)—Worship and love. I. title.
BM750.F63 1995
296'.092'2569442—dc20   95-21767

Manufactured in the United States of America. Jason Aronson Inc. offers books and cassettes. For information and catalog write to Jason Aronson Inc., 230 Livingston Street, Northvale, New Jersey 07647.

This book is dedicated as a prayer to God
for the uplifting of the soul
of my beloved brother Jakie

JACOB FREEDMAN — YAAKOV YISRAEL BEN REUVEN

May all who knew and loved him
Remember
his great warmth and humor
his many deeds of kindness and help
the courage and blessing of his good years
his hard work and business ability,
his great love of and care for his family,
the unique music of his soul when he sang with joy

Contents

Acknowledgments

To each and every rabbi and teacher of Torah who consented to meet with me, and whose words and thought are the heart of this work, I express my deepest gratitude.

The late Dr. Rivka Ashbel of Hebrew University, a member of the pioneering generation that helped build the modern State of Israel, first made me aware of how interviewing could be a means for both revealing a chapter of history and illuminating human character.

The Israeli writer Haim Chertok's excellent study of contemporary Israeli writing (*We Are All Close*) also served for me as a guide in the use of the interview technique.

In selecting the rabbis for the interviews, I was greatly helped by Jerusalem editor-translator-writer Chaim Mayerson and by Dr. Yaakov Fogelman.

Various stylistic points were clarified by queries to Professor Lawrence Besserman of the English Department of the Hebrew University.

My deep gratitude goes out again to Arthur Kurzweil and the staff of Jason Aronson Inc. Janet Warner has for a second time ably edited a work of mine. She has my great thanks.

Introduction

This work is a series of interviews with twenty distinguished teachers of Judaism. Each interview is an effort to reveal the individual's way of seeing and understanding his own work in service of God. In the course of this there is an attempt made to clarify the meaning of the concept *Avodat Hashem* (the service of God) and its meaning for the modern Jew today. The interviews, in seeking to understand the work of the individual, also throw light on the general situation of the Jewish people today.

Among those interviewed are: Rabbi Dov Berkovits, rabbi of Shilo and codirector of Yakar Institute; Rabbi Chaim Brovender, pioneer in English-language Torah teaching in Israel and codirector of the Ohr-Ha-Torah Institutions in Israel; Professor Emil L. Fackenheim, Fellow of the Institute of Contemporary Jewry at Hebrew University and one of the most important Jewish thinkers of the postwar period; Rabbi Gedaliah Fleer, teacher of Bratslav Chasidism and well-known figure in Torah outreach work; Dr. Yaakov Fogelman of the TOPP Outreach Center in Jerusalem, whose weekly *Parsha* sheets are well known throughout the English-speaking Torah world; Rabbi David Golinkin, dean of the Seminary of Judaic Studies in Neve Schecter and expert on responsa literature; Rabbi Irving Greenberg, founder and director of CLAL, National Jewish Center for Leadership and Learning, and one of the most original Jewish thinkers working today; David Herzberg, Jerusalem Torah teacher whose concentration in "learning" is Chasidism; Rabbi Mendel Lewittes (of blessed memory), world-renowned scholar in Jewish law; Rabbi Ze'ev Chaim

Lifshitz, founder and director of the ENOSH Institute and pioneering thinker in Jewish Psychology; Rabbi Nathan Lopes Cardozo, popular Torah teacher at Ohr Someyach and Jerusalem College of Adults, author, and thinker; Rabbi Abraham Ezra Millgram, Jewish educator whose anthologies on the Sabbath and the *siddur* have been among the most popular produced in the English language; Rabbi Chaim Pearl, distinguished Rabbi in England, the United States, and Israel and well-known author and scholar; Rabbi Nachum L. Rabinovitch, head of Birkhat Moshe Hesder Yeshiva in Maale Adumim, distinguished scientist, and Maimonidean scholar; Rabbi Aharon Rakeffet, widely respected Torah teacher and one of the foremost pupils and transmitters of the teaching of the Rav, Rabbi J. D. Soloveitchik z"l; Rabbi Shlomo Riskin, chief rabbi of Efrat, codirector of Ohr-Ha-Torah Institutions, and one of the most dynamic communal builders in the Jewish world today; Rabbi Meir Schweiger, teacher of Torah at Pardes Institute in Jerusalem; Rabbi Shubert Spero, Irving Stone Professor of Jewish Thought at Bar-Ilan University and one of the most profound Jewish thinkers working today; Rabbi Emanuel Quint, teacher of Torah, lawyer, and author of a highly respected series of commentaries on Jewish Civil Law (*Hoshen Mishpat*); and Rabbi Daniel Tropper, founder and director of the Gesher Foundation, which is devoted to bridging the gap between the secular and religious in Israel.

   The generating impulse for the present work came from two events, one private, the other public. In the course of seeking endorsements for a book of mine upon which I had worked for many years, and which contained my own personal answer to the question of "making meaning of one's own life," I came to meet and speak at length with a number of remarkable teachers of Jewish thought. In speaking to them, I understood that a further probing of their thought would deepen my own understanding of the basic questions of life. I also had the strong feeling that making the work of these teachers of Judaism more known would be a true act of service to the Jewish people. The idea thus came of interviewing a number of teachers of Judaism on their own lives and thought.

In one such interview with Rabbi Irving Greenberg, the public event was mentioned that gave added impulse to do the work. Rabbi Greenberg had been speaking about the 1990 Council of Jewish Federations (CJF) study, which had indicated that rates of assimilation in the U.S. Jewish Community were worse than even the most pessimistic experts had expected. As I sensed his great concern to find ways of helping the Jewish people, it came to mind that another aspect of the interviews should involve asking the teachers of Judaism more directly about the broader problems of the Jewish world as a whole. This meant asking many questions about the situation of Israel, the heart of the Jewish people.

In my previous work I had centered on the concept of "Creation" as the keynote in understanding the Jewish way of giving meaning to life. Yet even then, I was troubled by the sense that this concept would not speak to a great share of Jews who are involved in their daily lives with work not ordinarily considered "creative." Influenced by my daily study of Yitzhak Buxbaum's classic work *Jewish Spiritual Practices,* I had the sense that the concept *Avodat Hashem* (Service of God) might be more meaningful to many seeking to understand how to come closer to God. Moreover, as I was, in speaking with rabbis, speaking with those whose lives are specifically dedicated to the service of God, I believed it would be both necessary and worthwhile to explore their own theoretical grasp of the concept, *Avodat Hashem.* Thus, the whole question of the meaning of service of God is the central theoretical question of this work. In the course of the interviews, most of the teachers of Judaism were asked to speak not only of the main events of their own lives and work, but also about how they understood these events in relation to the concept, *Avodat Hashem.*

All the interviews were conducted in Jerusalem and the greater surrounding area. In choosing the rabbis who were to be interviewed, I in most cases simply turned to those from whom I had, in some way, "learned" in the past. The principle was simply based on my own personal intuition that these were teachers who had given, and could continue to give, much in "learning." In the course of nearly two and one half years, I came to investigate a good share of the English-language "learning scene" in Jerusalem. I discovered a wealth of people and institutions, and got the sense that there is a tremendous variety and depth of Jewish intellectual and spiritual work in Jerusalem happening now.

My regret is that I could not come close to encompassing this in one work. If I myself am impressed by the remarkable group of teachers who appear in this work, I am also humbled at the thought of how many great teachers of Torah, both known and not known to the general public, have not been included here.

I have other reasons for well-justified humility in regard to the result of this work. I am not a rabbi myself and am small in learning in comparison to each and every person I spoke with here. I simply am not, in many ways, on the level of these people, and I believe a more well-learned person could have conducted the interviews on a higher level. Moreover, if each interview does make some attempt at getting an overview of the rabbi's life and some key points in his worldview, it is obviously a small drop in the sea of what each one knows and has to teach. My prayer is that each of those who have been interviewed will not feel their own story misrepresented.

Again, I am a person who throughout his life has asked the question, "How does one live the meaningful life? – the good life?" In looking to these teachers of Torah, I have looked to those whose stories can hopefully be in some way exemplary for others. I tried to provide a certain insight into the lives of those who, in living in service of what is beyond them and in working to serve the Jewish people, have truly served God. My prayer is that their words here will be the same kind of help and inspiration for the reader as the meeting with them has been for me.

An Additional Word on the Method of the Work

The reader is being presented with a transcript of an interview and not my "interpretation" of that interview. In most cases the teachers themselves edited the manuscript, and in some, they rewrote it considerably. I myself tried to tamper as little as possible with the words of these teachers for fear of misrepresenting their views. As interviewer, my aim was to enable them to present their views as they best could. The reader troubled by the absence of a truly critical tone in most of my questions must understand that I approached each person interviewed as a student approaches a wise teacher and not as an inquiring journalist approaches a public figure he is aiming to test.

The interviews are presented chronologically in the order in which they took place, from February 1992 through August 1994. This is because thoughts and ideas expressed in earlier works often play a role in questions asked in later ones. And though each interview is conducted as a story of its own, there is the hope that, interview by interview, a cumulative meaning emerges that better illuminates the concept "Service of God."

There is no attempt on my part to represent all strains of thought in the Jewish world. Again, the selection is personal, based on people from whom I had, at some stage or other of my life, learned. I alone am responsible for bringing together these teachers in this format, and I pray I have not insulted or harmed anyone in doing this.

Each interview is prefaced by a brief description of the meeting itself and a few words about the teacher of Torah whom I interviewed. My words are inadequate to describe the joy and sense of sanctity I felt during these meetings. My prayer is that the reader will share this joy and sanctity in the course of reading this work and come through it in some way, however small, to greater service of God.

Rabbi Irving Greenberg

Rabbi Irving Greenberg has been a major figure on the world Jewish scene for the past three decades. A rare combination of communal leader and original thinker, Rabbi Greenberg is president of the National Jewish Center for Learning and Leadership. Rabbi Greenberg was one of the major figures involved in the establishment of the National Holocaust Center in Washington, D.C. Raised in an Orthodox family, his father a *talmid chacham,* he was educated in the Musar tradition and in secular studies at Harvard University. The integration of tradition and modernity is the subject of his major work to date, *The Jewish Way* (Summit Books). Rabbi Greenberg, whose Ph.D. is in American history, is a religious thinker for whom historical events are of decisive significance. Thus the two major events of modern Jewish history, the Holocaust and *lehavdil,* the founding of the State of Israel, are crucial in his rethinking of the Tradition. Rabbi Greenberg and his wife, Blu, are respected and admired by many in the Jewish world, not only for their intellectual contributions but also for their personal kindness and generosity. And in fact, it was such an act of kindness, Rabbi Greenberg's taking the time to read and endorse a manuscript of mine, that led to the conversation that moved me to do this work.

This present interview, while only a small sample of his thought, nonetheless reveals the primary stress he places on the concept of *tikkun olam* and on the use of human freedom in covenant with God for achieving the Jewish goal of creating a world of human dignity.

1

S. F.:   Could you briefly tell me the story of how you came to found the organization you now head: one that is well known through the Jewish world – CLAL – The National Jewish Center for Learning and Leadership? Did this work begin immediately after you finished your formal education?

Rabbi Greenberg: CLAL's roots are embedded deep in my life – at least as far back as the post-high school years. By luck, I stumbled into a refugee European *Musar yeshivah*, Bais Yosef Navardik, and went there for advanced talmudic study and, eventually, *smichah*. The *yeshivah* influenced me in many ways personally, including its emphasis on character building and its powerful missionary thrust to spread Torah to others. Yet originally, I planned to go into academia, and not the rabbinate. I essentially became a "professional Jew" in an unplanned way. While in graduate school I was approached by the Young Israel of Brookline to serve as their rabbi part-time. I threw myself into work – a sign of strong Jewish loyalty seeking an outlet. I finished the Ph.D. and went to teach history (general history, not Jewish) at Yeshiva University.

I then went to Israel on a Fulbright appointment to Tel Aviv University in 1962. Unplanned, I began to read and study about the Holocaust. Finally, I was religiously and emotionally overwhelmed by this encounter with the Holocaust and its aftermath. I determined to teach more in Jewish areas – preferably on this topic. After some pressure, Yeshiva University finally allowed me to teach a Holocaust course.

At Yeshiva, I was not really allowed to teach and find fulfillment primarily in Jewish studies. They were too proud of my Harvard Ph.D. in American history to give up the specialty easily. As a result of my frustration, I became open to alternatives. Riverdale Jewish Center approached me to fill in as their rabbi briefly; then they asked me to stay on and be their rabbi. I had seven wonderful years at the synagogue, but I became restless. I felt something had to be done to help Jewry cope with modernity and the growing loss of Jewish identity.

The more I reflected on the Holocaust, the more it led me to believe that healing Jewry from assimilation, or spreading Judaism, was not something that could be done just by the Orthodox. After the Holocaust, I think the idea that only the Orthodox were, or are, exclusively right becomes grotesque. Jewish unity and Jewish learning had to go hand in hand.

Finally, I decided that I was going to leave the synagogue, take a sabbatical for a year, and go to Israel. I wanted to write a book on the implications of the Holocaust and the rebirth of Israel. Just before finishing at the synagogue, I was approached by City College of New York (CCNY) to set up and chair a new department of Jewish Studies. A year earlier, I was asked to teach a course on the Holocaust at CCNY. During that year, they were trying to find a full-time chairman to set up a department. The school was close to taking a standard academic type for the job, but the students, who were deeply involved in the process, pushed for me to get the job. This was in the days of the student protests, and the student pressure had a disproportionate effect. The next thing I knew, they offered me the job. For the next two years, I taught and ran the department.

Years before, as one who had been deeply affected by the encounter with the Holocaust, I had read Elie Wiesel's work and felt that he had not received the hearing and recognition he deserved. For years, I had promised myself that if I ever ran a college department, I would approach Elie Wiesel to teach there. I was convinced that he would make a superb, unforgettable teacher.

City College wanted to retain and attract Jewish students at a time when open admissions was leading to a "Jewish flight" from CCNY. This was behind the push for Jewish Studies. They gave me some lines to appoint people – including the possibility of a Distinguished Professorship. This was in the early 1970s, when the old academic rules had loosened. Hiring writers, musicians, and artists was becoming acceptable. They agreed that we recruit Elie Wiesel to teach. Over the course of the year, the two of us sat around and talked. He had the same idea that I had been floating for years – to set up a study center to reach out to laypeople in order to help bring about greater understanding of the religious and ethical consequences of the Holocaust.

At that period, I was still "naive" in my faith and looked for–and often received–religious signals as to what to do with my life. (Now I am more skeptical of such signs as I have come to think of God as being more sophisticated in technique than I had given God credit for at the time!) Just then, Meinhardt Spielman, an alumnus of City College, died in the Philippines (I never found out what he was doing there), and he left a large amount of money to City College on the condition that it be used exclusively for Jewish students. That kind of testamentary provision is against New York State law: it is considered discriminatory. But City College was desperate over Jewish flight, and the president, Bob Marshak, who wanted to save the college's quality, thought that he could get the money for a Jewish Studies program. Since Jewish Studies was open to all students (and non-Jews, whites, and blacks took its courses), such use would be nondiscriminatory. On the other hand, the family would be satisfied that the essence of the intent was being met, since the bulk of the students were Jewish. I concluded that Divine Providence had signaled. Here was the money that could be used to start this center that I had been looking to establish all along.

We split the money in half: half was to be used to set up a Research Institute on Contemporary Jewry at City College, and the other half would be used to hire Steven Shaw, who was going to organize the lay outreach program. This would strengthen Judaism and put City College back on the Jewish map–which would attract Jewish students. Elie Wiesel would be the spiritual leader and I would be part of the brain trust. That's how CLAL got started.

As it turned out, there was a problem with Church and State. As the visibility of the program increased, some faculty and administrators began to complain that we were teaching religion with taxpayers' money. One day, the president of the university took me to lunch and suggested that I concentrate on the Research Institute. He promised to raise funds for it, while explaining that if we continued to stress the other program, namely, teaching Judaism to Jews, it could not continue to be part of City College.

We decided to move the program into an independent organization, the National Jewish Conference Center (NJCC). Elie Wiesel contributed his name but made it a condition that he not have to deal with the nitty-gritty. Steven Shaw was a great programmer and idea man, but he was weak in administration and fund-raising—as I was. The organization struggled to survive. Finally, I realized that I would have to work at it full time (and more) for NJCC to succeed as an organization (in later years the name became CLAL).

S. F.:   How is CLAL operating now?

Rabbi Greenberg: CLAL's primary work is educational. The program reaches mostly elite laypeople, mainly connected with Jewish Federations and United Jewish Appeal (UJA). I am feeling very critical about the organization's work now because of the recent survey data on the American Jewish community. The data shows that neither CLAL—nor any other organization—has prepared the Jewish community adequately to prevent the present rate of assimilation.

S. F.:   In a *Jerusalem Report* article, you indicated that not only is the rate of intermarriage and assimilation greater than expected but the *baalei Teshuvah* movement has had less effect than was thought; that is, that the American Jewish community is declining at an alarming rate.

Rabbi Greenberg: In 1968, I wrote an article called "Jewish Survival and the College Campus" about the coming assimilation. This concentrated on the assimilationist effect of the college experience. In college groups then, the intermarriage rate was already at 40 and 50 percent. Eventually, when college students became the whole marriage cohort of the Jewish community, such rates would spell disaster. However, once I became involved in CLAL, this awareness was in the back of my mind, as I was busy concentrating on the task of building CLAL.

Looking back now, I am very critical of myself. I had often criticized those who could not look objectively at their own organizational structures and see their failure to respond to the historical situation. But this is just what I ended up doing. I was persuaded that if I kept harping on the global needs, the specific program of CLAL would never be properly defined and supported. So, I consented to be consumed with the work of an organization that was not adequate for the dimensions of the global crisis that was coming, or with the needed communal response. The establishment is so typically wrapped up in setting up and maintaining its own structures that it does not deal with the big picture or the critical issues. Although I had vowed not to make the same mistake, that is exactly what I had done.

Because CLAL was successful in its own way—it reached out and touched a certain group of people—I had committed the same error that my predecessors had: I had not kept community's eye on the coming assimilation. When the CJF study came out, I berated myself—how could I have fooled myself? True, no one person could have changed this, but . . .

S. F.:   But haven't the *Baalei Teshuvah* movements, primarily Lubavitch, done a very great deal toward turning the tide, moving a lot more people back to Jewishness?

Rabbi Greenberg: Lubavitch tries hard, and they have achieved enormous visibility and institutional strength. But the right-wing Orthodox are so deeply immersed in premodern culture that they cannot transform the great majority's life-style to help it resist assimilation. The Lubavitcher and *Baal Teshuvah yeshivot* graduates have tremendous devotion, but they cannot get across the cultural gap. Unless we can upgrade Jewish life—culturally, religiously, conceptually—we will also not get across the cultural gap. The key question is how to develop intellectually and emotionally sophisticated values and connections to enable Jews to meet the challenges of freedom.

In Israel, the challenge takes a moral form more than a cultural one. In Israel there is a Jewish majority—which reduces cultural erosion, intermarriage, and so forth. Still, in the long run, if there is peace with the Arabs, the pressure of assimilation may well appear in Israel also. In America, the primary challenge is fashioning a Jewish identity, culture, and life-style that can win loyalty and nurture life in the presence of freedom and of alternative values and systems.

S. F.:   Do you think it's primarily a question of greater funding for Jewish education?

Rabbi Greenberg: I do not think that funding is everything, but funding could underwrite a good deal of the work needed to solve the problem. In the long run, the critical question is the compelling (or noncompelling) nature of Jewish belief and values. A combination of adequate and imaginative funding, recruiting effective people, and redefining institutional functions and people's ideas: all this will be needed to meet the test.

S. F.:   Do you think that there are any Jewish spiritual leaders or cultural figures on the scene, aside from Elie Wiesel, who are of the stature required to make an impact on the mass of the Jewish community?

Rabbi Greenberg: There is a shortage. This does not mean that there are no thinkers in Jewish life with valuable ideas. But few of the most positive Jewish teachers have substantial exposure in the media. If you talk about international stature and visibility there is Elie Wiesel, Cynthia Ozick, Natan Sharansky; it gets very thin after that. There are not enough positive models to get wide exposure. Compare the enormous coverage the pope gets in the secular media everywhere in comparison with that given the chief rabbi of Israel.

S. F.:   But isn't part of the problem that there are a lot of important cultural figures who are nominally Jewish and yet stand for everything that is against traditional Jewish religious values? How do we return our people to traditional Jewish values?

Rabbi Greenberg: We have to offer our own alternative, positive Jewish values. I think the idea that man is created in the image of God is the central Jewish value. That norm implies further concepts: perfection of the world (*tikkun olam*), justice, the concept of covenant, concern for peace and for human dignity. These values are at the core of the religion of Judaism. They must be offered to all Jews in the context of contemporary culture through models of Jewish living, namely, *mitzvot*. When these values are offered, there are takers. This is the key to renewal.

Unfortunately, the kind of *baalei teshuvah* we are getting now are convinced that you have to reject much of the technology, science, and the political and social values of modern culture. This approach will not work. The *haredim/yeshivah* world have no adequate leadership role for women; they cannot deal with the serious, modern intellectual critique of Judaism or with the presence of strong values on the other side. I turned on the radio this morning, and there was a news report. A Pepsi commercial had been banned in Israel because it plays off the idea of evolution. This is an embarrassment. Must one deny geology, biology, and science to be a religious Jew?

The prevalent *baal teshuvah* represents an extremist alternative to present life. There is such a big gap between the two worlds that people who consider becoming Baalei Teshuvah feel they have to reject all, or most, of the modern world. This is counterproductive. Such rejection is not going to ever be a serious option for the great majority of the Jewish people.

Were it true that there is no real possibility of remaining Jewish once one gets involved in modernity, then we would have no choice but to withdraw and build up the ghetto walls – intellectually and socially. But is this really necessary? Or is this the original right-wing, Orthodox religious weakness, now built up into a closed system and buffered by a lavishly funded outreach program – based on the internal value system and ideas of the ultraorthodox world? They create a type of Jew dependent on an intellectual, moral, and values shelter. The *haredim* can be compared to a fish that lives in deep water under constant pressure. Once it is raised up to the surface, it explodes outward and disintegrates.

We need a different model for the Jewish people's relationship to modern culture. I use the Mao Tse-tung image of the guerilla who swims in the sea of the people. Judaism has to learn to speak the modern system's language and to share its experiences – then it can transform society and culture. The *Baal Teshuvah* movement wanted to create its own private deep-water pressure chamber at a tremendous cost to the community as a whole. Ultimately, it is a self-defeating process. They save 2 or 3 percent: this handful is living off a dying general Jewish community that cannot and/or will not follow their model. I do not think the *Baal Teshuvah* movement offers enough yield in the long run to stem assimilation. Therefore, it is not the solution to the problem of Judaism and modernity.

S. F.:   But aren't there many religious Jews who are working well in both worlds, who have a place both in the traditional, religious world and the modern world? Isn't there, too, a greater openness to modernity on the part of increasing segments of the religious community? And can't these people be in the forefront of a movement to strengthen the Jewish people?

Rabbi Greenberg: There are positive elements in many groups. The *Haredim* are a good countercultural model – but they cannot be the answer for the majority of Jews. The *Haredim* have a tremendous contribution to make, but it would be greater if they would accept the idea that they should not try to define and control the religious structure of Israel.

The modern Orthodox community is a model of how to live in the modern world successfully as Jewish. This is the group to which

I feel closest personally. But this group has gone through massive decline. I have been depressed by the collapse: often I feel like a bird whose natural habitat has been decimated. The decline of modern Orthodoxy has been bad for the Jews. This is the group that is most needed to make the religious synthesis: this is the group that could be a natural bridge between Judaism and modernity. The collapse of the bridge leaves a dangerous and growing gap between classic Jewish religion and contemporary culture.

S. F.:   But aren't there signs pointing to a revival of modern Orthodoxy?

Rabbi Greenberg: Twenty-five years ago, modern Orthodoxy was the dominant Orthodox group. In these decades, it has lost its nerve and all but given up on itself. Its decline is institutional, theological, social – nothing less than the disintegration of the tradition of moderation. Modern Orthodoxy has a great contribution to make, but first it has to be rebuilt. It has to recover its own values, to assert them and teach them. In my judgment, modern Orthodoxy was excessively influenced – first by modernity in the 1930s, 1940s, and 1950s, and then by the swing to the right in the 1960s, 1970s, and 1980s. We need a renewal of modern Orthodoxy now, which must start with self-criticism – not self-abandonment. And this group must give up the notion that it is the exclusive savior of Jewry. Then it can make a great contribution.

S. F.:   From reading your book *The Jewish Way,* I know you place great importance on the value of each religious group but also see secular Jews as having an important role in the process of historical redemption. But I wonder how such Jews can really have a part in Jewish life when they do not understand the basics – *shemirat Shabbat,* for instance.

Rabbi Greenberg: Two points: first, *Shabbat* is extraordinarily beautiful – but how do you get people to see that? Not by putting down their way of living. The best way to teach *Shabbat* is by living it in the others' presence. Don't begrudge or belittle people who don't accept *Shabbat;* share it with them. Second, 90 percent of the Jewish people do not observe *Shabbat* in the Orthodox way. The Covenant entails more than *Shabbat,* and many of the 90 percent who do not observe *Shabbat* take responsibility for the Jewish people and their covenantal mission in other ways. If someone wants to claim that those who do not observe *Shabbat* are not Jewish, that is simply unacceptable to me.

I do believe that *Shabbat* is indispensable for Jewish living. But the only way to restore the *Shabbat* is by providing an attractive spectrum of *Shabbat* living models so people can hook into it in some way. Hopefully, then they can grow into the rest of it. This is my position: provide every variety of Orthodox *Shabbat* experience. Witness to people with your own life. Offer them every variety of Jewish experience. But many will still find Orthodoxy of any form too "far out" for them. The community should be set up as a conveyor belt, a continuum that is constantly moving. A person should be able to get on anywhere that appeals and then move to the next step in order to progress. The way it is now, the system is moving rapidly, but there is only one experience offered, so that the person either leaps on successfully or misses and falls into the gears below and is swept away.

S. F.:   Perhaps the answer for the Jewish people, and for all the assimilation, is simply to have all in the Diaspora move to Israel. Here, after all, even the most secular Jews have a kind of Jewish identity that those in *Galut* do not.

Rabbi Greenberg: That all Jews will come to Israel is not in the cards—short of a catastrophe. Such a catastrophe, God forbid, would be damaging, on balance, to the entire Jewish people.

True, the losses in the Diaspora are much higher than I expected at this point. I hoped that we would have a solid core of renewed Jewish community in America that, as part of its Jewish life, could do a lot for Israel. Such an outcome would have been quite constructive.

In general, I do not see why it is necessary for Israelis to knock Diaspora Jewish life or to predict (or hope for) its demise. If you love your own reality, you don't need to put down the others.

As a result of Diaspora and Jewish assimilation (and Israeli birthrates), the Israelis are on the way to becoming the majority of the Jewish world. Still, it is a tragedy for Israel when Diaspora communities die. If I were one of the policymakers in Israel, I would invest heavily in keeping Diaspora alive and flourishing. The rewards would be great – including *aliyah*.

This is a paradox, but it is true; the more Jewish the American Jewish community becomes, the more *aliyah* there will be. Day school graduates' rate of *aliyah* is seven times that of the general American community. The reason is obvious. The more Jewishness is important to the individual, the more the logic of coming to Israel takes over.

There is no point in seeing Israel and the Diaspora as competitors. The reverse is the case. When Diaspora communities grow strong, they strengthen Israel through support and *aliyah*. The stronger each partner becomes, the stronger the other one will be. In sum, the logic of Jewish history seems to be pointing to Israel as the emerging dominant Jewish community. But any process that makes Israel the sole surviving community will have weakened the Jewish people.

S. F.:   So, as I understand your thought, the emphasis must be on the Jewish people strengthening itself through creation in all areas of life.

Rabbi Greenberg: This the heart of Jewish faith. The Jewish people are to be a "light unto the nations" – and not just morally. Overcoming ethnic rivalries and poverty, moving a backward population into the modern, affluent world equitably and without losing their values; the dilemmas our world faces are at the heart of Jewish experience today. Jews are concentrated in the 5 to 10 percent of the world population that is the most privileged, the most educated, the most involved with developing policies to deal with these issues. This makes us an avant-garde. Someday – perhaps fifty years from now – when others catch up to us, they will appreciate us!

Israel has made great accomplishments, for instance, the creation and preservation of democracy under extreme conditions. No other democracy has faced such vicious threats to its own existence for five decades without eroding its basic democratic structures – yet Israel managed to do this. Also, in its treatment of the stranger, Israel on the whole has provided a positive example. In France, almost 20 percent of the national vote went to a party whose candidate promised to expel the Arabs. In France, the Arabs have not been identified with ongoing terror attacks or with twenty-two other nations that have sought to destroy the country through war and economic boycott. In Israel, the extremist group calling for "transfer," namely, expulsion, of the Arabs received only 2½ percent of the vote. The accomplishment is all the more remarkable in that the bulk of the Israeli population living in Israel during the founding years of 1948 to 1955 had lived previously in Eastern Europe and the Middle East – places where there was no democratic system or culture. Someday, the world will come and study how the Israelis did it.

Similarly, Jews are – and should be – leaders in every aspect of using modern life and productivity to upgrade the image of God for every human. American Jews are also pioneers in dealing with the challenge of freedom and affluence. A personal friend just gave and raised over sixty million dollars to build a superb children's hospital, which will serve the entire population of Israel, Jews and Arabs; it can, and wants to, serve the entire Middle East. That is the kind of leadership Jews should be showing. Other people will then learn from Jews, and Jews will want to be Jews.

S. F.:   When you think not simply of "improvement of life," greater good, but the ideal state and ideal relations between Jews and humanity, do you conceive all peoples flowing to the mountain of the Lord in Zion? Do you expect them to all accept, in one form or another, the vision of God and humanity given to the Jewish people?

Rabbi Greenberg: Christianity and Islam are serious religions, spiritually dignified. You don't have to become Jewish to be related to God. We want those religions to acknowledge and fully recognize Judaism and our role in the world. We need not convert them all to be Jewish. It is blessing enough that we have this chance to influence the world.

We must ask ourselves, "What is the Jewish message?" If Israel cleaned up its environment, healed its people, created jobs to give everyone self-supporting dignity, helped bring the Jewish past alive, lived by Jewish values, and upgraded the dignity of every man and woman in God's image, then Jews would have a persuasive message for humanity. That message will be heard—and followed—by using, borrowing, and adapting our models; the world will be redeemed. Then we will fulfill the promise "In you will all the families of the earth be blessed" (Genesis 12:3).

Rabbi Chaim Pearl

Rabbi Chaim Pearl has been the rabbi of both major Orthodox congregations in England and a major Conservative synagogue in the United States. Like most of the remarkable Conservative Jewish figures of the previous generation, Rabbi Pearl had an Orthodox education. But this alone does not explain the special quality of excellence and dedication that he displays in all he does. Often through the years, when I heard him as *shaliach tzibbur* (prayer leader), I was certain that this was the prayer of the Jewish soul crying out in the deepest way at the Gate of Heaven.

Along with his more than forty-five years of work as pulpit rabbi, Rabbi Pearl has authored ten books on Jewish subjects and edited a number of others. Among these are two books on Rashi; a work on Isaac Arama, *The Medieval Jewish Mind;* and his translation of Bialik and Rawnitzky's *Sefer HaAggadah, Stories of the Sages.* Rabbi Pearl is also the editor of the *Illustrated Israel Encyclopedia of Jewish Life and Thought.* Also forthcoming is his *Theology of Rabbinic Folklore.*

My conversation with Rabbi Pearl (and his correction of the typescript) took place in his home on Harari Street in the Tzameret Habirah district of Jerusalem, close to Mount Scopus.

The conversation was an express tour through the whole of Rabbi Pearl's career, and it concludes with his own moving statement of his conception of *Avodat Hashem,* in which he stresses the centrality of the *mitzvot* between man and his fellow human beings.

S. F.:   Could you tell me about your professional life before your coming to Israel?

Rabbi Pearl: Before coming to Israel, my experience for thirty-five years, from 1955 to 1980, was totally in synagogue work, with two leading congregations in England and one in New York. Although my first job was largely in education and youth work, subsequently it was mostly pulpit work. Looking back, I suppose I got a lot of my inspiration from the basic education I got from the age of fourteen in Talmud Torah. After the war broke out in 1939, I was a senior *yeshivah* student until the middle of 1940. Our *yeshivah* was very professional and attracted students who were planning to do more study when they finished. Rabbi Isser Unterman, who later became Ashkenazi chief rabbi in Israel, had great influence, but there were a number of other outstanding teachers. The impression was given that when I was ready for it, I would become a rabbi of a congregation. But when the war broke out, plans were upset and I took on a post teaching evacuated Jewish children in two hostel schools. And that's what I did at the beginning of the war years.

S. F.:   And after this, as I understand, you received your first rabbinical position at Birmingham.

Rabbi Pearl: There, I became assistant to Abraham Cohen, who at that time was one of the leading rabbis of Anglo-Jewry, a great scholar, and the editor of the Soncino Bible. I had the opportunity to watch him at work for four years, and I learned a great deal from him. I believe he was the greatest of the Anglo-Jewish preachers of his time and, too, a great communal leader. When he resigned from his position, I was offered his pulpit. I had not applied for it, since I thought comparisons would be made between him and his successor. But to my surprise, this did not happen, and the congregation was ideal. The congregation was unique in Anglo-Jewry in that it adopted a middle-of-the-way path, almost like that of a traditional Conservative synagogue. During those years, the Singer's Hill con-

gregation was a model in Anglo-Jewry, for its services were organized and intelligible. During the fifteen years I was there, I was able
to accomplish a great deal. Aside from a network of Sunday and
afternoon schools, I introduced the first communal *bat mitzvah*
service. Interestingly, even some of the strictest Orthodox families
enrolled their daughters. I taught this class myself, and the influence
on many of these girls was long-standing. My closest contacts with
the old Birmingham Jewish community and those who grew up
there have come from those graduates of the *bat mitzvah* class, who
by this time are middle-aged. There were, of course, of number of
major community and youth institutions that I helped strengthen,
including a B'nai B'rith lodge, a residential Hillel house, and an
active synagogue guild with a full adult education program.

S. F.:   I understand the Birmingham years were full and rewarding
ones. Why did you decide to move on?

Rabbi Pearl: My predecessor had been at Birmingham for nearly
forty years. While I had, in my years there, learned a great deal, I felt
I was, after a time, not making any new waves. When we celebrated
the centenary of the synagogue building, the president boasted that
in one hundred years, the congregation had had only three rabbis.
This remark was greeted by thunderous applause. My own reaction
was very mixed. On the one hand, a community leader who stays in
one place for such a long time sees two or three generations of each
family and becomes deeply involved in their lives. This deepens the
appreciation of the community for the rabbi. On the other hand,
nothing new happens. You have started the engine, it is on the right
track, but there is no new horizon. So, too, I felt that I myself was
becoming staid and needed some kind of change.

S. F.:   From reading your memoir, I also received the impression
that you were, in your own mind, too involved with the personal
lives of members of your congregation.

Rabbi Pearl: In 1958, the congregation suffered the loss of a number of prominent people, including youngsters, and this affected me, too, in a very deep, personal way. A rabbi, like a doctor or psychologist, has to, to a certain extent, be emotionally removed from the particular problem he is dealing with. Birmingham was a family community, and I, at that time, was too young and too sensitive. So despite the efforts of the community to keep me there, after fifteen years I decided to move. I received a call from the West End Synagogue in London, with an offer to succeed Rabbi Louis Jacobs, who was resigning from the pulpit. The West End Synagogue, while very prestigious, was a stiff, Victorian congregation. It included among its members Simon Marks of Marks and Spencer, the Seiff family, Viscount Samuel, the Montagues: the cream of Anglo-Jewry. I didn't see them in *shul* except on Yom Kippur, but they were members of the synagogue. I was foolishly attracted to this synagogue, which in many ways was the opposite of Birmingham. Nothing could change, and to be quite honest, my influence on the congregation was minimal. I suspect I had greater influence on the wider London community than I did in my own synagogue. So, when the opportunity came, after about four years, I made the move to a Conservative synagogue in New York City.

S. F.:   And this New York experience was, as I understand, a far happier one.

Rabbi Pearl: In New York, my job was in Riverdale, a lovely, pleasant community in the north Bronx. Interestingly enough, the standards of observance in the Conservative synagogue of Riverdale were higher than those in the Orthodox synagogues of West London. At that time, the West End had many of what could be described as NOOJ, nonobservant Orthodox Jews. And so, it was a pleasant surprise for me to come to the congregation and find higher standards of observance. I also came knowing Conservative philosophies, as I had been reading Kaplan, Heschel, Finklestein, and others for many years. Also, the community in Riverdale was a special one as it had a large number of Jewish Theological Seminary (JTS) graduates. I was told to do what I could to strengthen the synagogue. It was very hard and very rewarding work.

S. F.:   At the same time you were engaged in this pulpit work, you were also pursuing your scholarly researches?

Rabbi Pearl: This was not easy, and it made my days and nights even longer. Already at Birmingham, I wrote my first book, *A Guide to Jewish Knowledge*, which was published in 1957 and, incidentally, has been translated into Russian. This book is a guide to Jewish practice and the calendar. And the last two sections give a view of Jewish religion philosophically, and a bird's-eye view of Jewish history. Once having published the first book, I got the taste for other things. So when the *Jewish Chronicle* invited me to contribute to a series on Jewish festivals, I did two, one on Shavuot and one on minor festivals. And then, my Ph.D. thesis was on the commentary of Isaac Arama called *Akedat Yitzhak,* a massive work on the Five Books of Moses and the *Megillot.* I was invited by my tutor Isidor Epstein, who was head of the Jews' College at the time, to take on this research work. Both a leading philosopher and a talmudist, he was of extraordinary help to me. This became my fourth book. After this, I did the Jewish history for schools, which was published in pamphlet form. In London, I was also the editor of the *Popular Jewish Library,* which was an activity of the World Jewish Congress. I edited ten books for them, the first by Abraham Cohen on differences between Judaism and Christianity. And then I did two works on Rashi.

I had always wanted to write and had gotten into the habit of writing seriously in Birmingham. At first, I wrote every *Shabbat* sermon in full manuscript. In this weekly exercise, I followed the practice of my predecessor. It served three important purposes: it helped avoid repetition, it kept the sermon to an acceptable length, and it trained me to write clearly and effectively. I preached on other occasions, and this amounted to seventy or eighty sermons a year.

In America, the preaching was different: more personal, less formal. The bulk of the rest of the writing was done in New York: my first work on Rashi, and also the first volume of *Sefer HaAggadah*. Then, after my retirement, I wrote the second volume on Rashi here in Israel. This has now been published in Hebrew, Dutch, and a number of other European languages. I also was a contributor of a great deal of material to the *Illustrated Bible Encyclopedia*. I wrote about two hundred pieces for the one-volume *Encyclopedia of Judaism* and have just recently completed my editorial work on the English edition of the *Illustrated Israel Encyclopedia of Jewish Life and Thought*. Altogether now, there are ten published works. I also have to give a lot of my time to the *Jewish Bible Quarterly*, for which articles come in from all over the world.

S. F.:   There are many things I would like to ask you about your scholarly work, but one thing in your memoir particularly struck me: your ideas on sermon writing.

Rabbi Pearl: It's an interesting subject, and there are many views about it. I passed through a stage that many pass through, when I thought it all a waste of time. You might as well read them the telephone directory. But then, I often had the experience of people coming to me and saying how they had begun to act differently as a result of this sermon or that—a girl coming to break off an inter-marriage, people changing and beginning to eat *Kosher*. Once a man came after a sermon about Israel on Rosh Hashanah and decided to donate a million pounds. I have had *bar mitzvah* boys who, years later, came and told me what I had said in their *bar mitzvah*—a frightening thought. It is true that 95 to 99 percent of sermons have little effect. But it is sufficient that the sermon touches one or two people. The effect is like that of a gardener. You do not see the water under the ground, but if the watering were not done, nothing would grow. There are about twelve hundred sermons in all, which will go to the JTS Archive when the time comes. In Israel, I believe it's necessary to emphasize the *Musar* element of the sermon because of the troublesome times we are living through.

S. F.: Rabbi, when did you first come to Israel, and when did you decide to make *Aliyah?*

Rabbi Pearl: My wife and I first came in 1956 and then in 1958, and we tried to come every two years for a month or so. We had always wanted to live in Israel. We bought an apartment here in Bayit Vegan in 1974. After careful consideration, I retired at the age of sixty instead of sixty-five, so we will have, with God's blessing, a few more years here.

S. F.: These have been productive literary years. Have they met your expectations in other ways?

Rabbi Pearl: I have published three books since being here, and I am on my fourth now. As for other expectations, I was brought up in the Zionist model tradition of *kibbutz* socialist egalitarianism. Everyone works hard, and then at night, you dance around the campfire. There was that kind of attractive ideal. I don't need to tell you that the real Israel today is not like that. One problem I have is that the Conservative movement is not recognized. I have another problem, which I suspect you don't share. Israel has become too right-wing. Looking at the horrible hooligans at Bat Yam last week made my blood curdle.

S. F.: I agree with you about the wrongness of chanting slogans of hate. But what most disturbs me is that in the Jewish state, which after all was founded with the idea in mind that here Jews could be safe, there is murder of Jews for being Jews. Last week alone, two people were stabbed to death by Arab terrorists. Those rioters in Bat Yam were somehow reacting to the pain of their fellow citizen, Avi Rapp, whose fifteen-year-old daughter was murdered near their home – in the Jewish state, after all the struggle and suffering.

Rabbi Pearl: I think we agree that security problems are the number-one problem in Israel. We can agree that this is the first priority. But this does not diminish my concern over moblike action, even the possibility of dictatorship.

S. F.:   I suppose I am less troubled over this prospect because I know how true in Israel is the old saying, "Two Jews, three opinions." But I was wondering if you don't see a brighter side of Israel.

Rabbi Pearl: The kind of cultural and educational activity in the Hebrew language is one such bright side. Walking in the streets of Jerusalem, I sometimes sense how I am walking in the very place Jeremiah walked. Above all, the very miracle of the State of Israel itself, with Independance Day, Jerusalem Day. I think a very significant portion of the community appreciates deeply the fact that we are in Israel and understands the historical significance of this. But all the good does not free me of the worry over the negative things.

S. F.:   And one of the negative things is the relatively low level of religious observance of the community as a whole?

Rabbi Pearl: I think that the level of observance among the members of the Conservative community is that of a comparable Conservative congregation abroad.

S. F.:   Considering the great crisis over assimilation in the Diaspora, isn't this still another argument for urging Jews of the world to come on *aliyah?*

Rabbi Pearl: I think the day will come when the majority of Jews will be living in Israel. At the moment, 45 percent of all Jewish children born in the world are born in Israel. About ten years ago, it was 40 percent. Still, I am not one of those who argue for the negation of the Diaspora. We should be realistic and understand that most Jews simply do not want to come here. What are we going to do, simply have nothing to do with them? We are one people, "*Am Achad.*" The other point is that without the support of Diaspora Jews, and particularly American Jewry, Israel would be a more impoverished state. This may mean that the American Jewish community is going to remain a great center of Jewish life and thought for many years to come and that the world Jewish community will have two focal points.

S. F.: But the 1990 council of Jewish Federations (CJF) study indicates that the contraction of the American community is much more serious than imagined previously.

Rabbi Pearl: One can never tell. I recall in the 1960s listening to people talk about French Jewry as if it were finished. Today, France has the largest Jewish community in Europe. Jewish life has never been describable as a simple chart, a line going in one direction, up or down. Bialik once wrote that he was writing for the last generation of Hebrew readers. He should only know that his works today are read by more people than ever before. I believe the same kind of thing can happen with American Jewry. There is a tremendous communal power there, many with deep connections to Israel. I would not give up on American Jewry so quickly.

S. F.: Rabbi, you have, both in the Diaspora and in Israel, been contributing to the Jewish community for many years. Do you understand this work as *Avodat Hashem?* How do you understand the concept of *Avodat Hashem?*

Rabbi Pearl: Your question is not an easy one to answer, but perhaps I can divide it into two parts. There is the *Avodat Hashem* that is purely personal; that is, it relates to my own religious life. And then, there is the *Avodat Hashem* that is connected with the entire thrust of my work in the rabbinate.

Let me deal with these two parts separately. First of all, I think that every religious Jew punctuates a great part of his personal life with *Avodat Hashem*. As far as I am concerned, this happens on the occasions when I pray with sincerity and when I perform any *mitzvah* with *kavvanah*. I pray three times every day. I do this even when I am not in the mood because I know that good habit makes for character and second nature. When I do not pray with *kavvanah*, I realize the shortcoming and I know this is not proper *Avodah*. But there are very many times when I am able to pray with complete concentration and sincerity. The prayer comes from the heart, and I truly feel that such a religious exercise is *Avodat Hashem*. The old masters of prayer knew the importance of such prayer, and they were able to offer their prayer in total dedication and sincerity. We can only try to follow their prescription. I personally understand my own shortcomings in this, but I keep trying. What applies to prayer applies to the performance and observance of every *mitzvah*. The mystics used to say a *kavvanah* before observing a *mitzvah*. We still have a good example of such a *kavvanah* before the counting of the *Omer*. But the ideal should not be forgotten, and as far as possible, I try to perform the *mitzvah* with its full meaning clearly in mind.

Now, as to the other aspect of *Avodat Hashem*, namely, that which relates to my work in the rabbinate, I have always seen that as, first of all, being able to serve the community. And serving the community is ultimately my way of serving God. But serving the community from day to day, all the hours of my work, is my first objective. This breaks up into practical programs, the education of young and old, the organization and leading of services in the synagogue. It includes an attempt to strengthen the religious service. This is a little nearer to the idea of *Avodat Hashem* because it's the religious services, where the person feels closer to God, in love and praise of God, in asking the help of God. All of this is involved in *Avodat Hashem* through the process of maintaining the steady flow of religious service.

Avodat Hashem is, too, involved in the preaching in the synagogue that I have done for over forty years. This is part of the teaching of Judaism, which has always been for me a first objective. I have always tried to stress the "*Ahavat Haberiyot*" (the love of one's fellow human beings). The love of God and the love of human beings are two sides of the same coin. I have always found it essential to stress that to "Love your neighbor as yourself" is central to the love of God. In brief, I think my work has been, in all modesty, an attempt to serve God. And fate has given me the opportunity, over the last several decades of pulpit work, synagogue education, religion services, and sermons, to realize that *Avodat Hashem* through serving the community of Israel.

Rabbi Nachum L. Rabinovitch

Rabbi Nachum L. Rabinovitch is *rosh yeshivah* of Birkhat Moshe in the community of Maale Adumim. Formerly lecturer of mathematics at the University of Toronto, he served as principal of Jews' College, London, and has written extensively on the code of Maimonides. He served as associate editor of *Ha-Darom* from 1957 to 1983. He has been an authoritative spokesman for Religious Zionism.

Without question, the Rambam and his work stand at the center of Rabbi Rabinovitch's intellectual universe. And in our meeting, the Rabbi seemed far more comfortable talking about the Rambam than about himself. When I arrived at the *yeshivah* to interview him, I saw him tutoring one student at length. I had the sense that the giving of special care to each and every one of his students is at the center of his educational approach. From the interview the reader can get a sense of a man of great principle and dedication to Torah and to the Jewish people.

S. F.:   Rabbi, how would you describe your work as *rosh yeshivah?*

Rabbi Rabinovitch: It's very straightforward. I am involved in teaching young men Talmud and *Halachah,* the teaching of Torah and Judaism.

S. F.:   How did you come to your present position in Yeshivat Birkhat Moshe in Maale Adumim?

Rabbi Rabinovitch: I was a congregational rabbi and taught for many years at university, and then, afterward, was head of Jews' College in London. I visited Israel frequently, and when two acquaintances, Rabbi Sabbato and Rabbi Sheilat, told me about the founding of this *yeshivah,* I decided to make *aliyah.* This was fifteen years ago. The government had decided to build a large town in Maale Adumim, and the *yeshiva* was to be built for the community. I had decided to make *aliyah* a very long time ago but had to find a suitable niche. I have, *Baruch Hashem,* a large family. Today, they are all married, but I always had to be concerned about the material needs of existence as well as in finding a place in which I could make some contribution. It took some time until I found what I believed was the proper place for me.

S. F.:   Along with being an educator, you have a reputation for your scholarly work. What are the main areas of your interest?

Rabbi Rabinovitch: I have a strong interest in Rambam and have worked for a number of years on a comprehensive commentary to Maimonides' code. A large number of volumes of this work have been published already. In my scientific work, I have dealt primarily with the history of science and with mathematics. Here, too, my interest in Rambam plays an important part.

S. F.:   Do you come from an academic family? Did your family oppose your entering the world of science?

Rabbi Rabinovitch: My parents were not academics. They had come to Canada from the Ukraine before the First World War. I myself never saw any contradiction between Judaism and the academic world.

S. F.:   And along with your rabbinical training, you have a formal scientific education?

Rabbi Rabinovitch: I have a degree in mathematics and a doctorate in the Philosophy of Science.

S. F.: From my brief time here I saw how deeply involved you are with your students. How would you compare the students you teach here with those you taught in America, Canada, and England?

Rabbi Rabinovitch: In this *yeshivah,* we have some of the best students in Israel, along with some very good students from abroad. On the whole, students in this country are more mature than in America, or England for that matter. The army is the experience that pushes them to grow up. They come to us for two years after high school, after they have their *Bagrut* matriculation. They then go for a stint of army service, and when they return it is possible to see how much they have matured. The army experience is a very important component of their overall development. And it contributes, not only in terms of emotional maturity but also, I believe, to intellectual maturity.

S. F.: Could you please explain how you believe this happens?

Rabbi Rabinovitch: One of the important aspects of what I call intellectual maturity is the understanding that one has to fully make use of one's own resources. Usually, young people – for that matter, most people – do not know how to value the time at their disposal. "Work expands to fill the time available to do it." One of the things that people learn in the army is that both their physical and mental resources are much greater than they suspect. When life depends on it, the human being can work even after twenty-four sleepless hours. This lesson of the making use of our capacity more fully is an important one. The discovery that one's physical resources are much greater than imagined, that one's willpower to marshal these resources is also much greater, contributes much to intellectual maturity.

S. F.:   Rabbi, could you please say a few words about the program of the *yeshivah?*

Rabbi Rabinovitch: The objective of our type of study is to develop individual scholars, with each one trying to utilize his capacities to follow his own major interests. Already in the first year, there is a requirement to do an independent research essay. Almost every year, at least one or two of these are good enough to be published. As they go through our program, we continually evaluate their achievements. At a certain stage, there are more formal examinations for those students who are working for rabbinical ordination. And there is, too, a special examination for postgraduate students after they finish the *Hesder* course. There is also a program for training teachers. Again, though, the major evaluation is on the work they do as independent scholars.

S. F.:   In the five-year *Hesder* program, how is the time divided between the army and the *yeshivah?*

Rabbi Rabinovitch: The time actually spent in the army is between sixteen and eighteen months, this after spending two years in the *yeshivah.* They are inducted into the army after Pesach of the second year. After the army, they return for another *yeshivah* stint. Our students go wherever they are needed in the army. We have men in the paratroopers, in Golani, in Givati, in the tank corps. We even have two in the navy, which is rather unusual.

S. F.:   Students of a *yeshivah* who also serve in the army are realizing the Zionist religious ideal in the most vital way imaginable. This would seem to be the kind of integration Rabbi Kook would have dreamed for Israel. Are you, in your own thought and work, a follower of Rabbi Kook and his ideal?

Rabbi Rabinovitch: While I highly esteem Rabbi Kook, I do not see myself as his disciple because I am much closer to the Maimonidean view, which is to steer clear of mysticism.

S. F.:   But you do hold Rav Kook's view regarding the centrality of the land and people of Israel to Jewish redemption in history?

Rabbi Rabinovitch: I accept this, but not as the exclusive view of Rav Kook. Seeing redemptive processes in the return to *Eretz Yisrael* is, I think, the central message of Rambam's theory of Jewish history. This theory motivated the early Religious Zionist thinkers like Reines, who were careful to distinguish between mystical approaches and practical, this-worldly conceptions.

S. F.:   You mean, by a practical approach, *dunam* by *dunam?*

Rabbi Rabinovitch: Yes, *dunam* by *dunam.* But another side of it is that we see our responsibility as greater than do the mystics. The mystics see the hand of God doing the job and pulling us along. I believe we have to be much more conscious of the need to do things, to take action by ourselves. We must trust in the Ruler of the World that He will help bring success to our efforts. But we must not think we can do nothing and have all given to us. I think this difference in approach, by the way, also applies to a degree within the Religious Zionist group. There are some who tend to think the drama has a foregone conclusion, and others who believe we are participating in a Divine Drama, where we can make mistakes, where we must continually take responsibility for our action, where we must help ourselves in realizing the Divine Goal.

S. F.:   So you do not regard the outcome as predetermined at this stage, that the process of return is under way and must come to its logical and complete realization.

Rabbi Rabinovitch: I do not believe the outcome is predetermined in any stage. We should rather see ourselves engaged in a great adventure in which the Almighty can help us, but one that demands we take responsibility for our actions.

S. F.:   So the recent coming to power of a government that seems to want to unload a part of *Eretz Yisrael* is, as you understand it, a setback we have made for ourselves.

Rabbi Rabinovitch: I don't think that one can, on such immediate matters, make a judgment in the light of a religious outlook. I believe there must be a strict seperation between Torah institutions and any kind of political activity. This does not mean I do not have my own political outlook. But I do not claim that my views have a special validity because I have a role as teacher of Torah. In political matters, my views are as good or as bad as the next person's.

S. F.:   So you do not see the historical process of Jewish redemption as one in which the government of Israel becomes a theocracy.

Rabbi Rabinovitch: Definitely not. I have written in many contexts that I believe the government ought to be a civil government, which means that its jurisdiction is restricted. It deals with economics, social structure, international relations, politics, defense. But spiritual matters are not in the state's jurisdiction. Should the civil government wish to overstep the bounds of its legitimate jurisdiction, then Torah scholars must sound the alarm. It is the duty of spiritual leaders to warn against moral breaches.

S. F.:   And yet, you see the historical process as a spiritual one.

Rabbi Rabinovitch: Yes, of course. But Jews always had autonomy, even in the Diaspora until modern times, when the emancipation ended this. Under different regimes in various places, Jews usually had, to some degree, an autonomy. In all these communities until modern times, the structure was basically halachic structure with a two-pronged leadership: the lay leadership and the rabbinic leadership. And while it is true that they often influenced each other—frequently overlapped—the areas of responsibility were clearly distinguishable. Any study of the Responsa or *Halachah* literature over the centuries makes it very clear that there was a separation of powers and jurisdictions. I think that's essential.

S. F.:   But given the rate of assimilation in Western countries today, doesn't the whole process of returning them to Israel mean saving them as Jews? And shouldn't our ideal be to bring them all on *aliyah* as soon as possible?

Rabbi Rabinovitch: Let's not fool ourselves. The process of return to Israel is not going to take place overnight. The process of nation building is a process that takes generations. Israel cannot be secure in its identity and sense of common destiny unless we build it from the ground up. I also think it's important for the *olim,* those especially who come with little Jewish background, to be exposed and learn something of what Judaism is all about. Whether fortunate or not, the struggle for the spiritual face of Israel is going to go on for a long time. It takes many generations to fashion the ethos of a people. At the same time, we have to try and impart the living message of Torah wherever there are Jews. And there is no doubt that we have very powerful ideas, ideas that have fermented the whole of Western civilization. The last two hundred years of scientific and political turmoil have seen the loss and destruction of large numbers of our people. And this heightens the need to restore physical normality, as much and as soon as we can. In the first generations, all energy went necessarily into building the economic-political structure of the State of Israel. But now we need to devote energy to our spiritual foundations, to bring to bear the innate strength of our heritage, make life meaningful for Jews as Jews in the modern world.

S. F.:   And do you believe the autonomy models of the past have some positive elements from which we can learn?

Rabbi Rabinovitch: These autonomous communities ran on the principle of partnership, with everyone a partner in the common undertaking. This idea is not one that was very popular until the rise of modern political theory, and even today, this idea of halachic community is not well understood. The partnership had much to offer, with every community a voluntaristic establishment. Jews chose to remain Jews, though they had to take on themselves the internal burden of Torah and *mitzvot*, and the external burden of persecution. And they could never be certain when the next persecution would come. And yet Judaism, for them, was worth choosing. There is a tremendous power in Judaism, which has to an extent been diminished in the modern era, and which must be renewed.

S. F.:   Is part of this renewal through our being a light to the nations?

Rabbi Rabinovitch: I don't believe that being a light to the nations means making this our first priority. All humanity is our interest and nothing should be foreign to us, but before we are a light to the nations, we must be a light to ourselves. The light is important to us; every human being is important to us. To discover the light that radiates throughout all of existence, and to which every individual can relate, is the purpose of our being. And when we discover the light, we spread the light. Our sages say, "A lamp of one is a lamp for a hundred." If you really discover the light, then it shines for everybody. It is not going to be a greater light if you look for it for others first. You look for the light, and when you find it, you will have it for others, also.

S. F.:   Rabbi Irving Greenberg has the idea that Israel should be a light to the nations in most areas of life: in scientific work, in raising the economic level of the poor, in activities that would upgrade the spiritual level of "mankind." Is this the kind of light that you, too, are talking about?

Rabbi Rabinovitch: Yes and no. I am interested in helping the needy, not because it will serve as an example but because it's necessary and right for us and for them. If we can help others, we can serve as inspiration. And there's no doubt that if you consider Israel in comparison with the ninety other new nations that have come into being in the world since the end of the Second World War, Israel is an inspiration. Israel is one of the few that came from being a Third World to a First World country while maintaining and developing its democratic political institutions. The development of Israel is a tremendous example for those who wish to learn from it. Unfortunately, many of our neighbors are not interested in this kind of thing. If they were interested in the welfare of their own people, they could learn from us in many different ways.

S. F.:   You speak of a slow process of building. But do we have time, especially in the Diaspora? In the 1960s, intermarriage was 9 percent; now it's over 50. The Diaspora is aging and losing numbers.

Rabbi Rabinovitch: What you say is true, but I believe we must bear in mind two things in regard to Israel. First, Israel has been, and continues to be, at war. And, in spite of that, we have all the achievements, many things to be thankful for. I have very powerful stories of young people, one of whom was a colleague of mine and whose Jewish identity was completely unknown to me until the Six Day War, who have returned to Judaism. Another story is of a young person I met in Siberia, who listened to the report of the Six Day War there and was moved to returning to Judaism. The very existence of Israel is a powerful antidote to assimilation and indifference. It's not the all-powerful cure, but no cure can be fool-proof. It does seem to me that the ongoing development and, most especially, further spiritual development of Israel will be a powerful inspiration to Jews in Diaspora to maintain their Jewish identity. Another aspect of this is the demographic problem. It does not help to tell people that they should have more children because this is what Jewish history demands. The only demographic answer today is through growth in Israel. We must have more Jewish children in Israel today. And if we show to other Jews a living Judaism, this might inspire them too to care more for the young. After all, having children is, in the deepest sense, an expression of confidence in life. That people have become cynical, alienated, and selfish is unfortunate. There are more and more who mistakenly identify having careers with having no children. The far-out feminists talk about their children as being burdensome to the quality of life. But in fact, that way of thought is both wrong and dangerous. People who feel at home in the world have children; people who do not, do not. So, this kind of thinking is extremely dangerous for the Jewish people. The way to help is to provide that kind of spiritual self-confidence that enables people to confront the ultimate reality. The rule is, where there is a vital Judaism, there is a higher birthrate, and we see that in the much more self-confident development of the Orthodox community today than of the general Jewish community.

S. F.:   But in Israel, this is perhaps 20 percent, and in the United States, perhaps 7 or 8; is it too small a community to balance out what is happening to the whole?

Rabbi Rabinovitch: In Israel, the number is closer to 40 percent. So we have to reach out to wider circles. But there is no good in talking about those who are lost and saying this over and over. What we have to do is work on building up both Israel and Judaism as powerful stimulants to return to the Jewish people. And we should become less concerned about survival and more about making Judaism relevant, more about giving people spiritual roots and self-confidence. Survival should not be the first purpose except, for instance, when there has been a terrible accident and life hangs by a thread. But a normal person, if he concentrates on survival, is sad indeed. We have to bear in mind that if we make Jewish life worth living, instill Jewish meaning and values, then survival will come of itself. Historically, in this century, we as a people had the experience of the *Shoah*, where "survival" was the question. Today, in Israel, what is in question is hopefully more the material and, above all, spiritual quality of our people, which we must strive to elevate.

Rabbi Meir Schweiger

Meir Schweiger has been a teacher of Torah at Pardes Institute in Jerusalem for over fifteen years. He also teaches in Mahanaim, a cultural and educational center for Russian *Olim*. His courses in *Humash, Mishnah, Gemara,* and Ethics have made him, through the years, one of the most respected figures in the world of Outreach Education in Israel.

For close to five years, I had studied in the night courses of Rabbi Schweiger at Pardes Institute. I went back year after year because I found him to be, aside from a considerate, insightful person, the most remarkable teacher I had ever had. Each class with him became an intellectual adventure, a kind of mystery story, in revealing layers of meaning of the biblical text. In the course of this, there was frequently also revealed a deep understanding of the "human condition" and the particular situation one happened to be going through at the moment. I was always impressed, too, by how Meir managed somehow to include all his students, making each one involved in the reading he was leading us to.

Our interview centers more than anything else on what might be called an approach to education, to what is done in places like Pardes. But it also includes a definition of the meaning of *Avodat Hashem*, which I found in complete accord with the comportment and character of Meir. In this definition, what counts in *Avodat Hashem* is the individual's ability to understand that there is something greater than his own individual appetite and right, and to understand his responsibility to Jewish community and history as a whole.

This interview was conducted in the Har Nof district of Jerusalem at the then Schweiger home. Recently, the Schweigers moved to their new home in Efrat.

S. F.:   I know you have studied at Yeshiva University, at Kerem B'Yavneh, and at Yeshivat Har-Etzion. Can you describe what each of these experiences contributed to your development?

Rabbi Schweiger: I received in Yeshiva University the basic tools and techniques for studying. The emphasis throughout was on Gemara, and I was given an approach to how to analyze Gemara. In Kerem B'Yavneh, I received an environment in which I was enable to do independent study. At Yavneh, I began to apply the Yeshiva methods in order to achieve what I would call a breadth of knowledge. The year at Gush Etzion was not revolutionary but more a synthesis of Yeshiva and Kerem.

S. F.:   When did you first come to *Eretz Yisrael,* and when did you decide to make *aliyah?*

Rabbi Schweiger: The first time I came was in 1968 in a program called "Summer in Kibbutz." I had, at that time, probably already decided to make *aliyah.* Two years later, I was in Kerem B'Yavneh, where I solidified my desire. And I finally came on *aliyah* in 1972, while studying at Gush Etzion.

S. F.:   Were you married at that time?

Rabbi Schweiger: I was married four months before I came on *aliyah.* And when I went back to the states after my year at Yavne, everything I was doing was in preparation for *aliyah.*

S. F.:   And you began teaching almost immediately upon arrival?

Rabbi Schweiger: I began teaching in 1973, the year after I was in Gush Etzion. Rabbi Brovender was the head of a *yeshivah* that at that time was called Shappel's or Hartman's. I was in the *kollel,* which meant that I was studying and tutoring, though it was clear I was very much interested in teaching. So initially that year, I did quite a bit of tutoring, and in the following year, I began teaching full time.

S. F.: And how did you become connected with the institution where you have done most of your teaching, Machon Pardes?

Rabbi Schweiger: The last year I taught at Shappel's, 1976, one of my students was a fellow named Levi Lauer. I referred him to Pardes and he was later made its director. A month later, I came and asked him for a job.

S. F.: And you have been at Pardes ever since. Could you briefly describe the educational principles of Pardes?

Rabbi Schweiger: Our basic educational philosophy is the desire to expose every Jew, no matter what his belief or practice, to traditional texts, and to try to get him engaged as much as is possible in what could be called a "dialogue with the text." We want the person to reach his own conclusions in regard to whatever practical applications will come of this dialogue. We are not interested in approaching the text from a purely academic point of view as an abstract, intellectual exercise but would like to affect the person's observance. In Pardes, the notion of noncoerciveness is central, and the individual must choose the direction he would like to go. Pardes also believes very strongly in equal opportunities for education for men and women.

S. F.: Do you, as an Orthodox Jew who lives by *Halachah,* have any problem in teaching "mixed classes"?

Rabbi Schweiger: I do not necessarily have a problem with teaching men and women together in the classroom. However, when men and women study together, I think a certain intensity is lost because of the sexual component. All the disclaimers aside, this does come into play. On the other hand, I do not overall have a problem because I think the educational goal is to engage people in the text in a way that will involve them deeply in Jewish belief and practice.

S. F.:   Would you give a profile of the average student at Pardes?

Rabbi Schweiger: I would say, generally the average students are in their mid-twenties. They have already finished college and have an advanced degree. If they do not have such a degree, they have probably worked for a year or two. The average student tends to be bright, searching, and inquisitive. Generally, they are people who come from a minimal Jewish background and have no formalized Jewish education. Even in terms of Jewish practice, they have had minimal exposure to Judaism. And yet, they are people searching to increase their involvement with Judaism through an encounter with the text.

S. F.:   Do you have an educational philosophy that guides you in relation to the students?

Rabbi Schweiger: As an educational approach, I would like to encourage people to come up with original ideas and accentuate whatever is positive in what they have to say. I think part of the educational philosophy is showing that there is not necessarily one pat answer, one way of looking at a text. Many different ways may each bring an element of the truth. And maybe that's the advantage of learning together in a group, because each one is able to bring out a different, complementary point. I think part of my educational philosophy is to show how this complementary approach works. Part of the greatness of the Torah is that it has so many different dimensions.

I also am not looking at the text in a mechanical or technical fashion. I am approaching the text in order to understand what it says to my "reality." I am trying to get to the depth of the text because ultimately, it speaks personally to me.

S. F.:   I would say that as a student in your class, I saw how you, in reading the text, not only illuminated it but also gave insight into some vital question of life and reality. I did, however, find one problem in your classes: the tremendous gap between your own level in learning and that of your students, including myself. When you read a sentence from any text, you seem to have simultaneously in mind all *Tanach Mishnah Gemara* and appear ready and able to find worlds of meaning in it.

Rabbi Schweiger: I believe it relates to what I previously called having a "breadth of knowledge." There is no shortcut to this. It can come only through sitting and going through a great deal of material. Then, when students analyze any text, they will be able to plug into whole worlds of information.

One reason I encourage students who come for one year to continue is that only by the second year do they have "tools" that enable them to really go through the material. I believe that a person, no matter how original and creative, will always be limited if he does not have a broad background.

I should also say that relative to my students, it may seem that I have a great breadth of knowledge. But I myself feel I have a long way to go.

S. F.:   In learning *Mishnah,* the tractate *Kiddushin,* with you, I had the sense you were making interpretations that had not been done before. Is this right?

Rabbi Schweiger: I and a number of other people have developed a methodology in studying Mishnah that is, I believe, unique. And work has been done on ten or twelve tractates, but that's just a fraction of the whole *Shas.*

S. F.:   What is the basic principle of this method?

Rabbi Schweiger: Traditional commentaries work *mishnah* by *mishnah.* Our concept involves looking at each *perek,* or chapter, as an integrated unit. We do use the traditional commentaries but also try to make new connections and ideas that relate to *perek* as a whole.

S. F.:   Could you say something about the general effect that studying at Pardes has had on students?

Rabbi Schweiger: The overwhelming majority of students have a better appreciation of the religious literature, the text. But the degree to which they make the text a part of their lives really depends on what happens to them after Pardes. Those who stay in Israel find ways of continuing to study. I think a major problem with Pardes is that it addresses the need of individuals and allows them to develop at their own pace. But what ends up happening is that people feel a tremendous need to become part of a community, and yet Pardes has not prepared them for this. People have come a long way as individuals, but because they do not fit into any framework, they feel themselves misfits. The traditional Reform or Conservative framework is not serious enough in terms of its involvement with the text. Pardes does, I think, a good job of preparing students' individual development, but it does not prepare their communal development.

S. F.:   The numbers are not large enough for Pardes to form a congregation, a community of their own.

Rabbi Schweiger: At various times we have spoken of the idea, but it is a tricky business, even within Pardes itself. I have spoken of extracurricular activities, in which education is not only a classroom matter but also has to do with all kinds of life experiences. I have introduced *tefillot* into Pardes, and it has been a standardized form of prayer, which is basically Orthodox. If it's *Shabbat*, there's a way we do *Shabbat*. And many students did not want this. Whereas in previous years students suspended their belief, this year they did not.

S. F.:   Is it the question of the woman's role in prayer that is problematic?

Rabbi Schweiger: The question of the woman's role in Judaism becomes the basic dividing point. The idea of having women on the other side of the *mechitzah*, not actively participating in the service, is unacceptable to many people. So it appears that the only kind of community Pardes can be is a (quote) learning community (unquote). There are quite a few people who are attracted to what you might call traditional Orthodox Judaism and yet have a difficulty emotionally and intellectually with the question of the woman's role in Judaism. They would like to be part of the community and yet cannot, because of the woman's issue.

S. F.:   You, in work, are in a sense bringing assimilated Jews back to the Jewish tradition. You also have indicated that those students who make *aliyah* tend to remain connected with "traditional learning," while those outside Israel drift away. Is *aliyah* the answer to the assimilation problem?

Rabbi Schweiger: I certainly believe all the Jewish people should be in Israel and that *aliyah* should be high on the agenda. On the other hand, if I am assuming there will not be extreme anti-Semitism in America that forces people to Israel, then there will remain a large community there. What I have found in recent years is that we are getting students who just do not know anything, and my impression is that this is a reflection of the general American community. In general, I think the educational level of the bulk of the population is minimal. So again, I would like to see a more intensive effort. I would like to see people staying a second or third year. I would like to see Pardes set up a kind of teacher's training institute that would go to the States and would help make Judaism give content to people's lives. Money has to be put not into razzle-dazzle but into sustained educational programs. I would like to see Pardes reach a wide spectrum in American Jewry and broaden and raise their Jewish consciousness in such a way it will lead many to come to Israel.

S. F.:   This brings me to ask you about the way you perceive your whole effort and lifework in Jewish education. Do you understand your work as service of God?

Rabbi Schweiger: I do relate what I do to the idea of service of God. I would say in a simple and brief fashion that service of God has to do for me with the idea of subordinating myself to some Higher Authority – to some higher purpose and its realization – and this instead of focusing on what might be called my own self-fulfillment. The idea is that I exist to contribute to something much larger than myself. It has to do first of all with my service of God, and also with the idea of service to the Jewish people. And perhaps what I focus on in teaching is giving people the idea that the world does not revolve around them solely. This even touches upon the relation to the woman's role in Judaism. Many people who come from Western society see that the emphasis is always placed on the individual, on what you might call individual rights. I think the whole thrust of Judaism is to accentuate the concept of responsibility, how the individual is responsible to a much larger unit, whether it be God or the Jewish people. And this becomes perhaps the most difficult point with which people must deal at Pardes. How do I somehow strike the balance between myself as individual and myself as part of some higher entity? Is the bottom line my individuality, or is it that I am part of a much larger reality and that I have to subordinate myself to the larger whole?

S. F.:   And doesn't this also suggest that the problem of dealing with assimilation is the problem of returning people to a sense of greater responsibility to family, community, people, God?

Rabbi Schweiger: Absolutely. I think that the person who starts out with the idea of the individual as the absolute end of all naturally feels that he or she should be able to marry someone whether the partner is Jewish or not. I think here the only argument against this is to tell the individual that he is part of a larger community – the Jewish people – and he has responsibility to this. And I will add that this has also to do with the question of ethnicity. It's not to one part of the Jewish people who happen to come from or exist in a given area, with certain folkways. Our responsibility is to the totality of Jewish history.

S. F.:   So the education you are providing is not in knowledge alone but also in fundamental values?

Rabbi Schweiger: That's basic to Jewish education. The aim is to study the texts in order to get those values. And as I said before, I think it is difficult because having those values of subordinating my individual will to a Higher Authority is placing "limitations" on people's lives. And people today do not want to limit themselves. I mention this because it's paradoxical that people on one hand want to become part of a community, and on the other, fear subscribing to certain norms of behavior that are necessary for forming any community. But without the community, people feel they are in a vacuum.

S. F.:   In the context of the Jewish people forming a community that is responsible to God, do you understand our ideal role as serving as a light to the nations?

Rabbi Schweiger: The Jewish people have an opportunity to become a light to the nations, primarily in terms of what happens in the Jewish state. I have arguments with lots of people who say Jews need to stay in Diaspora, where they are a light to the nations. My idea is fundamentally that the light unto nations relates to the action of people as a whole, and not exceptional individuals here and there. When you have a people, you encompass every facet of existence. And so, when you have a state, it should, in its manifestations, reflect Jewish values, whether in terms of its educational system, social policy, business, or commerce. In every different aspect of the state's existence, our national values are reflected. To me that really means to be the model for the world at large. And this relates to why I advocate *aliyah*. I do not do this on the grounds of individual fulfillment but rather because I think this is the responsibility of every Jew to come and help create the ideal Jewish nation, which can be a light to the nations.

S. F.:   Isn't there a contradiction now between the ideal and real within Israeli society itself, with more and more people stressing individual entitlement? Do you see the possibility that we might lose the first opportunity that we have had in two thousand years?

Rabbi Schweiger: I think that on the theological level, we have to eventually reach the ideal. As to whether the present State of Israel will realize the ideal, I do not know. I think that we have been given an opportunity for the first time in two thousand years, and we, in many ways, are botching it up. I wouldn't take it for granted. I see that we could lose this and might ultimately have to return another time. There is no way that we can ever totally lose it. We will always have to come back. I think that we are in a situation where we have been given the opportunity, and we have, in some ways, let things go in the reverse direction. I believe when I first came here there was more a sense of idealism, and that now there is more of a desire to capitalize on the pleasure of the moment. I believe we must come back to traditional Jewish values and not just religious values.

S. F.:   When you think of the ideal state, is it the one in which all Jews live by the Torah? Is this the ideal we should be aiming at? Or is it perhaps something less difficult, in accordance with Franz Rosensweig's ideal that each should live to the degree of observance he can manage now? I could not put on *tefillin* yesterday; perhaps I will be able to tomorrow?

Rabbi Schweiger: I certainly believe that everyone should live by the Torah. But it's clear that if you are going to create an ideal society, there has to be something in common that all share, that unites us. The one thing we can share that can unite us is the Torah. On the other hand, it's clear to me that we are very far from the ideal, and I don't envision that ideal being realized in my lifetime. But I certainly can see there is a process that is set in motion that can begin to create what I would call the common language to begin to work toward that ideal. I have said before, this has a lot to do with education. If you can create a framework where people see that Torah, that Jewish texts, are something they must relate to, even if interpreted in different ways, then at least we can have a basis for creating a common language. And this can bring us together as Jews. I doubt that ethnicity – bagels and lox Judaism – can do this.

Rabbi Chaim Brovender

Rabbi Chaim Brovender is one of the American pioneers in the upsurge of Torah teaching that occurred in Israel after the Six Day War. He is today, with Rabbi Shlomo Riskin, codirector of the Ohr HaTorah network of institutions and *Midreshet Lindenblum*. Among his many activities is the teaching of Torah in the former Soviet Union. Rabbi Brovender, in the choice between the academic career on which he was originally set and the teaching of Torah, chose what he regarded as the more satisfactory and intense way of educating, the teaching of Torah.

Though I had heard many people speak of Rabbi Brovender's teaching, my first real opportunity to hear him came in a public lecture he gave in the Israel Center on Strans Street, Jerusalem, in which he spoke about the meaning of Redemption in our time. In our interview he speaks primarily about his conception of Jewish education. In being asked about the Jewish people's situation today, he makes clear his belief that assimilation has gone beyond reversal point in the Diaspora and that the real hope for the Jewish future is in Israel. I found Rabbi Brovender challenging and independent in thought. I spoke with him at his home, from which there is a magnificent view of the new district of Ramot and the surrounding hills of Jerusalem. The combination of the new districts being built and the ancient, terraced hillsides seems to give concrete and pictur-esque meaning to the process of Redemption that Rabbi Brovender is so involved in helping to realize.

S. F.:   How do you understand your way of work in teaching?

Rabbi Brovender: I believe that I am giving students the means through which to integrate Torah learning in their lives. One component of this is providing them with the required "information." Fortunately, the Jews are blessed with a great deal of things we have to know about in order to understand and live Jewish lives. And this connects with what I have always felt to be the most important component in teaching, the integration of Torah learning to a Jewish life-style or plan for living. In order to make this integration, the individual not only must have competence in learning but also must know how to enjoy this learning and to apply it in his life.

S. F.:   And where are you teaching presently?

Rabbi Brovender: I teach in Yeshivat Hamivtar, which at present has a mixture of students of varying backgrounds and levels of learning. This *yeshivah* originally began as primarily for "*Chozrim B'Teshuvah*" students, but today it is more oriented to those with richer backgrounds in Torah. I also teach women, again of various backgrounds in learning, at an institution called "Midreshet Lindenblum," which when founded was called "Bruria."

S. F.:   There has been a tremendous growth in women's learning of Torah in Yerushalayim. How would you compare the "levels" of learning between the men and the women you teach?

Rabbi Brovender: Peer pressure and community pressure direct men to make tremendous time investments in Torah studies, to become "*bekiyim*" as halachic experts. Generally, no such interest or pressure is involved in women's learning. However, the experience of integrating Talmud Torah into one's life as a creative aspect of one's Jewish commitment is required of both men and women alike. Women even have a certain advantage in this in that they are not compelled to spend so much of their time in a framework where all learning is Gemara-based. But fundamentally, I have no reason to think there is any difference between the capacity of men and the capacity of women to study Torah.

S. F.:   Could you say something about the programs of studies at the various institutions in which you teach?

Rabbi Brovender: Yeshivat Hamivtar as *yeshivah* places its emphasis on learning Gemara, though the program includes Torah, *Chumash,* "*Mipharshim,*" and Jewish Thought. In general, I think more in terms of the teachers than the curriculum. It is important for teachers to teach things they like to teach and to learn themselves. There are subjects such as Rav Kook's Philosophy, or the *Tanya.* What is important is that the students feel they are studying with a teacher who is not simply going by rote over material but really learning himself.

S. F.:   So you yourself do not simply repeat the same courses year after year?

Rabbi Brovender: No, I may repeat, but I try to teach new material with this. I above all try to teach that which I am interested in. For many years, I taught the Ramban's *Commentary on the Chumash.* This year, I taught the *Kuzari,* which I hadn't taught for many years. Again, this is different from something like a high school curriculum, where you are compelled by an external source to finish certain requirements. Here, what is important is creating a deep, personal involvement and commitment on the part of the students, both to the learning process and to Jewish life.

S. F.:   Could you tell me about your own background and how you came to teach in Israel?

Rabbi Brovender: I studied in Yeshiva University before coming to Israel. My and my wife's involvement in B'nei Akiva is what led us to come. As soon as my studies were over, I did what just seemed the reasonable thing to do, came to Israel on *aliyah*. I studied in the Itri Kollel. I studied at the university, where I did a doctorate in Semitic Linguistics. Though I taught at the university for a while, once I became involved in Torah teaching, it was far more compelling to me. I had always been interested in a university career, and when I was young, I thought that would be a reasonable option. I always liked to study and was interested in knowing from a wide variety of areas. But the pleasure from teaching Torah was overwhelmingly more great than that from teaching at the university. Also, the contact with students at the university is not so intensive and ongoing as at Yeshiva. I had never planned it this way, but the teaching of Torah became the center of my life.

S. F.:   I know you have had many excellent students who have also become teachers.

Rabbi Brovender: There was a time when all the teachers of Yeshivat Hamivtar and Bruria were students of mine. It was a very remarkable *zecus* (privilege) to have students of mine teaching at these institutions. Today, things are more spread out, bigger. But that experience of having a faculty that consisted exclusively of people I had taught was a special and unique one. We were almost the same age, young, working together, good friends, building together. This was a very good and romantic period of my life. Today, the institutions, including Ohr HaTorah, where I am associated with Rabbi Shlomo Riskin, are so much larger that it is impossible to rely for faculty only upon those who have come up from the ranks.

S. F.:   Your work in teaching Torah in Yerushalayim comes at a time when most students of Jewish life feel that there is accelerating assimilation of the Jewish people in the Diaspora. Do you have any suggestions for what can be done about this?

Rabbi Brovender: There is a sense in which nothing can be done. The Jewish people have created for themselves a situation that is devastating. In order to be an Orthodox Jew, it is not enough to pay lip service to Judaism. It is necessary to be willing to take upon yourself the rigors of years of study and the association with an exclusive faith community. The *baal teshuvah,* however admirable individually, are, taken together statistically, a drop in the bucket. Historically, it's of no great relevance. I am not judging by the souls, the *neshamot* who are being saved. It's of endless value: and anyone who can make contact with another Jew and attach him to Torah is doing something deeper than the sea. What might, however, turn the tide for the community as a whole is that the Torah Jews have larger families and send their children to religious schools at an earlier age. I don't see any other way. Israel is the only hope for the Jews in the modern world. Jewish values do not hold water in America. Orthodox Jews know that their children are not satisfied being Orthodox and modern in America. In America, you are forced to be like everyone else. In Israel, your Jewishness is assured. However, what is so difficult about Israel relates to the spirit of the Jewish Tradition. It is painful that people of Jewish background know so little about Torah and *mitzvot* and yet claim to be Jews. Many of these people lead us in battle; are vital to the society economically, materially, make a real contribution to Jewish life in this way. In America, someone who makes a great contribution to the society at large, even if he is of Jewish origin, would not, I think, today be necessarily thought of as being a "great Jew." To be a great Jew today in the Diaspora, you have to have great Jewish knowledge, have to be connected with Jewish values and society. Another difference is that in Israel, we still have time. The next generation of Jews in Israel will still be Jews. This will give people who are interested the time to develop new methodologies for Jewish learning that we do not have today. It will give us time to try and reach those not committed to *mitzvot.* In America, the Jewish community is going toward a polarization in which the middle is disappearing.

S. F: And you do not give any hope to university programs of Jewish Studies, which have grown so significantly in the past twenty years?

Rabbi Brovender: Jewish Studies in the university might provide a fitting obituary to Jewish life in America. It's "Wissenschaft des Judentums," and as Zunz said, "You'd be giving a decent burial to the Jewish Tradition." You wouldn't say that every university department of American Indian studies is helping their revival. In the life of a community, academic interest is not a major element. What you have in the Diaspora in the United States is a large community of people who want nominally to be Jewish but are not willing to commit themselves to a Jewish way of life. A person who is not religious in America but somehow still feels he is Jewish has a choice. He can watch his children intermarry or he can move with them to Israel. The *Baal Teshuvah* movement is not going to save his children, and the chance that his children will, on their own, find meaningful Judaism in the midst of existing and nonexisting Judaism is a difficult gamble to make.

S. F: Is there within Israel a faith community that you believe has the right path for the entire Jewish people? Do you favor a pluralism of observance or one predominant faith community in Israel?

Rabbi Brovender: I find myself comfortable and associate with one specific community, but the truth of *am Yisrael* is always going to be a pluralistic one. Communities will present different aspects of the truth. However, when I speak of "pluralism," I am talking about those who can pray at the same *minyan*. I am talking of Satmar and the followers of Rav Schach or of Rabbi Lichtenstein. I don't see any reason to overcome this sort of necessary and positive pluralism. There are those who understand their primary responsibility in terms of *chesed,* going into the army being part of the overall fabric of Israeli society. However, I don't consider that Jews who cannot *davven Minchah* together are part of the solution. I rather understand them as part of the reality that has to be dealt with.

S. F.: I am not sure I agree with the idea that the differences between Jewish communities that pray together are so small. Between those who see the State of Israel as the first light of redemption and those who have no sense of obligation to its defense, there is a long way.

Rabbi Brovender: I don't think that's true. Faith communities in the modern world have difficulty in expressing their own particular kinds of faith. All the communities we have been talking about have a high-profile relationship to God but choose various ways of expressing this. One community might choose to emphasize "Talmud Torah" and another, "*Eretz Yisrael*," but no community would say that either of these is not part of the Covenant. For reasons that may not necessarily be profound, such as the language you speak at home or the land you made *aliyah* from, you choose a particular form of commitment. But when you look around Israel, you do see Jews from various communities living together, not expelling each other. They have arguments and fights from time to time, often over trivial things. Actually, the ability I have to put up with my brother's lack of consideration of me is much less than for a guest who comes for a couple of days. I expect more from my brother. He's got to be compassionate and understanding. And when the chips are down, there's no doubt to me and my brother that we are in the same boat, that we at critical points are involved in the same enterprise. While one community may well have a well-developed vocabulary about the State of Israel, another may lack this. Yet both communities are involved with each other, want to build their families and community life. And the religious as a whole do not leave Israel. You can argue all you want about whether or not to say "*Tachanun*" on Israel Independence Day, but it becomes trivial when set against the historic fact that so many Jews have returned to the Land of Israel. It is trivial when considered against the situation where you have chosen to live your life in the Land of Israel.

S. F.:   So you understand that all these different religious communities are working, within their own way, to contribute to the process of Jewish history, which many of us see as a process of Return as Redemption. But how, precisely, do you understand this redemption? Does it, for instance, involve the rebuilding of the *Beit Hamikdash?*

Rabbi Brovender: There is a theoretical redemption that will be in the end of days. Religious Jews do not doubt the rebuilding of the Temple and the service (*Avodah*) therein. This part of redemption occurs at the end of days. There are different opinions about the character of theoretical redemption. But these are not so much our concern today. We are today living redemption. It is not as if we were in seventeenth-century Poland and the Redemption was merely a dream. Then we could worry primarily about whether it will be Mosheach Ben Yosef or Mosheach Ben David. At that time, a few might gather together and go to live in abject poverty in *Eretz Yisrael.* But by their action, they would not convince anyone they were living in a redemptive period. What we are doing now, in this period of history, is living Redemption. We have lived it so much in the past forty years that we tend to overlook it. It may sound like preaching, but it's true. We have now an *aliyah* from all over the world, even from Russia, which we, for many years, thought was completely lost. The fact that Israel is slowly coming to be the largest Jewish community in the world, the power that Israel represents in the Middle East, also is part of this historical process. This does not mean that this is guaranteed or that we are free of threats of destruction. It doesn't mean I believe we should be foolhardy about our power. It is just that when one places this in the perspective of what the Jews have suffered through the generations, there is something remarkable in the transformation.

S. F.:   I see you connect the specific events of Israel's modern history with the divine redemptive process.

Rabbi Brovender: There's a kind of remarkable process taking place, which we can understand if we look back at our dreams of one hundred, or sixty, or four years ago. The establishment of the State of Israel is a remarkable turning point in this process. Lending a hand to the redemptive process is, I think, the critical issue of our time. The question of what the Redemption will look like at the end of time concerns us less. We know this does not mean it's all going to work out smoothly and easily just as we want it to. We can mess up, and as I have said, there are no guarantees in history. We are looking now at a process of redemption to which we ourselves need to be very sensitive. We should ignore it simply because there are so many signs of it. We, as those who live by *mitzvot*, have to be sensitive to the fact that we are involved in a process that is redemptive by its very nature. And that today things are happening that no one could ever have imagined.

S. F.:   And you understand that this redemptive Jewish process will lead toward teaching all the world the word of *Hashem:* "From Zion will go forth the Torah."

Rabbi Brovender: First you need Tzion. The Jews have to become a faith community, and this when today, 80 percent of the Jews are nonobservant. So our task is for the 20 percent to lead others to turn again into being a community of *mitzvah* doers. However, if someone has a particular ability and there's a need to present Jewish points of view to non-Jews, they can do it.

S. F.:   You don't think it's a first priority to reach these other peoples?

Rabbi Brovender: The Rambam said that the Messianic Era will be made possible through Christianity, and Islam, that they are teaching the belief in the validity of the Old Testament. The Rambam said that while we are studying Torah, Christianity and Islam are teaching hundreds of millions Torah values. The education of just one Jew is a massive undertaking, especially when everyone wants his child to be a *talmid chacham*. If we are engaged in this remarkable goal of educating Jews, we cannot also be expected to educate the world.

S. F.:   But there is another problem for the Jew in learning, the division between Torah studies and all other forms of learning. Do you have your own particular rule as to how to divide the time?

Rabbi Brovender: This is a difficult subject, which would require another long conversation in itself. When I was growing up, there was the assumption that in order to be good at what you were doing, for instance, in medical research, you had to be totally dedicated to it. I know the stories we read about people who come up with new ideas concern those who are totally involved in their own fields. So if you are trying to think of a curriculum for a universally learned personality, I am not sure I would know what that means. I think what education does, or should do, is to open up a variety of doors and enable students to make good decisions. I think that sometimes what is called *"Yeshivat Tichon"* education involves so much time, so many slots in learning, that it prevents the student from doing that. My feeling is that education should somehow be something that opens doors and even allows the student to close doors for himself if that's what he wants.

S. F.:   So general nonreligious studies is not something the Jewish people should be afraid of?

Rabbi Brovender: I am not talking about being afraid. If I said to somebody, "Don't go to the university," it would not only be because I thought as an individual he did not have the character to deal with nonreligious society. But this would not be because of fear of university classes.

S. F.: To go back for a moment to another aspect of the relation between Jewish and non-Jewish worlds. Do you have a sense of what Israel as a modern state should be giving the world?

Rabbi Brovender: The State of Israel is engaged in fighting for its existence. Our problem is that we do not have the leeway for ideology. One reason peace is important is that it enables you to develop different energies. A beleagured state has little to offer. But as a history, as a tradition, as a collection of ideas that kept us together, we have a tremendous amount to offer. But so long as our own existence is our first concern, we will have difficulty transmitting this to others.

S. F.: Some have said that for years, Israel in its stand against terrorism and violence, in maintaining morality while struggling to stay alive, did set an example for the world to follow.

Rabbi Brovender: I am not sure that's true. Surely there are Jews who are special people and who have acted humanely. But whether we as a state are different from others? I imagine that we have acted in various ways at various times.

S. F.: I believe in comparison to any other people who are fighting for their lives constantly, provoked, attacked, that Israel has shown a higher standard in moral behavior.

Rabbi Brovender: I drive by Dehaishe three or four times every day. They put up a kind of corrugated fence. No one can look out, or in. Is it as bad as Sarajevo? What is exemplary about states of war? If you are in a state of war and subjugating a population, it really does not make it possible to be a "light to the nations."

S. F.: So you believe a peace process of some kind is an absolute necessity?

Rabbi Brovender: It's critical for us to get back expressing ourselves in the way we have always thought of ourselves. Again, the war is not something we wanted. The enemy is responsible. I am not living in a fairyland kind of situation. We are more civilized than other people at war. But I don't think we are doing anything we have to be ashamed about. I think the security forces and army are doing the right thing. I don't find fault in that. But your question was, "Is there a message for others in our action?" I don't think there is a message.

Rabbi David Golinkin

Rabbi David Golinkin is presently chairman of the Vaad Halacha of the *Masorti* movement in Israel and serves as dean of the Seminary of Judaic Studies. He also writes a column for *Moment* magazine in which he gives halachic rulings on contemporary moral and ethical issues.

I met with Rabbi Golinkin in his study at the *Beit Midrash*. An intense and thorough response to every question was what I expected of Rabbi Golinkin, and I was not disappointed. In our interview he describes his present work activities and defines his own approach to the writing of responsa. His emphasis is on serving the Jewish people, and he finds fault with those who live in learning alone without making any real contribution in the world. For him, teaching is a means to "doing," and the main thing is not the Midrash but the "*Maaseh.*" This interview was conducted in the summer of 1992.

S. F.:   Could you describe your present work activities?

Rabbi Golinkin: I am dean of the *Beit Midrash*, the Seminary of Judaic Studies, which means that I supervise all the academic programs, including the rabbinical school program, the educational program, the program for Russian *olim*, the M.A. programs, and the programs for rabbinical students from North and South America. In addition, I teach a number of courses every year. One is a year-long course in Practical *Halachah,* which consists of a survey of the *Shulchan Aruch,* mostly *Orach Chaim* and *Yoreh De'ah.* A second course I will teach is a course called "Polemics in the Responsa Literature," in which I take specific issues and compare the responsa of Conservative, Orthodox, and Reform rabbis. A third course I teach is "Modern Approaches to the Study of Talmud," which is a survey of various modern critical approaches to the study of the Talmud. In addition, I devote a lot of time to serving on the *Halachah* Committee of the *Masorti* movement. I have served on this committee since it was founded, and I am now its chairman. This summer I edited the fourth volume of our *Teshuvot.* I also have a column in *Moment* magazine, which appears a few times a year in which I answer readers' questions on halachic concerns. These are usually ethical questions because the editors of *Moment* are more interested in ethical than ritual issues. One column was on whether Jewish law requires us to tell the truth to a person with a terminal diagnosis. Another column was called "Should You Give *tzedekah* to Everyone Who Asks for It?"

S. F.:   Could you tell me something about your background and education?

Rabbi Golinkin: I was born and raised in Washington, D.C., where I went to a very good Orthodox day school called the Hebrew Academy of Washington. To this day, I am very thankful for the fact that my parents sent me in spite of the considerable cost and the tremendous inconvenience, as we lived in Arlington, Virginia. I don't study Torah with Rashi now on a regular basis, but I still know Torah with Rashi from having studied it there for so many years. Shortly after graduating from the Hebrew Academy, we moved to Knoxville, Tennessee, and I went to public school there for a year. I also studied on the side with my father, who is a Conservative rabbi, and with an Israeli who taught me Hebrew literature. But I wasn't satisfied with the Jewish education I was getting there, so my parents and I decided I would spend the following year at a day school. We chose the Akiba Hebrew Academy in Philadelphia, a nondenominational day school of excellent quality, which I enjoyed a lot. And then, when I graduated from high school, I came to Israel for a year and studied at Beit Midrash L'Torah, which is a modern Orthodox *yeshivah* run by the Jewish Agency. There I studied Talmud intensively every day for about sixteen or eighteen hours a day, and that is where I truly learned how to study Talmud. After that, I was scheduled to go back to the States but wanted to stay in Israel, so I did my B.A. in Jewish History at Hebrew University. My specialty was Medieval Jewish History, though I studied all periods of Jewish history. When I finished Hebrew University, I began rabbinical school at the Jewish Theological Seminary (JTS) in New York, and after spending the required year there, did two years here at Neve Schecter. I returned then to New York for a fourth year, and at the same time began my Ph.D. in Talmud. I stayed there two more years because there was a residency requirement. Then we officially made *aliyah* in 1982, and I began to teach at Neve Schechter and, later on, at the *Beit Midrash* – eventually finishing my Ph.D.

S. F.:   One of your principal activities as chairman of the *Halachah* Committee is making rulings that, in effect, decide what is *Halachah* for the *Masorti* community in Israel. This committee, you said before, was founded in 1985. How did they deal with responsa before that time?

Rabbi Golinkin: Before then, if there was a question in Israel it might be sent to the Law Committee in New York. But basically, each rabbi decided issues on his own, a situation that led us to understand that we needed a committee that would respond to the problems and questions specifically related to life in Israel. I volunteered immediately without understanding that in time, it would become a major interest in my life. In the beginning, Rabbi Theodore Friedman was the chairman of the committee, with Rabbi Reuven Hammer and myself as the other two members. Eventually, we added four more members because we felt the volume of questions required this.

S. F.:   What happens when there is a contradiction between a ruling you make and one made by the committee in America?

Rabbi Golinkin: We are considered the halachic authority for the *Masorti* movement in Israel. We never raised the question of deciding *Halachah* for the Jews of North America because there is a Law Committee there that has been in existence since 1917. A number of people on the Law Committee there opposed the creation of the committee here because they view themselves as the authority for the entire Conservative movement. We have explained to them that the conditions are totally different here than in North America, sociologically and otherwise. Furthermore, there is the Zionist aspect of the matter. The Jews of Israel should not be dependent on the Jews of the Diaspora for halachic decisions.

S. F.:   Do you feel the halachic rulings you make here have any influence on the larger Jewish community here, which is overwhelmingly Orthodox? And what kind of effect do your rulings have on your own *Masorti* people when the great majority of them do not live strictly by *Halachah?*

Rabbi Golinkin: As far as the impact outside the Conservative movement, I would imagine the impact is very little. Obviously, the members of the movement here get them, as do Conservative rabbis both in Israel and without; also major libraries get them. But the chances of an Orthodox rabbi owning a copy are rather slim. There are certain Orthodox rabbis to whom I sent the *teshuvot* to because I want them to have them. Professor Daniel Sperber, who wrote a two-volume work on *Jewish Customs* has a chapter on *kitniyot* (legumes) on Pesach in which he quotes my *teshuvah* on the subject. To what extent other Orthodox rabbis might be influenced, I have no idea. Each time a volume of responsa appears, we send it to the newspapers in Israel. The secular newspapers are not interested in anything of a Jewish nature, and the Haredi newspapers are only interested in attacking us. The *Jerusalem Post* reviewed the *teshuvot* because the *Jerusalem Post* is interested in Judaism. So, unfortunately, the effect on the Orthodox has been minimal for both technical and polemical reasons.

As for the influence on the *Masorti* movement, I get feedback from time to time. Kibbutz Hanaton follows our *teshuvah* on *shemitah*. I know many people have been bothered by the issue of Tishah B'Av, whether to fast a half day or a whole day, who found my responsum convincing and now fast the whole day. Many people have told me they changed their minds after they read our *teshuvah* allowing women to have *aliyot*. I also wrote a *teshuvah* proving that women may recite the Mourner's *kaddish*. Many women have thanked me for that. On many *teshuvot* we have gotten a lot of reactions. To what extent the rank and file have read the *teshuvot*, I do not know.

S. F.:   Do you conceive the work you do as service of God? How do you understand the concept of service of God?

Rabbi Golinkin: That is a very difficult question. First of all, I conceive of my work as service of the Jewish people. In other words, I think the main reason I spend most of my time now writing about *Halachah*, and not Talmud, is that I feel *Halachah* is much more relevant to Jews living today. I love studying Talmud. It's a lot of fun. But a person can study Talmud for twenty years and still not know how to live a Jewish life. I know many people who have studied Talmud for many years, who when asked a question in practical *Halachah* do not know the answer. I feel that's one of the big mistakes in *yeshivot*, that there is this incredible overemphasis on Talmud at the expense of everything else. You have *yeshivah* students who, after years of studying Talmud, do not have basic answers in *Halachah*.

S. F.:   I am surprised you say that, because I often sit with religious laymen between *Minhah* and *Maariv* for a *shiur* in *Mishnah Berurah*. And they know their *Halachah*.

Rabbi Golinkin: At *yeshivah* there is little emphasis on *Mishnah Berurah*. It is something you do on your own time. This is inherited from Lithuanian *yeshivot,* where you could study the Babylonian Talmud for years, to the exclusion of all else. My belief is, then, that in writing *teshuvot* both for the *Halachah* Committee and for *Moment* magazine, where I reach a wide audience who know nothing about *Halachah,* I do a service to the Jewish people. Second, to be challenged by the halachic sources and see that they are relevant to the questions of the day is also a service to the Jewish people. People think Halachah is irrelevant and outdated. The fact is that most so-called modern questions have been dealt with one way or another in our sources. Last year I wrote a *teshuvah* during the Gulf War about whether we could read the *Megillah* early since it was dangerous to go out at night. Rabbi Ovadia Yosef was asked the same question in 1944, when the British imposed a curfew on Jerusalem. Whoever was caught outside then might be shot, so the ruling was that the *Megillah* could be read early. So there are very few questions that have not been dealt with.

In addition, reading a *teshuvah* brings the person into contact with the Talmud, with *Halachah,* with Jewish history, and really gets the person involved in Judaism. It's not something theoretical or static but practical and very much alive. So I feel, first of all, that writing *teshuvot* is serving the Jewish people. Is it a way of serving God? I don't presume to speak for God. In any case, most of our halachic tradition is not from God but from human beings. All of the responsa and hundreds of codes that have been written during the past two thousand years–few claim that they are divine in origin.

S. F.:   But isn't there a point where you have to decide that there is something divine in origin, lest you be left with the claim that all is only human invention? For the Orthodox, both Written and Oral Law are Torah, the words of God.

Rabbi Golinkin: I think from the point of view of authority, the Torah has the most authority and should least be tampered with. Something from the Babylonian Talmud is next in authority, and that is certainly the basic document of Jewish Law. But once you pass the Babylonian Talmud, I think you have a tremendous amount of leeway. Just because the Rambam said something does not mean it is authoritative. Frequently, you have halachic authorities who disagree with him. I'll give you an example. In a *teshuvah* that I recently wrote about women rabbis, I have a chapter on women and the study of Torah. The Rambam takes a very strict position, following Rabbi Eliezer, who says it is forbidden for women to learn Torah. Most modern Orthodox authorities take the Rambam and try to find loopholes. Rabbi Eliezer says, "He who teaches his daughter Torah, it is as if he had taught her frivolity or lechery." Some Orthodox rabbis claim the restriction is only on teaching your own daughter and that you can teach other people's children, or that it meant only the Oral Law and not the Written. But Rabbi Eliezer and Rambam are not the only positions on the subject. In the Mishnah, Rabbi Eliezer is arguing with Ben Azai, who ruled that a man is obligated to teach his daughter Torah. I said, there's an alternative position: that of Ben Azai. In light of the fact that women today receive a thorough secular education, it would be absurd for them not to receive a thorough Jewish education. So many times when I write *teshuvot* I skip over the medieval authorities and go back to the Talmud, which is ultimately the major source of *Halachah*. I see what the primary sources have to say on the subject and do not necessarily follow all the later commentaries. So certainly in our *teshuvot* we give more weight to the Talmud and Tannach than to the later authorities. And again, when dealing with authorities, we give more weight to the *Rishonim* then to the *Achronim*, which is the opposite of what the Orthodox do. Thus, for example, there is a *teshuvah* on eating legumes on Pesach. There are dozens of *Rishonim* who deal with the subject and say it's perfectly permissible to eat *kitniyot* on Pesach. On the other hand, those who forbid *kitniyot* do not know exactly why it's forbidden and suggest different reasons. So, by going further back in Jewish history in the halachic process, you have much more flexibility to deal with issues in a more sensible fashion.

S. F: In my own way of thought, I suppose I would want to say that work that serves the Jewish people serves God. But I would like to know something of your own inner feeling about this.

Rabbi Golinkin: I think the way the Jewish people serve God is by doing. In other words, studying *The Guide to the Perplexed,* however fascinating and interesting it is, is not in my judgment the true service of God. To me, service of God is performing *mitzvot.* I believe the way you feel God's presence is by performing the *mitzvot,* making *kiddush* on Friday night, putting on *tefillin,* giving *tzedekah.* Last night, I was at a wedding of one of the students of our *Beit Midrash,* and we were dancing and singing. There was religious joy in everyone's face. To me, that's serving God. There was a sense of the joy of performing a *mitzvah.* That's why writing *teshuvot* is important. You are teaching people how to live as Jews, and by living as Jews, they come closer to God, to Jewish Tradition, to the Jewish people and spirituality. But I don't believe spirituality is something you can teach people. You can teach people how to do, and then they, by doing, reach a level of spirituality.

S. F: Thank you very much, Rabbi Golinkin. I would like to shift emphasis a bit and ask you a question about the communal problems of the Jewish people. I know your work is primarily in Israel, but nonetheless I know, too, your connection with, and concern for, the Jewish people everywhere. Can you briefly give your views on the assimilation problem and what you feel might be done in response?

Rabbi Golinkin: There is rampant assimilation in the United States. And it is no surprise when you consider that America is one of the freest and most assimilationist societies where Jews have ever lived. I do not know what the intermarriage rate was in the Golden Age in Spain, but the influence of Spanish culture on Jews was very great. Any book on the history of Spanish Jews will show parallels to what's happening today. And the rabbis complained about the same things they complain about now. So what's happening now is not without precedent, though it is perhaps more extreme. The only answer is Jewish day schools, more education. The part-time solution of Hebrew schools, for four hours a week, has been a failure. To what can this be compared? In the 1970s, I worked with deprived children in the Shmuel Hanavi neighborhood. I worked four or six hours a week, hoping to transform their lives. There was no way I could undo in a few hours what was done in their homes for the rest of the week. The same is true with Hebrew school. I taught Hebrew school in the United States. Half the time they did not come because they had a piano or tennis lesson. There's no way that a child can come out with a strong Jewish identity in such a system.

To me, the major emphasis in Jewish education in America should be on the day schools. The percentages are still low, but they have grown greatly in the past twenty years. The other major emphasis should be on Adult Education, which has a lot of people involved in it now. I know that Yitz Greenberg of the National Jewish Center for Learning and Leadership (CLAL) has a whole network of Adult Education. The Melton School also has one. My father, Rabbi Noah Golinkin, has been teaching adults in the United States how to read Hebrew for the past fifteen years, with tremendous results. He initiated the Hebrew Literacy Campaign of the National Federation of Jewish Men's Clubs. Now he has a program called "While Standing on One Foot," which is being used throughout the United States in which adults learn how to read the *siddur* in one day. According to an article in the *Encyclopaedia Judaica Yearbook* last year, one hundred thousand adults learned to read Hebrew using my father's books. I think that because we have an entire generation of American Jews who did not receive any Jewish education, we have to simultaneously teach both parents and children. As far as mixed marriages, I have no simple solutions. It's a serious problem, with most families bringing up their children in a state of religious confusion.

S. F: Has anyone turned to the *Halachah* Committee in relation to the question of patrilineal descent?

Rabbi Golinkin: Here it's not a major issue. I would unequivocally answer that the Jews, for two thousand years, have followed the *Halachah* that descent is through the mother. There's nothing to discuss. This is also the position of the Conservative movement in the United States.

S. F: Do you see the Reform decision in support of patrilineal descent as a danger?

Rabbi Golinkin: I think that in this issue the Reform movement has acted in a very irresponsible fashion. There are thousands of Reform Jewish couples whom I do not consider married. There are thousands who have divorced and do not have *get*, a Jewish bill of divorce. I don't know if it's going to form two Jewish peoples, but it's going to cause a lot of problems in the future. Frequently, a Reform Jewish convert comes to a Conservative congregation and wants to join the synagogue. The rabbi asks diplomatically about their conversion and lets them know they are not yet Jewish. Frequently, they have to have circumcision or immersion in a *mikveh*. There's no simple solution unless the Reform movement wakes up and says, "We should not do these things!"

S. F: Are you in contact with rabbis of the Reform movement, and do you discuss questions of *Halachah* with them?

Rabbi Golinkin: It is ironic that the Reform movement in the States, which is much more left-wing than the Reform movement here, has published ten volumes of responsa. So even though they do not consider *Halachah* officially binding, they are very interested in *Halachah*. The questions they raise are important and interesting. Their responses are sometimes odd. Rabbi Freehof particularly will go through a whole *teshuvah* and tell you what the *Halachah* has to say on the subject, and then his last sentence will be, "But we are Reform Jews. So we don't do that."

Here in Israel, my counterpart is Rabbi Moshe Zemer, who writes many *teshuvot*. He has a volume of *teshuvot* called *Halachah Shefuyah* (The Sane *Halachah*), and it was published by Dvir in 1993.

S. F.:   Do you regard your responsa as binding on Conservative Jews in Israel, or are they merely a kind of recommendation?

Rabbi Golinkin: I certainly do not feel as if our *Halachah* Committee is a Chief Rabbinate or Council of Torah Sages, as in the Haredi world. When Harav Moshe Feinstein wrote a *teshuvah*, it wasn't just binding on the person who asked him, it was considered binding on all the *haredim* in the world. I do not think that is our role. There's no precedent for that in Jewish history, except the Sanhedrin. I think the person who asked us the question is required to do what the "ruling" says. I would hope that many *Masorti* Jews would be influenced by our *teshuvot*, but I don't consider the *teshuvot* binding on everyone.

S. F.:   Rabbi, I know in one of your rulings you made a decision that does contradict the ruling of the Law Committee in America, on the question of whether it is permitted to drive to synagogue on the Sabbath. Could you explain this?

Rabbi Golinkin: The majority of the Law Committee in the States decided in 1950 that it is permissible to ride to the synagogue on *Shabbat*. I explain that the conditions of the United States in 1950 and Israel in 1990 are like night and day. The rabbis who wrote the lenient *teshuvah* stressed that it's not only that they want the people to be able to go to synagogue, but that without going to synagogue, these people are not going to celebrate *Shabbat* in any way whatsoever. In other words, other than *shul,* they have no observance of *Shabbat* at all. Furthermore, in 1950 a large percentage of American Jews worked on *Shabbat.* They had stores and kept them open. So the question was not whether to stay home and observe *Shabbat,* or to ride to *shul.* The question was whether you were going to drive to your store on *Shabbat* or drive to the synagogue. So the question was an entirely different question, and the justification an entirely different justification. Here in Israel, what justification is there for driving to synagogue when every neighborhood has a synagogue? Every Jew knows how to read Hebrew here and can open a *siddur* if he wants. The sociological situation is completely different. In fact, if the Law Committee in the United States were asked the question today, they might come up with a different answer because even there the situation has changed greatly.

S. F.:   I have just one more question. How can the *Masorti* within Israel do more to reach out to the secular majority?

Rabbi Golinkin: I think the only way to do more is through education. I am an active member of our *Masorti* congregation in East Talpiot. The synagogue is successful and we have beautiful *tefillot,* but it has attracted few native-born Israelis. Time after time, we have a *bar mitzvah* family who come for six months, tell us how wonderful it is that we are so accepting and tolerant, but after the *bar mitzvah* invariably leave.

I think the only way to reach secular Israelis is through the school system. The *Beit Midrash* is actively involved in the Tali school system, for which we write the curricula. And the fact is that a large percentage of students studying for an M.A. at the *Beit Midrash* are secular. They may not be interested in Jewish practice, but they are interested in learning about Judaism at an advanced level.

S. F.:   But isn't your viewpoint that there can be no Judaism without practice?

Rabbi Golinkin: There are a lot of Israelis who want to know about Jewish history, about Talmud and Midrash, without necessarily wanting to follow the *Shulchan Arukh*. One of our students from Kibbutz Beit Hashita wrote a wonderful paper on the history of the *Halachah* of "Redeeming of Captives." She views this issue as relevant today. Should we exchange terrorists for hostages? – For Israeli soldiers? Does this mean that she is going to *davven* three times a day? No. But she thinks that our sources and our traditions should influence the major decisions of our lives. This particular student observes *kabbalat Shabbat* in her house. They light candles and recite *kiddush*. To what extent the learning is going to turn into practice in the long run, I don't know. But I think the least we have to aim for is an Israeli public that is not ignorant of the Jewish Tradition.

To say that the main thing is that practice does not mean you cannot study. It has to come from both directions. You can teach a child to hold a *lulav*, and hopefully from that he will want to learn the tractate of *Sukkah*. Or you can teach the tractate of *Sukkah*, and from that he will want to learn how to hold a *lulav*. So I think the *Masorti* movement has to get involved in a big way in primary and adult education. We are doing some of those things, but not enough. Just based on my own experience in our synagogue, if we put all our eggs in the basket of *tefillah*, we are not going to reach the masses of Israelis.

Rabbi Daniel Tropper

Rabbi Dr. Daniel Tropper is the founder and director of Gesher foundation, an educational institution for bridging the gap between secular and religious Jews in Israel. He is also a regular contributor to the *Jerusalem Report,* is heard frequently on Israeli radio, and is a well-known lecturer.

Over twenty-five years ago, Rabbi Tropper understood that the secular–religious gap would be one of the major problems facing Israeli society in the future. Through those years, he has educated thousands to better understanding and tolerance of those whose worldview is different from theirs. Rabbi Tropper believes that the problem has nonetheless intensified and taken on, in the past year, ideological-political dimensions.

In his response to the question of doing *Avodat Hashem* in his own work, he makes it clear that no profession, no group, has a monopoly on the concept. He democratically gives examples of various forms of *Avodat Hashem* in the modern world. He also gives a fair and hardheaded, yet warm and appreciative, evaluation of Israel society, and how far it has come in the years he has lived and worked in Jerusalem.

I met with Daniel Tropper in his office in the Gesher building on King David Street in Jerusalem.

S. F.:   How would you describe your present work at Gesher?

Rabbi Tropper: At Gesher I am now trying to develop a religious–secular dialogue that will promote a sense of unity in a
country presently moving in the opposite direction. We live today
in a society that is more and more intolerant, where people do not
wish to hear the other side. Here, in the middle of this, is a Don
Quixote yelling: "No matter how great our differences, we must find
a way to work together for our common good. And this is true
because our differences will be seen to have been small if our
disunity leads to some great future disaster."

S. F.:   Are you referring primarily to the religious–secular division
in Israel?

Rabbi Tropper: I am referring both to the religious–secular division and to the political division. Today there is a great overlap
between the two. Ninety percent of the religious population is
rightist, and probably 90 percent of the secular intellectual population, leftist. Between these two groups is a large middle ground,
which can go either way. But the two strong ideological axes – the
political and the religious – are bound together, the right with the
religious and the left with the secular. And it is this overlap of the
two ideological elements together that makes the situation dangerous. The ideological dimension is strongly intensified by the fact
that for both those in the Religious Zionist camp and those in
Chabad Chasidism, the political process is connected with their
idea of religious Redemption. There are also innuendos of this in a
more subtle way in the *Haredi* religious camp as well. And for the
secular in Israel, being leftist does not mean, as it once did, a
traditional labor-socialist position but rather being connected with
a fashionable kind of cultural cosmopolitanism. For this kind of
secular leftist, there is almost embarrassment in any kind of partic-
ularism. There is a strong need to feel a normal part of the worldwide scene. The sources of division are thus varied and run deep.

S. F.:   What kind of programs do you have at Gesher to bridge the gaps?

Rabbi Tropper: Most of our programs are for youth. In a society in which here-and-now problems are so great, this might for some seem a wrong kind of strategy to adopt. I can imagine people saying that we should focus our efforts on those presently making the crucial decisions. But I have learned in my twenty-five years of doing this work that such an approach is not the most effective in the long term. Through these years, tens of thousand of young people have gone through our programs and have, in time, become part of the decision-making apparatus of the country. People who have gone through *Gesher* programs are today working in the Knesset, are assistants to ministers, and are working in education throughout the society. Another good reason for this decision to work with youth is the basic fact that young people are more impressionable than those whose views have already been formed. A third reason for working with youth is a practical one – their accessibility. We can bring together adults in the tens, or sometimes in the hundreds, but not in the thousands, as we can with youth. Moreover, the amount of time and effort to bring together adults, who always have diverse schedules, is large and therefore also a factor. On the other hand, by making arrangements with schools, it is possible to work with large numbers of youth fairly easily. We have worked with the help of the Ministry of Education in organizing programs and have been able to run programs for tens of schools, thousands of youngsters, each year.

S. F.:   What is the format of these programs?

Rabbi Tropper: Our seminars for youth are three-, four-, or even five-day retreats. Sometimes we work with the religious and secular separately, and at other times we have mixed groups. We have discovered that the retreat environment is the healthiest one to work with, partly because of its informality. The group leaders

are only a few years older than the students and therefore close
to their problems. It's not a school and there are no tests, so
the atmosphere is not threatening. Because the students do not have
to meet someone else's expectations, they are more ready to open
up. The first day of the seminars are often, and I say this par-
enthetically, "wasted" because the students let off steam, speaking
out the usual platitudes. On subsequent days, they are able to get
down to the "gut issues." Our experience has shown that brief, one-
or two-day programs generally do not work and that the four- or
five-day program is better for getting them to really think about the
issues seriously.

S. F.:   And as I understand it, there is no effort to induce the
nonobservant to move toward observance.

Rabbi Tropper: No, that is in no way part of our agenda. Very
occasionally, we have to deal with suspicious secular parents thinking that we are out to make their children religious, or suspicious
religious parents thinking we are out to ruin their children. Both
sides in such a polarized society are naturally wary of exposure to
each other. But on our retreats, strong leaders are always there to
help educate and inform, not to convert. There are no hidden
agendas or programs. And the fact that we have been working under
Ministry of Education supervision for close to twenty-five years is, I
believe, the best evidence of the integrity of our operation.

S. F.:   Rabbi, how did you first become involved in this work?
What is your own educational background?

Rabbi Tropper: I grew up on the Lower East Side and had an
Orthodox education at the Rabbi Jacob Joseph School. I then went to
Yeshiva University, where I was a biochemistry major. Though I
liked science very much, after a year of studying at Rabbi Kook's
yeshivah here in Jerusalem, I changed career direction. Upon return
to America, I began simultaneously to study for both rabbinical

ordination and a doctorate in Jewish history. Upon receiving both of these, I came back to Israel with the thought of entering the academic world. But as a group of us had conceived the idea of Gesher and wanted to begin to put it into practical operation, I agreed to postpone my academic plans for a year or two. The postponement has now gone on for twenty-five years. As they say in Israel, there is no more permanent solution than a temporary one. One facetious way of saying this is that now, "Rather than teaching history, I am trying to do something far more difficult, to make history." Writing academic articles is a lot easier than trying to change people's ideas and attitudes. Gesher actually began because a group of about twelve or thirteen people who had studied in Israel strongly felt the religious–secular polarization. We put out a brochure of seventeen pages describing the problems we saw and giving our prognosis for the future. Much of what we had predicted has come true. Though we could not have guessed the coming of cable and satellite television, we did understand that the introduction of television was going to further Westernize Israeli society and deepen the polarization. We believed that there had to be introduced a force that could educate, and so moderate the divide. We sensed that the moderating force could not come from within. We tried to bring in a solution from outside. But of course, the outside became the inside, because through the years I have come to become more Israeli. Now most of my friends are Israeli, and Gesher itself is very Israeli.

S. F.:   The central concept around which this series of interviews is built is the concept of *Avodat Hashem*. How do you understand this concept? Do you think of your own work in terms of it?

Rabbi Tropper: First of all, let me answer by saying, "Yes, I do consider the work I am doing as a kind of *Avodat Hashem*." But *Avodat Hashem* is a very difficult concept to fully comprehend. When we, for instance, are concerned with *mitzvot* in the Torah, it is apparently easy to understand the concept. God said putting on *tefillin* is a *mitzvah*. And as I believe Torah is given on Sinai, it's clear to me that obedience to that commandment is serving God. This is a very clear directive, nonthreatening to the ordinary religious person, and fits well in the whole context of the *shul*-going person's life. *Avodat Hashem* becomes, however, much more complex the minute you leave the narrow confines of what is today called "religion" and walk out into the real world. This, by the way, touches upon one of the real problems in the way Western governments, and particularly the government of Israel, are organized. The moment you have, as in Israel, a Religious Ministry, which deals primarily with *shul*, *tefillin*, and rabbis and a separate Ministry of Social Welfare, which cares for the needs of poor people, you have a real problem. If it were up to me, the proper definition of minister of Religion would be prime minister, namely, one who would deal with the total fabric of life and society's problems. In this world outside the *Beit Midrash* you enter a gray and nebulous world, where directives are not clear. And I believe there is a very good reason for this. There is no way that a written code of laws can cover every possible situation. In one sense, this is a technical problem, but the real meaning of it is much deeper. If God had wanted us to be robots, He would have provided us with all the answers beforehand and so deprived us of any opportunity for freedom of choice. But the moment God wanted us to be human beings and have the Divine Image, *Tzelem Elokim*, God had to leave us a gray area where we are able to grapple with issues on our own. God gave us this incredible ability to shape our own world and life through our own free choice. Examples abound in the modern world, and the area of medical ethics is particularly instructive. There are in medicine some very difficult life-and-death issues and decisions. We enter areas where we must try to understand the definition of God's greatest gift to man, life. On the one end, at what stage is a fetus a life? At the other end, at what point do we consider a life to have ended? There are major decisions to be made here.

For the religious person, true guidance is often given to us by the *poskim*, those who decide Halachah. And their decision, besides being based on sources and precedents, often reflects their own sensitive ethical and moral personality. And yet there are differences of opinion. The same kind of situation often applies in the educational area. The question may be how to develop an appropriate religious educational system for a certain community. The question may be whether to be open to the world or to lock oneself in and cut oneself off from what may be considered a corrupt world. If one decides to be open to the world, all kinds of subquestions develop. What does being part of this world mean? What is my true attitude to Torah studies—and to making a living? Is mathematics something that God wants me to study? This is not a technical question. It's a real question of *Avodat Hashem*. If I want to be a person who serves God and lives in God's world, I need to understand what God wants of me. I must also ask what kind of spiritual personality God wants me to develop.

Now, so far as my own education and view go, I do not aspire to be a mystical personality cut off from reality. To me, to serve God means to be a very sensitive human being, committed to working in this world for the good of others. I see our mission as working in this world to change reality. I have often taught the first chapter in *Bereshit*. Man is the last creature who is created. Man is created in the image of God. He is given free choice. He is created with the power to control the rest of the world. In other words, man is not created as a neutral being but rather as an organic, if special, part of the rest of Creation. As for the Jews, we have greater demands placed upon us. The dialectic in the Torah is between two great events, the Creation and the Revelation, the first being universal and the second particular. The Jew must be involved in both; he must live by *mitzvot* and must demonstrate committment to changing the world for good. I hope that in the work I am doing, I have found the way to do both and to develop a true *Avodat Hashem*.

Now in my own work, I make use of a certain potential I have, and which I developed. I seem to be able to do this kind of work better than other things. I am not a businessman who spends most of his time earning and then gives some hours to "learning" or "helping others." I am what might be called a "professional Jew," and I see this as something God has guided me to. I would not, however, ever make the judgment and say that I am more *oved Hashem* than anyone else. Each person has his niche and has to do what he can do authentically and well. God is not going to ask a businessman, "Why were you not an educator?" but rather: "What kind of businessman were you? Were you honest? Did you use your free time for good?" He is going to ask the educator similar kinds of questions: "Are you in it for the honor only, or are you honestly trying to help people?" The clear point is that each has his own unique *Avodat Hashem* to do.

S. F.:   Thank you. In your work, you are in close touch with a variety of sectors of Israeli society. Is the society, in your judgment, making use of its God-given freedom wisely? Or is it, as certain social critics think, simply moving away from any special Jewish role and racing after general Western cultural trends?

Rabbi Tropper: There is no question that Israel is moving in an accelerated manner from a kind of parochialism to a sense of stronger connection with the rest of the world. We are witnessing a worldwide process of mass communication and mass travel, opening up every society to Western culture, primarily American culture. It's true that Israel, like any young country, was extremely nationalistic at its inception. Political nationalism made for a certain cultural nationalism. Nationalism is not "in" in Israel today, certainly not among the intelligentsia. Just as they are moving away from a particularly Jewish commitment, so they are moving away from what is Jewish culturally. This is connected to the whole panoply of choice, which has been opened up in the modern world. The most conspicuous example of this is in the world of media. People do not sit and watch television as they once did. They sit with a remote control, changing channels. They leave one program, watch another, watch many programs at once. They have seemingly lost the commitment to one specific thing.

S. F.:   Sociologist Elihu Katz said that since the inception of cable in Israel, and with it, the world of multichannels, television viewing, which first went dramatically up, has now gone dramatically down. People get tired and confused from so much choice and withdraw from it.

Rabbi Tropper: I think that what happens is that in some cases, the abundance of choice drives people crazy and deprives them of their ability to be committed to anything. Someone once defined a liberal as one "tolerant of everything except commitment." I think this is a problem with which Israel, like all Western societies, is going to have to deal. To return to the religious context, I believe God wants man to have freedom. I think freedom is one of man's most important values. But something has to balance this freedom because, when taken to the extreme, it becomes perverted. Taken to an extreme, freedom means a loss of all sense of obligation and ability to give to others, a loss of all sense of authority. If a society cannot educate its people to have some kind of obligation to what is beyond the individual self, it is in trouble. Israel is now moving more in this direction, more in the direction of the typical Western society. The saving grace for Israel is that it is still a very strong ideologically oriented society. Its political and religious sense of commitment can be a counterbalance to excessive individualism. The problem is that in today's society, often the religious ideology, instead of serving as a counterbalance, serves to further distance and polarize. Part of the mission of Gesher is to help see that this does not happen.

S. F.:   Isn't it true that in Israel today those religious Jews who have traditional values such as *chesed* and *gemilut chasadim* are more open to secular individualistic Western society than are secular Jews to traditional Jewish religious values?

Rabbi Tropper: I would tend to agree with you. I believe the religious are more exposed to the secular culture than are the

secular to the religious. But after all, Israel is, as all Western governments are, a secular government with a secular culture. Certainly
the media, which today is a fundamental source of education, is
secular. In the religious schools, the secular curriculum is over
50 percent of the material, while in the secular schools, the religious
material is probably 20 or 30 percent. This is a very difficult and
serious problem. There is no way we can open the secularists to the
message of their Tradition when they regard it as an anachronism.
Even those who have the dream of one day having a religious
society understand that the time is not right, that to put it on
the public agenda would be counterproductive now. The secular are,
at this point, too uptight about this. They have to be made to feel,
first of all, that there is something worthwhile for them in the
Tradition. The history of religious coercion in this country has been
counterproductive and has turned many people away from religion
who might have been opened to learning about it. In this, I believe,
one most productive way of operating is through personal, individual contacts.

S. F.:   Do you have friends who are secular Israelis?

Rabbi Tropper: I have. But it's not fair to take me as an example.
After all, I have people working with me here from a variety
of backgrounds. Moreover, my social agenda is largely determined
by the fact that I have ten children. My social life is built around
the house. But in general, I would say that my closest friends
are religious.

This is a phenomenon that repeats itself over and over, of our
associating with those from similar backgrounds. I simply share
much more with my religious friends. We read, trade articles, and
there are even certain jokes I can tell only to a religious person.
Nonetheless, I believe it is important to push in this society for
greater closeness with others. And just as I know much about
secular culture, I believe it is important for the secular to learn and

know more, to be educated in the religious culture. Otherwise, the cultural unity of the Jewish people is in danger.

S. F.: As someone so intimately involved in the daily struggle to educate the people of Israel, what do you see now as vital steps in this process?

Rabbi Tropper: The Jewish world must first of all admit its own failure. The leaders must admit that they have sinned and face the need to try to correct a bad situation. We have a word for that: "*teshuvah.*" The great promise of Torah is that *teshuvah* is possible. No matter how bad a situation is, how low you have sunk, you can come back. And God is waiting for your return. The human being has this incredible ability to rise from the lowest abyss to the greatest heights. The story of Eliezer ben Durdaya in the Talmud is the classic example of this – how he saved his whole world in a moment of repentance.

The Jewish family is in serious decline. We have made mistakes and must do something urgently about Jewish education. The American Jewish leaders, instead of being forthright about this, have in the past preferred half-measures. I believe that if American Jewry were willing to face the problems and come up with new programs, they would be able to save what is savable. I believe there are many American Jews who are very talented and very committed Jewishly. My program would be to bring them to confront the issue. And then, I am sure they could handle it better than I.

S. F.: When I asked about the present situation of the Jews, I also wanted to hear from you about Israel. Do you believe that the State of Israel is serving now as "light to the nations"?

Rabbi Tropper: I think it is. The fact of its very existence gives pride and dignity to Jews all over the world. There is a lot to be proud of in Israel on every level, economically, socially, militarily. It is a democracy, a very decent country that exemplifies high moral standards. With all our complaints about Jewish education here, it is far better than anywhere else in the world. I don't think Israel is anywhere near being the kind of society it should be. Were we to still have some of the ideological fervor we had twenty or thirty years ago, it could radiate a lot more light. But I don't consider Israel in any way a disaster. In many ways, there is much that has been done here, of which the Jewish people can be proud.

S. F.:   Do you believe that Israel, in order to become an ideal Jewish society, must achieve a situation where all Jews are observant of Torah?

Rabbi Tropper: I want this, but I am also a realist. I have to separate what I personally aspire for, and my own program in Gesher. I think that as a religious Jew, the true way to achieve spiritual fulfillment is for all to do *Avodat Hashem.* However, in Gesher my aim is to do only one thing, to wake people up and start feeling, in some kind of authentic way, the promise of our Tradition. I want the Jewish Tradition, the Torah, to be again an open book to the secular in Israel. I want to move them out of their narrow conception of Jewishness and see the Tradition in its true breadth. This is not making anyone a *baal teshuvah,* though obviously, I believe this is what God wants. I have no messianic visions for myself. I don't see myself or my organization as responsible for that. But I do want to bring the secular and religious in Israel to greater understanding of each other and of their common Tradition and hope.

Rabbi Emanuel Quint

Rabbi Emanuel Quint was a leading New York lawyer before making *aliyah* to Israel and devoting himself to the teaching of Torah. In the past several years, he has written and published a number of volumes on *Hoshen Mishpat,* Jewish Civil Law, which are highly popular throughout the English-speaking Jewish world. Along with the classes and lessons he gives, Rabbi Quint is well known in Jerusalem for the semiannual lectures (Chol HaMo'ed Sukkot and Chol HaMo'ed Pesach) where he shares the platform with Rabbi Adin Steinsaltz. My first real acquaintance with Rabbi Quint's teaching came from such a lecture.

Rabbi Quint, in our interview, spoke of his effort to reach people at all levels of learning in his teaching of Torah. He was wary of large, self-aggrandizing definitions and seemed happier dealing with stories of particular cases. Not only did his great learning shine through the interview, so did his particularly warm and kind personality. I had the sense in meeting with him, and talking briefly with both his wife and himself, of people devoted to helping others and serving the community, people devoted to *gemilut Chasadim.* Our interview took place in the Quints' beautiful home, not far from the Nature Museum in Emek Refaim in Jerusalem.

S. F.:   Could you please tell what the main stages of your education and work-life have been?

Rabbi Quint: After college and law school, I practiced law for many years and was a founder of the firm Quint Marx and Chill. While studying in college and law school, I simultaneously attended the Rabbi Jacob Josef Yeshiva and received *semichah* from that school. My wife and I made *aliyah* on July 1, 1984. Two of our daughters were already living here, and we believed we could be of help to the Jewish people in Israel. My wife and I are engaged here in a wide variety of voluntary and charity activities.

S. F.:   In Israel, your main activity has been teaching Torah?

Rabbi Quint: Yes. Teaching, lecturing, and also writing.

S. F.:   I know you have published a number of volumes on Jewish Civil Law. Could you tell me more about the course of your work in writing?

Rabbi Quint: When I was living in America, I wrote, in collaboration with Professor Neil Hecht of Boston University Law School, two volumes called *Jewish Jurisprudence*. In Israel, I am the editor of the Council of Young Israel, "Rabbi in Israel" book series. Three volumes have been published.

Since making *aliyah,* I have written several volumes of a series on Jewish Civil Law published by Jason Aronson Inc.

As for teaching, I was a volunteer *rosh yeshivah* at Yeshiva University in America, where I taught *Hoshen Mishpat* in their *chaver* program. Since coming to Israel, I have taught *Yoreh De'ah* at the Yeshiva University Gruss Kollel, when Rabbi David Miller was on a sabbatical. (He is a tremendous *talmid chacham.*) I also taught *Hosen Mishpat* there for a few years.

Rabbi Adin Steinsaltz and I established the Jerusalem Institute for Jewish Law in order to teach those who have not had experience in "learning." I am pleased to say that many of these students make great progress in learning. The students come from all walks and classes of life. Rabbi Steinsaltz and I also participate in a semiannual forum in English on the first days, respectively, of *Chol HaMo'ed Pesach* and *Sukkot*. The subject of these lectures is business ethics and civil law in *Halachah*.

I conduct a weekly, hour-long class in Talmud for men and women and an all-night learning *shiur* on Hoshanah Rabbah. I also lecture at various schools and institutions such as the Israel Center, Young Israel, and synagogue weekends and forums.

S. F: Rabbi, the main concept of this present work is *Avodat Hashem*. Do you consider your life devoted to *Avodat Hashem?* How do you understand the concept itself?

Rabbi Quint: *Avodat Hashem* permeates all aspects of Jewish Law, ritual and civil. Hopefully, every time we study and act in accordance with Jewish Law, we are serving *Hashem*. Man's logic might sometimes lead him to different conclusions in Civil Law from those of the Torah, but we have to realize that the word of *Hashem* is reflected in the Torah, both Written and Oral, and the subsequent codes, commentaries, and responses. When we conduct ourselves according to His Law, we are serving Him.

S. F: Do you feel that in Israel you serve God in a better way than you would outside Israel?

Rabbi Quint: I wouldn't say that. I believe a person can serve *Hashem* anyplace they happen to be. I never criticize anyone who does not come on *aliyah* because I understand he may have his own special reasons. But I do believe I can make more of a contribution to Jewish life here than I could in America. On top of that, I have the special privilege of making any *mitzvah* performed here a "double *mitzvah*." I not only put on *tefillin*, I put on *tefillin* in *Eretz Yisrael*.

S. F.:   You have been here for more than ten years. How has Israel developed in this time?

Rabbi Quint: I think that Israel has developed, and is developing, tremendously day to day. The Jewish population continues to grow. There are more *yeshivot*, synagogues, Torah classes, hospitals, clinics, roads, material goods available. There are more places to eat out, more cultural events, more study groups, welfare organizations, volunteers, more of all that is required for the Jew to have a complete life in his homeland. The Talmud relates a statement that when the first man wanted to have bread, he had to first plow, then sow, then water, harvest, winnow, grind, and bake. Now one can go down to the store and buy a loaf of bread without going through all the earlier stages. So, too, those who are living here now have a tremendous amount available to us, which has come as the result of earlier efforts of others. Therefore, we should try to do all that we can so that the next generation will find this country an even better place than we found it.

As for the political situation, I have strong opinions and misgivings, but that is not part of your question. I give the people with whom I disagree the benefit of the doubt and assume that they have the benefit of the country in mind when they make decisions. Very often, I am convinced that their decisions have nothing to do with *Avodat Hashem,* but I would hope their actions are motivated by the love of the people of Israel.

S. F.:   Many of those I have spoken with in these interviews are involved in *Avodat Hashem* of strengthening the Jewish community in its struggle against assimilation. Do you yourself have any ideas about what must be done now to fight against the growing assimilation in the Diaspora?

Rabbi Quint: I think the greatest challenge is that most Diaspora Jews lack a Jewish education. I recently read an article that had a survey showing there will be about two million Satmar *Chasidim*

in upstate New York by the year 2030. So from one end of
the spectrum, we don't have to worry. Lubavitch, too, is making
a tremendous impact. Young Israel in the past had a bigger impact,
but they are still working. Yet all these religious groups are isolated cases in a desert. I have many friends who are active in
Jewish communities, and they tell me there's a sense of children
growing up without the first feeling of Jewish belonging. Years
ago, a man in America might go to work on *Shabbos* and yet feel
deeply Jewish. The old Bolshevik leaders of this knew Jewish
culture. The new, nonobservant Israeli youth do not have the
slightest notion of what it means to be Jewish. They have no sense of
Jewish values and do not have a *Zeyde* who can tell them what he
remembers of his Jewishness, or a grandmother lighting candles on
Friday night. In America, many Jews are surprised when their
children marry non-Jews. They don't realize that they did nothing
to make their children know and feel a distinctive Jewish identity.
While Lubavitch or Young Israel may influence some, here and
there, to make *teshuvah,* a much larger number are simultaneously
being lost to Judaism.

And yet I do not lose hope. I remember the incident of Elijah
the Prophet. He declares that "I am alone left." And yet the generation
after his boasted that every Jewish child knew all the laws of the
most difficult tractates. *Hashem* can cause a major breakthrough and
turnaround in a moment if we are worthy of it.

S. F.:   You have mentioned the education problem in Israel. Are you
concerned by the religious–secular divide here?

Rabbi Quint: The Guttman Institute just published a survey
showing that a great majority of the people of Israel observed at least
some of the laws of Judaism. I am certain that the percentage of
observant Jews is highest in Israel in comparison with all other
states in the world. There are certain traditions that Jews have
received from their grandparents and continue to maintain.

S. F.:   Here the Jewish calendar shapes the life of the country, whether we are conscious of it or not.

Rabbi Quint: When I watch the news on television, I realize I am in a Jewish State. The Hebrew date is on the screen. If it is during the counting of the *Omer*, this is mentioned; at Friday, in the afternoon newscast, the listeners are wished *Shabbat Shalom*. The regular weekday radio programs begin and end with selections from the *Tanach*.

S. F.:   I know that most of your activity now is in the educational area. Do you believe that a Jewish society should be educated according to one main stream of thought?

Rabbi Quint: It has to be multifaceted, enabling each person to find his own way. I personally would like to see more teaching of feelings of the heart in the nonreligious schools, so that young people would feel that they are not only Israelis but also Jews. I was walking with a rabbi the other day when he saw some some obviously nonobservant young men acting rowdily in the street in Yerushalayim. He commented that if they had Jewish values, they would not be so rowdy. I agreed they should have more Jewish values but reminded him that in a year, they will be in the army protecting those who attend *yeshivot*. They are, in their way, helping to strengthen the Jewish state. Still, I would like them to have more Jewish education.

From the other side, I had a meeting with a secular professor who said he could not believe people were still foolish enough to believe in the coming of the Messiah. I replied that he wouldn't dare tell this to about a billion Catholics and hundreds of millions of Protestants who feel strongly about their Messiah. It's just that he knows so little about Judaism that he easily belittles it. This is because he has no real Jewish education.

S. F.:   Another of the rabbis I spoke with in this series of interviews, Rabbi Nachum Rabinovitch, said that we of course believe in

Moshiach and the concept of Redemption, but it is wrong for us to rely on that in such a way as to believe that the historical outcome is inevitable and we ourselves have no responsibility for what happens. We must think instead in terms of how we can take responsibility, shape the world for good.

Rabbi Quint: I absolutely agree with the statement of Rabbi Rabinovitch, who is a great scholar. To describe free will is, of course, extremely difficult, if not impossible. All great philosophers have had little success in this. Last week, I had a meeting with an outstanding Catholic theologian who quotes Jacques Maritain, who claims that free will and God's ominiscience are two links of a chain, a chain that mankind cannot forge together. I agree with that. God gives us instructions on how to act, and we have to do the best we can to follow those instructions. The Prophet says of God, "My thoughts are not your thoughts." We, in performing the *mitzvot,* add *kedushah* to the world. We have to look at the world as equally balanced between good and evil, and as if the next *mitzvah* we perform will tilt the scales toward the good.

So I agree with Rabbi Rabinovitch. We have to, and God will give us that divine help we need, *"Siyata d'Shemaya."* He will help us to do whatever we can to help the process of the Messiah's coming.

S. F.:   So the Jew, even when events do not go his way, even when history seems turning against the ideal, must not lose heart?

Rabbi Quint: I would agree. One must not lose heart. We pray for rain, for worldly goods. We pray in our synagogue for the country and that God should give good counsel to our leaders.

The question brings to mind a difference in outlook between a woman and a man. Rabbi Meir, who was vexed by a neighbor, thought of praying for the neighbor's undoing. Rabbi Meir's wife told him that instead of such a prayer, he should pray that the neighbor would become righteous and stop vexing him. Rabbi Meir did, and the neighbor changed his ways. Similarly, we have to pray that if there are leaders we feel need to change the direction in which they are taking the country, we should pray for them to make this change.

S. F.:   Rabbi, I know you have a wide circle of friends in Israel. Do they come mostly from the people you knew in the States?

Rabbi Quint: Few are people I knew in the States. Our friends here are, by and large, what in Israel are called Anglo-Saxons from the States, Canada, South Africa, and England. We have many good friends here. And in truth, I don't really miss anything. We went from a marvelous life there to an even more marvelous life here. Moreover, three out of four of our children reside here. And hopefully, my son, my daughter-in-law, and their children will soon come on *aliyah*. Except for his two children, all my other grandchildren are *sabras*.

S. F.:   Could you say something about the method of your literary work?

Rabbi Quint: I must do a tremendous amount of research. At any one time, I have as many as thirty to forty volumes in front of me. I begin the research with the earliest sources, the *Mishnah* and Talmud, and the commentaries thereon, and the various codes such *Alfasi, Rambam, Asheri, Tur*, and the *Shulchan Aruch* and its commentaries. I also employ the responsa literature, including the latest volumes of modern scholars. Certainly, the *Aruch Hashulhan* by Rabbi Epstein, who died in 1908, is of great help.

S. F.:   Do you get a great deal of response from your readers?

Rabbi Quint: I get many practical questions in writing, by telephone, and in person. I also get many questions from people from all walks of life, who have theoretical questions about certain things I wrote.

S. F.:   What is the difference between the answers you give and the answers that would be given by *posek*, a decisor?

Rabbi Quint: I usually conclude my answers with the suggestion that the questioner consult with the practicing rabbi in his synagogue. If a rabbi asks me a question that was asked of him, I tell him what I think and then suggest that he also consult certain sources that I suggest, and very often, when pressed I say, "I think I would handle the matter in the following manner." If a question has to be decided on the spot, I am not loath to give an answer, and if I do not know the answer, I so state.

S. F.:   Do you have a rav of your own?

Rabbi Quint: In matters of ritual observance, I turn to Rabbi Solomon Sharfman, who was the rabbi of the Young Israel of Flatbush, where I *davvened* from 1960 to 1984.

S. F.:   When recently I spoke with your friend Rabbi Shubert Spero, we spoke about the possibility of deriving all Jewish morality from one principle, "walking in the ways of *Hashem*." Do you believe all the Law could be unfolded from this principle?

Rabbi Quint: Rabbi Spero is a true scholar and wonderful gentleman. The Talmud, toward the end of tractate *Makkot*, speaks of 613 commandments that can be restated and, for homiletical purposes, broken down into smaller units, concluding at last with the one ideal of walking with God. The walking with God means to me to follow all the 613 commandments: one walks with God when he does not eat non*kosher* food, when he observes the laws of *Shabbat*, when he does not act dishonestly in business. I do not think that to walk with God it is sufficient to be a nice person according to humanistic standards without paying attention to the commandments. When we put on *tefillin*, we do not know what it does for the universe, but God knows. I don't believe there can be a basic morality without following the Torah.

S. F.:   You mention the *Moshiach*. How do you envision the world will be changed by the coming of *Moshiach?*

Rabbi Quint: We do not have a fixed eschatology of what will be in the time of the *Moshiach* or in the end of days when resurrection of the dead will occur. There are many views on all of these subjects, and who can say which view is superior. I think that according to all views, life on earth will be better than it was before. I like many of the statements of Maimonides, who says that life on earth as we know it will continue, but with one great difference. The nations of the earth will live with the Jews in peace so that we can develop our own destiny as people of *Hashem*. We will have more time to devote ourselves to do the bidding of *Hashem* and be better human beings.

Only God knows what will be when things happen. But I am certain that when God sends *Moshiach,* it will be something beneficial for the Jewish people.

S. F.:   Do you look forward to a time when all the Jews of the world will be observant?

Rabbi Quint: That's a very difficult thing to anticipate. God created the world, including the concept of *teshuvah,* repentance. Thus, there cannot be 100 percent observance by all. Rambam and Tosafists differ as to the meaning of the Talmud teaching that the place occupied by *Baal teshuvah* is unique.

Recently, when someone told me he was a *baal teshuvah,* I responded that I hope that I, too, am a *baal teshuvah.* The Gemara tells us that only four persons died without having sinned. Thus, all of us must do *teshuvah.* Only God knows if a person is religious. The person himself may not know. Only God knows what is in the hearts and minds of man. Nobody can be like Moshe Rabbenu, and yet even when he was alive there were sinners. Hopefully, *Moshiach* will cure many of our spiritual ills and set us on the right path, and there will come a time when most Jews are Torah observant.

S. F.:   Do you notice any difference in your *davvening* in time?

Rabbi Quint: As one gets older he gets closer to meeting his Maker and taking his final exams in the heavenly testing grounds. As one gets older, he gets weaker and more illness prone. The prayer in *Shmoneh Esreh* for health takes on greater meaning. The *davvening*, especially on the *Yomim Nora'im*, takes on much more significance. I find that I approach things differently now. Friends are getting older and getting ill. One feels more compassion as one gets older. One begins to think of the next world. How will I get there? The *davvening* takes on a new dimension.

S. F.:   Do you have a special prayer in which you feel your service of God is greatest?

Rabbi Quint: Yom Kippur. I stand the entire *davvening*. My seat is next to the front wall. I bring my own *shtender,* put my *tallit* over my head, face the wall, and become more or less oblivious to all that is around me. I try to concentrate only on the *davvening* and my relationship with God, and on how I may make amends for all the things I should have done better, and for things I should not have done at all. I try not to let anything disturb me. Two years ago, I felt a tapping on my back. My son-in-law told me that my daughter had just given birth to a son. I had a new grandson born on Yom Kippur. I think that was one of the few times I spoke to anybody on Yom Kippur. I make it a practice, from the time I leave my house to go to the synagogue for Kol Nidre until I arrive at home after Neilah, and Maariv after Yom Kippur, not to speak to anyone. Who knows what I am going to say and to hear? Perhaps it is *leshon harah*. I find the *davvening* in our *shul* to be very inspirational on Yom Kippur.

As for the daily *davvening*, this too is inspirational. In the middle of Shmoneh Esreh I may say a prayer for the sick, who don't even know that I am saying the prayer for them. I feel that it's between me and God. When I say, *"Yerushalayim Ircha,"* even after being here ten years in Jerusalem, it still makes me excited. I very often say: "God, let's finish with all this nonsense and make Yerushalayim the city that You said it would be. Our city to worship You."

Every single *davvening* is different as to where I place my emphasis. Lately, it has more and more been for peace, *Oseh Shalom*. *He* will make peace, not some diplomats in a hotel. God will make peace for us.

Rabbi Nathan T. Lopes Cardozo

Rabbi Nathan T. Lopes Cardozo teaches at Ohr Sameach Yeshiva and at the Jerusalem College for Adult Education. The author of *The Infinite Chain: Torah Masorah and Man* and the recently published *Between Silence and Speech: Essays on Jewish Thought,* he is a popular teacher in the area of Jewish thought. Born in Holland and educated at Gateshead in England and at the Mir Yeshiva in Jerusalem, he has been a leading figure in the *Baal Teshuvah* movement in Israel. Rabbi Lopes Cardozo lectures widely throughout the Jewish world.

I met with Rabbi Lopes Cardozo at his home in the religious district of Bayit Vegan. Courteous and friendly, he spoke English with just a trace of a Dutch accent. Our talk touched upon, among other things, the two worlds, the *Haredi* and the Modern Orthodox, in which the rabbi lives. As one who made the long, slow path to *teshuvah* through wrestling with the greatest of Jewish heretics, Spinoza, he shows a particular understanding of those on the edge of the modern world who are returning to traditional Judaism. He too contends in his thought with the wise and correct way for the believing, observant Jew to be part of the modern world. In this, Rabbi Lopes Cardozo gives the impression of being a "thinker" who is, all the time, struggling with basic issues and seeking deeper understanding.

S. F.:   I know you have been teaching in Israel for many years. Could you tell me something about the process of your *aliyah?*

Rabbi Cardozo: We are here about seventeen years. I always have the feeling that I should have been born in Israel, and that Titus spoiled it all when he forced my ancestors to live in Babylon, Spain, Portugal, and, since the sixteenth century, in Holland, where I was born. I have the sense that was all a big mistake.

S. F.:   Nonetheless, I know you did some preparation for Israel when you were abroad. What is your educational background?

Rabbi Cardozo: After high school I studied at Gateshead Yeshiva in England. I then returned to Holland for a while and then came to Israel, where I studied at the Mirer Yeshiva and Kollel. By that time, I was married with children. As I had for years taken courses in general philosophy and other disciplines, I enrolled in a Ph.D. program at a not particularly well known university, Columbia Pacific University. My dissertation there was on the relationship between the Written and Oral Torah and the philosophical implications of this. A shortened version of the dissertation was later published as a book by Targum and Feldheim Press. Since then, it has been translated into Russian, and I am presently working on a Dutch translation.

S. F.:   Could you describe your present schedule of work activities?

Rabbi Cardozo: For over fourteen years I have been teaching at Ohr Sameach Tannebaum College for Jewish Studies. This is a remarkable institution devoted to educating nonreligious students in the Jewish Tradition. The students come from all over the world. There are professors on sabbatical, lawyers, physicians, business-people, even Reform rabbis, and from age eighteen to seventy.

I had also been teaching in Neve Yerushalayim College for Women, but I recently stopped so that I can devote more time to writing. By the time this interview appears, my most recent book will have been published. I also now give classes at Michlala Jerusalem College for women. I am sometimes a guest lecturer at Hebrew University's overseas program, Weizmann Institute. There is also a weekly class with the Jerusalem College for Adults of my friend Rabbi Dr. Shalom Gold. This is for a mixed, somewhat older crowd, and I enjoy it immensely. I also spend a few months of the year on lecture tours to the United States of America, Canada, South Africa, Switzerland, England, and my home country, Holland. I find that both exhausting and most refreshing.

S. F.: Is there any particular subject to which you devote your lectures?

Rabbi Cardozo: My main field is Jewish Philosophy and Weltanschauung. As I do not come from a religious background and struggled to find my own way to Judaism, its worldview philosophical outlook has always most concerned me. I find this a fascinating world and lecture on many different topics. Of late, I have been speaking about the halachic status of God and His integrity. I am working on lectures on Socrates' fatal cup (was it right for him to drink it?) and Spinoza's attitude toward the *Halachah*. In my thought I have been deeply influenced by Rabbi Samson Rafael Hirsch and Rabbi Joseph Ber Soloveitchik, but chasidic thinkers such as Franz Rosenzweig and Abraham Joshua Heschel have also had their influence, though I might not totally agree with their way of seeing things.

S. F.: How do you understand the concept *Avodat Hashem?* Do you see your own life and work having meaning in relation to this concept?

Rabbi Cardozo: Philosophically, I think *Avodat Hashem* really means to see the fingerprint of God in all things, including ourselves, and to translate this perception into a certain way of life. In other words, I understand the concept not as a mere abstract idea but as an imperative that I must translate into my own life experience. Personally, I think this means that we often find ourselves living a paradox, the paradox of religious life in a largely secular world. I think part of this means trying to make sense out of this and find what is of value in the secular world that can deepen and enrich the Jewish way of life.

S. F.:   Rabbi Kook was, I believe, of all Jewish thinkers in modern times the one who did most to stress the value of the secular for the religious, especially in the Land of Israel. Are you a student of his?

Rabbi Cardozo: I would not really regard myself as a disciple of him, or, for that matter, anyone else. But I have read a wide variety of writing on this subject.

S. F.:   Do you have some special approach of your own in teaching secular students Judaism?

Rabbi Cardozo: I do not have a simple answer to this question. I am troubled enormously that something as beautiful as the Jewish Tradition is doing so badly today in making its message known. I am involved in what is called the *Baalei Teshuva* movement, and I believe that not only is it small but it probably is not doing as well as it was a few years ago. The major problem, as I understand it, is that the Jewish Tradition is taught in many places as if it has value for the past only, as if it does not speak to us today. We are working basically with old texts, *Chumash, Mishnah, Gemara,* and it is necessary to translate these texts to address the concerns of those living today. Judaism is not only a tradition but a living experience, and this is what we must help students know. I also believe that in Israel we tend to place too much emphasis on, let's call it, the "ritual aspect" of the Tradition. We speak too much about the precise ways of keeping *kashrut* and *Shabbat* and not enough about the *mitzvot* involved in human relationships between man and fellowman. We must emphasize to many, even in the religious community, that our Tradition is one of demand for the highest ethics and morality. If we do that, and if we then succeed in presenting a different image of traditional Jewish life to the nontraditional world, we may have a much stronger impact on it. I know that many Israelis have no sense of this aspect of religion. They believe religion to be outmoded, and the religious to be a special-interest group who do not concern themselves with the well-being of society as a whole. I believe that Orthodox Jewry, of which I am a part, has for years been failing to live up to its own standards and that the larger Jewish community has paid the price for it.

S. F.:   Many observers point to a growing Orthodox community, which has a higher religious and general professional level than ever before. Can't this group have a greater impact on the world Jewish community in the future than it is having today?

Rabbi Cardozo: There has never before been a religious revival quite like the one we are having today. But when it is seen in global terms, it is small. The amount of people we draw back into the community is very small in comparison to those we are losing. Also, there is another problematic side of the situation today. Many who return to religion are simply trying to escape from a hard and difficult world. I would not go as far as Freud when he spoke about religion as an opiate to the masses, a kind of wishful thinking, but there is some element of truth in this in relation to some of those who return. And this is in contradiction to the Jewish idea that our task is to be responsible in and for the world. One of the most important points Rav Soloveitchik made was that religious life should not be an escape but rather a confrontation. We can get away with this for one or two generations, but if we do not at some point begin educating youngsters to confront the world, we are going to pay a price for this in time.

S. F.:   The closing off does, I think, work in certain ways, and we can see this in the great growth of certain chasidic communities. I think that one more evidence of your realizing the ideal of being open to the world community is given through your contribution to the building of Efrat. I wonder which community you personally feel close to and are connected with.

Rabbi Cardozo: I live on the borderline between the *Haredi* community and Modern Orthodoxy. I don't know how much of one leg stands in one community and how much of the other in the other. This does not make life easier, for often I disagree with both communities. I have a lot of friends in both camps and personally believe both are needed. I believe you need those who follow Rabbi Kook, and I believe there is something to say for Satmar as well. I know them all and am not ready to affiliate with one to the exclusion of all others. Socially, it means I, at times, feel very lonely, because there are few people who understand where I am coming from and what I have to say.

S. F.:   I think you also probably feel lonely because you come from a community that was decimated during the Second World War. Do you maintain ties with the Dutch-Jewish community?

Rabbi Cardozo: I come, as I said before, from a non-Orthodox, an assimilated, background. My father was a big Spinoza-ist, though he later became more religious. I read a lot of Spinoza, still read a lot of Spinoza, and find him a most interesting figure, the most interesting *apikoros*.

S. F.:   A disturbing and attractive figure for the Jewish people, one who, I suspect, helped more Jews lose their religious faith than any other person. And paradoxically, a heroic moral figure on his own terms.

Rabbi Cardozo: The damage this man did was unbelievable. He was the most daring philosopher, and yet one who may have deliberately misread Jewish Tradition.

S. F.:   You know Will Durant's comment about him, "He was the only one of the great philosophers who lived in accordance with his own teaching"?

Rabbi Cardozo: I, through reading Spinoza, became religious, because I had the sense that when he attacked the Tradition there was much he was hiding about it. This led me to begin searching myself through the sources, and so I owe a great debt to Spinoza for helping bring me to the Jewish tradition. I wonder if this is of help to him in the *Shemayim?*

S. F.:   The example you present of coming out of a rigorous Western philosophical thought and moving through the power of mind back to the Tradition is one that hopefully can be of inspiration to many young Jews questing to find their way. Do you use your own example in your teaching?

Rabbi Cardozo: I do a lot of that, speaking to my students of the intellectual problems that bother me, speaking of Spinoza as the one who brought me back. In a paradoxical sense, many of my *shiurim* are built upon his attacks on Judaism. I quote his critical statements, and then I show how to refute them. I have very little difficult understanding where a student is coming from, even when he is an atheist, because I was not far removed from there once myself. This makes my life as a teacher much easier. And it's one aspect of the teaching I tremendously enjoy, speaking to those who are where I was intellectually years ago.

S. F.:   For yourself, was there one great moment of intellectual insight that served as a turning point? Or was it the traditional process of *teshuvah*, which, ideally for the Jew, goes on all the time?

Rabbi Cardozo: It was very slow and painful. I was living in a real paradox of knowing the non-Jewish world well and believing it, too, has a lot to say. It took years before I was capable of sorting it out. And I am not sure I am completely out of it yet.

S. F.:   In your book *The Infinite Chain,* you speak about the Noahide laws, the relation of the Torah to the non-Jewish world. What do you believe the role of the Jewish people is today in relation to a world so varied, a world of tremendous poverty and tremendous wealth, a world of so many creeds, including various "monotheisms"?

Rabbi Cardozo: I have a liberal approach much like that of the Rambam, which is different from that of some other Jewish philosophers. I believe the Orthodox world does not take enough notice of the non-Jewish world. I do see a need for a wall between us and the rest of the world; but now the wall is too high.

S. F.:   I believe in the special role of the Jewish people in transmitting the idea of God, and the higher morality that is bound up with this, to other peoples. But I also say, "All Creation is from *Hashem,*" all that is true and beautiful and good. Surely other peoples contribute to this. But the world is so vast. How do we understand the purpose of God in relation to each of them?

Rabbi Cardozo: I also ask myself, "Why are there so many, for instance, millions of Chinese people walking around without really relating to 'monotheism'?" I have been thinking a lot about that. I believe that every culture and every religion, even when it's not monotheistic or when we would call it *"Avodah Zarah,"* has a divine purpose. I suppose that when God creates these people, there is a purpose that, from the divine perspective, makes it worthwhile.

S. F.:   This is an age that many speak of as being without "isms": postcommunism, postsocialism, postcapitalism, post- this and that. Isn't it still the Jewish people's task, perhaps even most especially at a time when so many are questing for a faith, to present the word of one God to mankind?

Rabbi Cardozo: The problem is that we have to first put our own house in order. We religious Jews first have to become a light to our own nation. As to being a light to others, in a sense we haven't even started yet. Lubavitch has done something in this regard. I think there is a failure in religious education, which is also an ethical failure. We live too much in and for ourselves. I say to my students: "If there is a problem in Bosnia, if something goes wrong in Bangladesh, that human problem is, too, a Jewish problem. How can I, as a religious Jew, go to bed with a clear conscience when I know that in other parts of the world people are going through horrible suffering?" I think our responsibility for our fellow humanity is a central teaching of the Jewish Tradition that is not stressed today.

S. F.:   Finally, Rabbi, how do you see the State of Israel in terms of its realizing traditional Jewish goals? And what do you believe should be done to bring the reality closer to the ideal?

Rabbi Cardozo: I think Israel is a much better society than it is presented as being in the media. In the communities within Israel, there are a lot of remarkable things going on, charity institutions, care for the sick. I think this good side of Israel rarely makes the news. But there is really much more at stake. A modern state cannot exist on the basis of charity institutions alone. If we want to make a real Jewish State out of Israel, we will have to give our younger people and students opportunities to study secular disciplines within a Jewish religious framework. One of the great mistakes of the *Haredi* community is the fact that it does not stimulate its younger people to become physicians and scientists. We cannot build a modern, balanced religious state if we do not build religious universities and academic institutions. If the situation continues, the religious will become even more dependent on the nonreligious. This is, in my judgment, very unhealthy. All of us must strive for proper *yeshivah* education, but we who are deeply immersed in the Jewish Tradition must make certain we contribute to the ideal Jewish State about which we have dreamed so long. This means we have to start thinking about a new kind of religious institution in which we teach secular topics without religious compromise. It won't be easy, and it is one of the great challenges of our religious leadership. In accordance with this we have to give our future rabbis an opportunity to study history, philosophy, and science so they will know how to relate to the secular Jew when they come to him for advice. I have seen an enormous communication problem between many Israeli rabbis and their congregants. It is time we started thinking in terms of educating young rabbis so they can be influential within the academic world. It is time we started thinking in terms that will enable the important truths of Judaism to serve Israeli society and the Jewish people as a whole.

Rabbi Mendel Lewittes z"l

Rabbi Mendel Lewittes (of blessed memory) passed to a world that is wholly good in July of 1994, approximately two months after having gone over and returned to me the corrected typescript of this interview. Jason Aronson Inc. has published several of his books, including *Jewish Marriage, Jewish Law,* and *Religious Foundations of the Jewish State.* During his last years in Israel, he was the editor of the annual magazine of the Chief Rabbinate of Israel, *Shanah b'Shanah.* He also gave two popular classes in the Talmud Yerushalami. Before coming to Israel some twenty-five years before, he had occupied a number of rabbinical posts and been one of the leading Orthodox rabbis of Canadian Jewry.

Rabbi Lewittes was a kind, considerate, and learned person. Our interview only touched upon the main stages of his long career, but one point I believe is important and does stand out in it. Rabbi Lewittes loved being a teacher of Torah and especially a teacher of young people. One of his proudest accomplishments was the school he had founded in Montreal. When he spoke of his own service of God, he gave the sense that teaching, and the role of teacher, was most important for him. One who knew him much better than I, Yaakov Fogelman, wrote of him: "He blended high-level secular education, deep commitment to *Halachah,* and an open, tolerant, constantly questing mind. He was dignified, soft-spoken and kind, yet the first to speak out courageously against evil." A large and devoted family and many colleagues, congregants, and friends now have his memory and good works as a legacy.

S. F.:   I know, Rabbi, you have had a long and distinguished career in the rabbinate. What are its principal stages?

Rabbi Lewittes: A word first about my educational background. I started out in a sort of modern Hebrew school, then later transferred to Rabbi Yitzhak Elchanan, which later became part of Yeshiva University. I went through their high school and received my bachelor's degree in the first graduating class of their college. Upon receiving rabbinical ordination, I began working, first in a small town in Pennsylvania. Shortly after marrying, I went on to a position in Portland, Maine, where I was not only the sole rabbi of the town but the first English-speaking rabbi they had ever had. There were three synagogues in the town, and I was rabbi of all three. As there was no other rabbi in all the state of Maine, I became, for a while, sort of the "chief rabbi of Maine." Later on, a colleague took a position in Bangor, and I left that part of the state to him. At that time, the Portland community was like a European *shtetl,* consisting largely of old-timers who had come from Europe. For example, on Thursday women would go to the market to buy live chickens and would go to the *shochet* house, where I would examine to see if they were *kosher.* I, of course, examined the *shechitah* in the abattoir. I remember one significant incident when a government committee came to check the *shechitah,* and I succeeded in showing them that our system was much more humane, less cruel to the animals, than that employed by the non*kosher* system.

My three older children were born in Portland, Maine. After a time, I felt the need for a larger congregation and community and accepted a position in Boston, at one of its leading Orthodox synagogues. This was when Rabbi Soloveitchik (of blessed memory) was there, and we had very cordial relations, in part because I had been a *talmid* of his father, Rav Moshe Soloveitchik, and knew his family. In fact, at *yeshivah* I had more or less been the personal secretary of Rav Moshe Soloveitchik. After being in Boston for seven years during and after the war, I was asked by my wife's family, who lived in Montreal, to accept a position in the Young Israel of

Montreal, which was just then expanding into a new neighborhood. This was, I understood, an opportunity for me to build up an entire new Jewish community. And the fact is, when we established the synagogue, a building contractor almost immediately began building new, big apartments close by. Under my leadership, the Young Israel of Montreal became the leading Orthodox congregation of the city. After surveying the Jewish educational institutions of Montreal and discovering that all the *yeshivahs* were of the old Lithuanian type and the community schools were without religious education, I organized and established a Jewish day school, which followed a Religious Zionist program. This school in time became extremely successful. In Montreal, I was also the chairman of the Association of the Jewish Schools, the chairman of the Religious Affairs Committee of the Canadian Jewish Congress, and the head of what was then called the Board of Jewish Ministers. I represented the Jewish community in communal events, such as the opening of Expo '67 and the opening of the Montreal subway system. As the Montreal Jewish community was expanding into the suburbs, our congregation took an interest in establishing suburban synagogues that would be Orthodox. We even went so far as to help organize an Orthodox synagogue in Ottawa. I worked a great deal during that time.

Before the Montreal years, when in Boston, I had taken courses at Harvard and there received my master's degree in Semitics and began working on my doctorate. I was there assigned by the late Professor Wolfson to translate a volume of the Rambam. This was eventually published by Yale University as *The Book of Temple Service*. Through this time I was also a regular contributor to local Jewish weeklies and the general press. Over the years, I developed my own particular style of writing and was eventually able to go beyond short articles to larger works, also publishing "sermons."

S. F.: And after the Montreal years began the Israeli phase of your work?

Rabbi Lewittes: The time had come after 1967 to make *aliyah* to Israel. One of my children had already settled here and is still living in Jerusalem. Then, a younger daughter decided she wanted to come to Israel from Stern College. Also, there was a change in the educational setup in Montreal, and my school's merging with another meant I did not have an educational institution to care for. So, after thirty-five years in the rabbinate in North America, I decided the time had come to settle in Israel. Fortunately, through my wife's family's help, I was able to come without having to accept a paying position. Here I could devote myself to writing. In the beginning, I gave much time to one institution, Otzar HaPoskim, the Institute of Jewish Law. I also gave lectures on a voluntary basis to army groups and to women's groups on *Parashat Hashavuah*. I initiated a popular *shiur* at Hechal Shlomo, and to this day I give *shiurim* there on Talmud Yerushalmi. My latest venture is as editor of the annual published by Hechal Shlomo, *Shanah B'Shanah*. As for my writing, I frequently review books on Judaica for the *Jerusalem Post* and have recently completed a book on Jewish marriage.

I am very fortunate that two of my children live here in Jerusalem, so that we have *nachas* from our grandchildren. My older two children live outside of Israel, one in Toronto and one in New York, and we also visit and see our children and grandchildren. We thank God that we are blessed with grandchildren as well, so that we are *adam zocheh l'shnei shulchanot* (a man who is fortunate to be blessed by having two places of sustenance).

S. F.:   Thank you, Rabbi. I would like to ask you whether through the years you have understood your life and work in terms of the concept *Avodat Hashem*.

Rabbi Lewittes: The work of the rabbi as I conceived it was primarily in Jewish education, teaching and explicating the ideas of Jewish thought. In this, I was often able to inspire to greater religious observance, with the children often having a positive effect on their parents' level of observance. But also, the work of the rabbi is pastoral work. I always found that people deeply appreciated visits of the rabbi when they were in hospital. I remember one incident when the hospital rabbi had not made arrangements for blowing the *shofar* on Rosh Hashanah. After our services, my son and I walked there, and I blew the *shofar* in the corridor. This was deeply appreciated. And this kind of kindness is, of course, central to the rabbi's task.

Avodat Hashem means, too, *Avodah B'Lev* (the Service of the Heart), and this is very difficult to live up to. It also means living by the *Halachah,* and the teaching of Jewish Law has been one of my main concerns. I have published to that purpose a volume on the development of Jewish Law that has appeared both in English and Hebrew. Unfortunately, I believe that the present day rabbinate often fail to accommodate the *Halachah* to the requirements of observant Jews living in the modern world. The late Rabbi Herzog, and before him Rav Kook, had wanted to make certain *takkonot,* but the rabbis refused to cooperate. A positive development, though, is the action of the younger rabbis, who have created institutes such as Tsoment for dealing with agricultural problems. I decry the tendency today to add *chomrot* (further severe restrictions) on the *Halachah.* If we want to attract more people to observance, we have to make the Law more pertinent and relevant. I am also unhappy with the hostility on the part of the nonreligious toward the religious. What is really lacking in Israel today is that the regular schools do not provide an education in the Jewish Tradition.

S. F.:   Both in what you have said to me today and in reading your sermons, I understand that a central concern of yours is educating young people to religious observance. There are, as you have just indicated, great problems in this in Israel today, and even greater ones in the Diaspora. How do you see the situation of the Jewish people today in this connection?

Rabbi Lewittes: I once characterized Jewry as a pin headed in one direction and pointing to another. The nonreligious today seem to

be becoming more nonreligious, and the observant, more observant. That is, there seems to me, a widening gap between the two
poles, and this for me is not a healthy situation. On the other hand,
the deepening observance on one side would seem to be a guarantee
of a viable traditional Judaism in the future. You must remember
that when I was a young man in the rabbinate, the common
sociological faith was that "Orthodoxy is passé" and that in another
generation, it will not even exist. That prophecy of doom turned out
to be mistaken, and today there is a vibrant, thriving, observant
Jewish community. One problem, however, is that it is a small
percentage of the total community. Still, it has gained great respec-
tability in the greater Jewish picture among the nationwide organizations. But another deplorable phenomenom is the division within
Orthodoxy itself, between Religious Zionism and the Aguda. Both
of us live by Torah and educate to religious observance. It is difficult
for me to understand why the so-called *Haredim* do not recognize
the gifts God has given us in our history. If we are not grateful
(*makkir tovah*), this is very unfortunate. Our aim must be to
overcome the divisiveness and become what the Prophet calls "One
people in the Land."

S. F.:   In regard to this historical gratitude or, rather, ingratitude of
the people, your friend Rabbi Shubert Spero has written that in the
Oslo Agreement, the government of Israel did what the Jewish
people never, in their worst suffering, agreed to do, to relinquish
their "right" to part of the Land of Israel? How do you understand the
situation of Israel now?

Rabbi Lewittes: I believe that what contributes to the sorry situation is the fact that a great share of the religious Jews of Israel have
not recognized the religious significance of the establishment of the
Jewish State. If they would recognize the religious significance of
Israel and become more involved in it, this would be greatly for the
good. As for the present political reality, we have a marriage of
convenience between two extremes, *Meretz* and *Shas*, leaving the

middle parties on dry ground. As for the Oslo Agreement, I do not
see that it leads us to anywhere but disaster. I believe it must be
changed in time.

As a strong believer in *hashgachah* in God's providential supervision of the world, I believe God adopts a very special strategy with
Israel. God gives us a great amount of latitude, of choice and
freedom. You must do and act for good, and if you do not, it will be
your responsibility and you will have to suffer the consequence. But
then there is a limit to this also, for when we go beyond a certain
breaking point, God intervenes and prevents it from going any
further. One great example of this is at the very beginning of our
history when we were slaves in Egypt. Jews were slaves for generations and suffered greatly. They began then to assimilate, and
deteriorated until they reached what our Sages called the forty-nine
Gates of Impurity. At this point God intervened, saying in effect that
in order to save them it is necessary to act for them. This is, in a
sense, my feeling about the present situation, that we may deterio-
rate to a certain point but then that at that point, God will help us to
find a new way of acting and of saving our situation.

S. F.:   At such a time of difficulty for Israel, it may seem senseless to
ask you the following question. Nevertheless, I would like to hear
your answer to it. Do you believe that the State of Israel can, in the
years ahead, serve as a light to the nations, that we can serve God in
this way?

Rabbi Lewittes: "First improve yourself, then you can improve
others." So our Sages tell us. Unfortunately, we are not in a position
where we have improved ourselves sufficiently in order to become a
light to the nations. In our society, we are not sufficiently moral.
When Avraham emphasized the universal aspect exclusively, that
did not work out. And God had to come down to Yitzhak and
Yaakov so that we could become more particularistic. Our Sages say
that when we say the *"Magen Avraham"* blessing of the *Amidah* we do
not conclude with *"Magen* Abraham, Isaac, and Jacob," we conclude

with "*Magen* Abraham," that is, with the universal aspect. That's the end, the close, the coming of the Messiah. But until we ourselves become an illustrious example to the world, that cannot happen. We can speak about our present state as the "beginning of the light of Redemption," but it's certainly not messianic. It is for us to pray and to work for this ideal state, and through this perfection of ourselves, to become the model for others.

Rabbi Shlomo Riskin

Rabbi Shlomo Riskin is one of the most dynamic leaders of modern Orthodox Jewry. In his American years, he was known, among other things, for revitalizing Lincoln Square Synagogue and contributing greatly to the renewed interest in Judaism of large numbers of young people. Even more remarkable is the transformation he made to being the communal builder and leader of the community of Efrat in Gush Etzion, just six miles south of Jerusalem. His description of how the building of Efrat came about is a central part of this interview. Rabbi Riskin is also a popular columnist whose weekly commentary on the *parshah* appears in 250 newspapers. In Efrat he is building not only a community but a network of Torah institutions for all ages, which is likely to make a major contribution to shaping the Israel of the future.

My first interview with Rabbi Riskin was in his car on the way from Efrat to Jerusalem. My second, which was much shorter than I would have liked, took place in his office. As communal rabbi, teacher, and lecturer, Rabbi Riskin is in demand and busy all the time, working at a remarkably intense pace. His energetic character is reflected in what might be called the upbeat tone of his speech. He is one of those people who does more than ten average people and yet is always running behind the new demands placed upon him. He gave me the impression of being a tremendously devoted rabbi, teacher of Torah, and builder of Jewish community values.

My regret was that my interviews just give a brief hint of the remarkable treasure of wisdom and learning that Rabbi Riskin has to give.

S. F.:   Could you describe the main stage in your transition from innovative spiritual leader in America to community builder and spiritual leader in Israel?

Rabbi Riskin: In 1975 there was a major symposium held in Kibbutz Lavi, which featured religious thinkers from both Israel and America. At the conclusion of the conference, each of the Americans was sent to a *kibbutz* for *Shabbat.* I was sent to one of the *kibbutzim* that had been first built in Gush Etzion in the 1930s and 1940s, Ein Tsurim. This *kibbutz* had been destroyed on May 13, 1948, with the fall of Gush Etzion. Before this, I had not been all that conversant with modern Israeli history, and here, through meeting with the family of Yehuda and Zehava Naiman, who became my close friends, all this changed. He told me of his having been in the *kibbutz* during the time of its fall, of his time in Jordanian capitivity, and of his deep love for the *kibbutz.* Through his recounting of the modern history, I learned to appreciate the Gush and its background, and I subsequently visited it a number of times. In fact, the next summer I came back as scholar-in-residence, and in the summer of 1976, I met a remarkable individual named Moshe Moshkevitz, who had been in the Gush in the 1940s. He had been a member of "Massuot Yitzhak," and his life had been saved only because during the fall and massacre he had been on a special mission to Cyprus. He had always dreamed of founding a city in the Gush, and had even called it in his mind "Efrat." The name Efrat was, of course, a reference to the biblical story in which the matriarch Rachel was buried in Bethlehem on the road to Efrat. As there was a cemetery in the area from Bronze Age times, it seems likely that the city of Efrat had been located in this place.

Unbeknownst to me, Moshe Moshkevitz came to a lecture of mine in New York, after which he was filled with enthusaism. So when I was back in Israel, he approached me and brought me to the spot of his proposed city. There he said to me: "They once asked Meir Dizengoff, the first mayor of Tel Aviv, how you become the mayor of a city in Israel. And Dizengoff replied, 'You build the city, and then you become its mayor.' Now I need a partner in building the city of Efrat." We shook hands and I *davvened Minchah* on the spot. And I believed profoundly that a city would develop on that spot. He was, at that time, already chairman of the Judean Mountains Development Corporation, and I became a member. In New York, I established an organization called *Reshit Geula* (The Beginning of Redemption) and began speaking of the dream of building a city some seven and one half miles south of Jerusalem, the city of Efrat. It would be situated between Jerusalem and Hebron, between the city of the Messiah and the city of the Patriarchs and Matriarchs, between the city of the Jewish future and the city of the Jewish past. Subsequently, I returned every summer as scholar-in-residence at the *kibbutz*, all the while working on the building of the dream. In 1981 came the ground breaking, and *Erev* Pesach 1983, the first family moved in. The last days of Pesach that year, my wife and I came for the first prayer service. That summer we made *aliyah* with our family.

I should add that the previous year I had established the Ohr HaTorah institutions, beginning with the high school for boys. I appointed a director general, David Freund; a *rosh yeshivah*, Shimon Golan; and a principal, Meir Krause; and we began the first public building in Efrat, the *yeshivah* for boys. So when I came in the summer of 1983 that month of *Elul*, we had our first class in the Neveh Shmuel high school of Ohr HaTorah, and this was the beginning of the network of schools.

S. F.:   Can you briefly describe the development of Efrat in the past ten years?

Rabbi Riskin: The development has been nothing short of miraculous. We now have close to a thousand families, with another five hundred families on the way. There is a beautiful elementary school of eight hundred students, the beginnings of a junior high school, kindergartens, nurseries, day-care centers that have nearly a thousand children. And there is also the Ohr HaTorah network, the high school for boys, with three hundred students, and the school for young women, which is just five minutes away.

S. F.: Rabbi, I sense that you are involved in every detail of what's going in the building and community life of Efrat. Could you describe your typical day?

Rabbi Riskin: My typical day begins with a *Daf Yomi shiur* from 6:30 to 7:15. There are generally twenty-five to forty participants. We have gone through *Shas* once, and we are now halfway through the second time. Then I usually *davven* with the sixth, seventh, and eighth grades and afterward give them a short Dvar Torah. After that, I go into one of the high school classes; I try to get into every high school class at least once every two weeks. Being in the classes enables me to get to know the students, and I provide for them *Ha asherah* (enrichment) on the theological and moral implications of the *suggiot* that they are learning. As the rabbis are in the *shiur* I give, it enables them to learn my own methodology in Gemara. After this, there is the work in the office, which involves my rabbinical duties for the community. In the afternoons, I teach *Hashgachah* one day a week at Yeshivat HaMivtar. One day a week, I teach a general lesson for the older boys of this *yeshivah*. And one day a week, I am at Morasha, which is our kind of Yeshiva University for post–high school graduates. Also, when various groups and seminars come to Efrat, I show them around. In the evenings, I teach in all the women's schools. In the evenings I also teach various *bar mitzvahs* and *bat mitzvahs*. Generally, I begin the day at 4:30 every morning and rarely get to sleep before 11:30.

S. F.: Rabbi, it would seem your whole life is dedicated to the service of the community of the people of Israel, to *Avodat Kodesh, Avodat Hashem.* How do you personally understand this concept of *Avodat Hashem*?

Rabbi Riskin: The best way I can explain it is by telling a story. In 1970, I was on a mission for the State of Israel and for the U. S. State

Department to the Soviet Union. My main job was to start up five underground *yeshivot*. By the time I got to Riga, the Soviet KGB was following me closely; four goons were with me everywhere. When I was in the synagogue on *Shabbat*, after the Torah was returned to the Ark, someone whispered to me that I should go down after the service to the basement. My hope was that the KGB officers would think of their lunch and not accompany me. Down there, it took awhile for my eyes to adjust to the darkness. There were somewhere around fifteen people, and a table was spread with vodka, honey, and sponge cake. They sat me at the head of the table and, thirsty for Torah, they asked me to speak. I gave them a *Dvar Torah*, we took some vodka and cake, and we sang *niggunim*. Then they asked for more Torah. There was more vodka, more song and dance. This went on for nine rounds, and after this, two things happened. First, I said I was out of "*divrei Torah*," and second, the room went from black to pink. I had, until that point, felt Tishah B'Av, and now I felt "Purim."

But then I turned to one of those present, Reb Yisrael, and said to him: "I want to bring something back. I want a *dvar Torah* from you." The *parshah* was *Ki Tetze*, which includes the injunction about "not delaying the payment to a day worker." This, in turn, refers to the Gemara in *Kiddushin* 39b, about there being no reward for obeying commandments in this world. Now, it would seem on the surface that there is a contradiction here. On the one hand, we are talking about not delaying wages, and on the other, we are saying that the reward of a *mitzvah* is another *mitzvah*. Now I should say here that this discussion was going on when at any moment the door could be opened and we all could be dragged off to prison. In the Soviet Union, then, to have a *kiddush* and to give a *dvar Torah* was against the law. Now the Gemara we were discussing at that moment illuminated our situation even then. If you look at the Gemara in *Baba Metzia*, the Gemara distinguishes between a day laborer and a contractor. A day laborer is paid at the end of his day's work, but a contractor, only when he finishes his job. Now Rav Yisrael explained the real meaning of what we were saying there is that in reference to your work for God, we are not day laborers; we are all, instead, contractors. Man is created in the image of God, and our task is one that is lifelong, that we cannot expect to complete in any one moment. I think this had special meaning then when one considered how long these people had waited to hear words of Torah, and how long those who had kept to the Torah had labored in the Soviet Union without reward.

So the most critical question a person can ask in regard to the service of God is whether he is using the unique strengths that God has given him to serve God and to perfect God's world. When we say *Alenu* each time, we make a reference to this, to the perfection of the world of *El Shaddai*. To serve God, each of us has to do his own little bit to perfect the world. And often we cannot know, even after ten or twenty years, whether we have done correctly. In regard to my own service of God, then, I moved to America from Israel because here I felt I could better serve life, serve God.

S. F: Rabbi, both in America and in Israel you have served God and the Jewish people through leading many individuals to *teshuvah*. How have you been able to succeed in this?

Rabbi Riskin: I have just said that everyone must use the faculties he has been given. But I would correct you: it is not me who leads people to *teshuvah*, but rather the Torah itself. I do understand how to explain Torah in a way that becomes attractive, but it is the Torah's teachings that are decisive. As to my own efforts, this in effect began in Lincoln Square, where I gave a crash course in Judaism. Now in the Ohr Hatorah Institutions, in the Rabbinical Seminary, many of my peers are involved in the teaching. We now have over thirty rabbi teachers throughout the Jewish world. Since I have come to Israel, I do a great deal of speaking during three months of traveling to South and North America, South Africa, England, Australia, New Zealand. I try to strengthen the teachers we have in different places, and when I am there, to understand how they are developing. I do the best I can in every way I can. But I would say the most important way I carry on this effort is through the work of my students.

S. F.:   In relation to this process of *teshuvah*, what steps do you believe now should be urgently taken to narrow the gap between secular and religious Jews?

Rabbi Riskin: I am not sure that in Israel the gap is increasing. There's a fascinating new study by the Guttman Institute that proves there is in Israeli society a continuum in relation to religious observance, and in the people's relation to Jewish civilization and culture. As I understand it, the most important task of the Jewish community is to produce rabbi educators who can serve as a bridge between religious and not-yet-religious Jewry. There is in Israel no developed concept of a rabbinate as a moral and ethical voice that stands outside the political realm. As for those living outside of Israel, I would recommend that communities should ensure that every Jewish high school student has a year in Israel and that the student during that time be exposed to the fullness of civilization that is Judaism, including Jewish literature and Jewish life on festival days in the Land of Israel. If we can take just these two practical steps we will come a long way.

S. F.:   Is it really possible to differentiate the religious from the political in the Land of Israel? In your *Shabbat Teshuvah* lecture this year, you addressed what may seem for some a political question when you endorsed Rambam's answer and said that any place Jews live and work on the land is sanctified by them, and thus not subject to political negotiation.

Rabbi Riskin: There is nothing alien to Torah, and everything is under the umbrella of Torah. But there has to be a division between the religious and the political. In Israel I do not think it serves religion at this particular point to be involved with political parties. Perhaps at the start of the State of Israel, the parties were critical to making an expression of the religious point of view. Now I believe religious parties have become counterproductive. The element of coercion turns the general population against religion. To take an example, now every child born in a nonreligious *kibbutz* is circumsized. Believe me, if the religious parties in the Knesset pushed through legislation requiring circumcision, a large number would stop performing it.

S. F.:   But these religious parties have constituencies with real needs. I do not know how you manage in Efrat without such party support.

Rabbi Riskin: We are independent. I believe that if there were no religious parties, the great number of people who have *Masorti* traditional religious interests would have those taken care of through their belonging to the larger parties who want their support.

S. F.:   So many people, the great majority within the religious community in Israel, have been tremendously shaken by the Oslo Agreement. Yet when I last heard you speak, I sensed a calmness in you.

Rabbi Riskin: I am certainly concerned and believe the government is making certain tragic mistakes. However, I have ultimate faith in the Jewish nation. The fact is, at the announcement of the agreement, 80 percent were for it, and as I speak to you now, 40 percent are. I don't think that in the long run, the government of Israel can work against such a large majority.

S. F.:   One last question. How do you see the community of Efrat developing in the years to come? Do you favor there being one Jerusalem municipality that includes, on one side, Gush Etzion Efrat, and on the other, Maale Adumim—a greater Jerusalem concept?

Rabbi Riskin: Efrat will, in the years ahead, reach Jerusalem. Its communal and educational institutions will continue to grow. And it will become a Torah center providing religious and educational leadership in this land for the twenty-first century. We hope we will produce people who will provide a moral and ethical voice for Israel and mankind.

Rabbi Aharon Rakeffet

Rabbi Aharon Rakeffet (Rothkoff) is a dynamic and innovative teacher of Torah. He obtained a Ph.D. in American Jewish history and is the author of the *Silver Era in American Jewish Orthodoxy* and *Bernard Revel: Builder of American Jewish Orthodoxy*. One of the youngest *rosh yeshivot* at Yeshiva University, he gave up his high position to realize a lifelong dream and come on *aliyah* to Israel. A devoted student of Rav Soloveitchik, he has labored for many years to make the Torah of the Rav better known in Israel. Rabbi Rakeffet, as a student of modern Jewish history, has pioneered in teaching young people ways of understanding how to live a devoted Torah life in the modern world.

I spoke with Rabbi Rothkoff at the Israel Center on Straus Street in downtown Jerusalem. A person of great enthusiasm, he in effect did the interview for me, often anticipating my questions before me. I was especially moved by his spontaneous answer to my question on whether he thought of his life in terms of *Avodat Hashem*. The answer literally leaped at me: "All I am is *Avodat Hashem*." Our interview centers on the teaching Rabbi Rakeffet has done through the years and on his conception of the teacher as highest Jewish role. His distinction between the *Sofer Mosheh* and the *Moreh Mosheh* and the higher place that the Tradition gives to the latter reflect the central role of teaching in his own life and work.

S. F.:   Could you describe your present teaching activities?

Rabbi Rakeffet: I am presently teaching at the Yeshiva University, Gross Kollel, in Jerusalem, where I give two major *shiurim* a week. One class is on the dynamics of the Halachah and is a combination of *yeshivah* and *Wissenschaft* approaches. *Baruch Hashem,* I have this year started the third cycle, and God should help me finish it, and start again. When I "learned" in Lakewood, Rabbi Aharon Kotler had a seven-year cycle on *Shas,* with *chiddushim* for his *shiurim,* and this was a model for me. The second *shiur* in on the teaching of Rav Soloveitchik. When I came on *aliyah* over twenty-five years ago, there was little knowledge of his teaching, and yet there was a great hunger to know more about his work. A few years later, David Hartman came on *aliyah* and started talking about Rav Soloveitchik, and about the same time, Pinchas Peli started talking about him. As a very close student of the Rav, I thought there was distortion, and people were getting more of Hartman and more of Peli in the respective classes than Soloveitchik. So I began in 1977 to give a course on the Rav, which in time developed into a three-year course. I take it for granted that my students are familiar with the Rav's publications, but the course does not center on them but rather on *Torah SheB'al Peh* (Oral Torah). I heard from the Rav over a period of forty years. I speak about the Rav as Rosh Yeshiva, as philosopher, as American, as Zionist, as Agudist, as human being, about everything I know the Rav was. I try to give it as honestly as possible, and I call it *Mishnat Rav Soloveitchik.* I would like to think it is 99 percent Soloveitchik and 1 percent Rakeffet. I can't say it's 100 percent the Rav because I am only a human being. This class is different from any other I give. Every *shiur* is reconstructed exactly as he gave it. If I say something of my own, I will always let that be known.

My other teaching now is in a school that I helped organize called Midreshet Moriah. We started seven years ago with fifty girls, and today we have four candidates for every one of our eighty-three beds. It's sad because a lot of good girls are not taken. I had taught at Michlalah for many years and was happy to bring with me to

Moriah most of the Zionist or semi-Zionist faculty. Midreshet Moriah, where I now give three classes a week, has become a premier school. Of the classes I give here, one I do twice because of the great demand for it. This class developed in 1971 at Machon Gold at a time when there were very few classes for overseas students, particularly girls. The class I taught at Gold that year was one of the finest I have ever had and included Beis Yaakov, Flatbush, Central, and Ramaz girls. I was young and popular then, the way Haim Ramon is today. Incidentally, I resent the cult of youth worship in our society. I know I myself may have had more strength then, but I was much less knowledgable, a lot stupider. In any case, the girls in this class came to me and said, "Rebbe, we are unhappy because we have questions no one is answering." So I gave them a paper and told them to write down the problems bothering them, and on the basis of this began a new class. This class is now a year long but should be even longer. And it is always being updated, as the girl of 1995 is not the girl of 1971. This course is basically one man's attempt to explain what it is to be a Jew in the modern world. I say to them two things: "If you do not want to live in the modern world, don't come to this class, and also, "If you don't want to really learn Torah, don't come to this class." I am a funny guy; I am not a *chabadnik*. If you want to learn with me, come, I'll be your best friend. But I'm not here to change anyone. I tell everyone, "The Torah is going to go on, with or without you." The first unit deals with the concept of rabbinical authority. The second and, by far, most popular unit, fortunately or not, deals with marriage and sex, and with how to have a happy marriage in today's world. Today there are numerous books on these subjects from a Torah point of view, but when I began it was a groundbreaking activity. I'd like to believe that those who take my course have less divorce than those who do not. In this unit I also deal with the relationship with parents. The second involves marriage, and questions of mourning. The third unit is concerned with *aliyah*. In this unit, I tell my students that those who are sitting here in Yerushalayim as if it were China should please not attend. I try to scare them away, but fortunately, no one gets scared away. In this unit I deal with the Holocaust, with problems of Religious Zionism. Also, I deal with the Haredi community. A fourth unit (which I stressed in the 1970s but don't anymore) is on Reform, Reconstructionist, Conservative Judaism. I tell my students that they are not going to hear one negative word from me, that all they will hear is the absolute truth. By the time I am finished, they have no problem understanding why they are Orthodox Jews. I round out this series with a unit on faith and biblical criticism. What has happened is that with so much divorce, the lectures on "happy marriage" take more and more time.

S. F.:   Rabbi, could you tell me about the way you made *aliyah?*

Rabbi Rakeffet: I see *Hashgachah Pratit* (Divine Providence) in all my life. When I came on *aliyah,* I have to admit now, I was "small in faith" in that I wanted to be certain of having a job. I was a young man at the time and was a *rosh yeshivah.* I may have been the first *rosh yeshivah* to leave Yeshiva University on his own free will. You must understand the meaning of being *rosh yeshivah,* of being able to teach Torah, how most people would pay for the privilege of teaching Torah. In 1969, I signed a contract with *Encyclopaedia Judaica* to become a staff editor in Israel. I was qualified because I had a doctorate and a contract with the Jewish Publication Society for the first real Orthodox book they ever published, my work on Bernard Revel. I was just what *Encyclopaedia Judaica* needed, someone knowledgeable in Shas and Poskim, with a doctorate in Jewish History and the ability to write in English. I came on *aliyah* on July 5, 1969, went to work a week later, and have never been unemployed in Israel since. I was, in one sense, happy with the encylopedia and wrote many articles for it, but in the course of time, I missed my students and teaching. To put it simply, during this time I was a *Sofer* but not a *melamed.* Moshe Rabbenu is called in the Gemara from *Sotah "Safra,"* but the Rav always said Moshe Rabbenu's greatest title was *HaMelamed Torah L'Am Yisrael* (Who Teaches Torah to the People of Israel). So in 1969, Machon Gold was opened up, and its first dean, Whitey Horowitz (who knew my brother and was acquainted with my published writings in *Jewish Life,* where I had more publications than any other author) invited me to teach. For me it was like manna from heaven. And I went on to teach there for twenty years. I put my life into the place, influenced hundreds of students. At a recent Bnei Akiva reunion, so many came over with tears in their eyes, thanked me and hugged me. I had great *nachat* from this, for there they were with their wives and children, and I understood I had influenced their lives for good.

When I began teaching at Machon Gold, I taught a course called "The Saga of Torah in Modern Times." This course has to do with the question of how we, while coming out of the ghetto, remain Torah Jews. I deal with *Hochmat Yisrael,* Mendelssohn, Napoleon, the Counter-Reaction. I also deal with the chasidic answer to modernity, and my favorite lectures are an analysis of the chasidic world halachically. You can hear in this course the echos of my rebbe, Rav Soloveitchik. The second term was on the Vilna Gaon, Haim Volozhin, the Musar movements, and then there is a unit is on German Orthodoxy, Rav Hirsch, and Rav Hildesheimer. I never have time to finish the final unit, which is on Torah in America. You must understand that all the previous things I have spoken about I do not know about as an expert. The only thing I have a doctorate in is the history of Jews in America. But here I followed the Rav, who always said: "Never lecture on what you know. Lecture on what you do not know, and that way you will master knowledge." One year I remember him saying: "Why Massekhet Niddah? Because I haven't looked at it in thirty years."

I also taught, beginning in 1971, a course on responsa literature in Michlalah. The first year I covered *Geonim* and *Rishonim* and the next year *Achronim.* I actually published a textbook with a selection of *teshuvot* spanning over one thousand years. And one more course I gave was an introduction to the Oral Law, in which I dealt with a lot of problems people are dealing with today. Rav Herschel Schacter just published a volume on many of these problems.

I taught for all those years, and nonetheless, to a certain degree suffered because I always dreamed about the *rosh yeshivah* I had been in the 1960s, when I taught Talmud five days a week. Then I lectured in Gefen, *Gemorra Perush* (Rashi), and *Tosfot*. I never got back to that, though teaching in the Kollel has been great compensation. And in fact, when *Encyclopaedia Judaica* was completed and they offered me a fat contract to continue, I declined because I wanted to go back to full-time teaching. At one point, there was nothing I wanted more than to be the rebbe of Beis Midrash L'Torah (BMT). But I don't believe I suited the image they wanted. They saw me more as a professor of Jewish History. They used to call me "Professor," but I said, "I do not need titles, but if you want to give me a title, please call me 'Rabbi Rakeffet.' "

S. F.:   Rabbi, as a student of Jewish history, how do you see the situation of the Jewish people today?

Rabbi Rakeffet: The situation is great today, and it's horrible. A month from today, I will be in New York speaking in honor of my childhood friend Rabbi Herschel Schacter. We grew up together in the Bronx, and in those days when I went to *Shul* there was no one between the age of thirteen and seventy there. So on the one hand, what we have today is tremendous, in Israel, in America, Canada, France, Belgium, and even Russia. Hundreds of thousands of people are engaged in prayer and learning. The chasidic world today is so much greater than it was just after World War II. In 1950, when the previous Rebbe died, Lubavitch was a few thousand people. Now it's a movement all over the world, with tens and tens of thousands. And we have the variety, "the knitted skullcap of Bnei Akiva," and the various groups of the Haredi world. In one sense, it's unbelievably good.

On the other hand, there is great tragedy. It's politicians like Haim Ramon. When *Shas* threw its support to these absolute leftists, anti-Torah people, they held a conference and its guest of honor was Haim Ramon. They began *davvening Minchah* and he stood there as if it were as meaningful to him as a Chinese warlord's dance before the tomb of Mao Tse-tung. He stood there without a *siddur*, without understanding what was going on. Not only that, but a non-Jew would show the courtesy of finding out what was going on. The element represented by Ramon does not even care to find out. The tragedy in short, is assimilation. In the United States, there is not a house that has not lost someone to assimilation. My wife and I come from families that have been in America for one hundred years. We have over one hundred souls from our two families walking the streets of Israel. About everyone who came on *aliyah*, we can say, "Here all of you are living today." In America, there is not in the fourth generation one Jewish marriage yet. And so the tragedy. The Jewish people have revived themselves after the Holocaust, and yet we are now suffering a "spiritual holocaust." Intermarriage is 50 percent in America, and in ten years it will be 70 percent.

S. F.:   What do you think can and should be done?

Rabbi Rakeffet: I don't know if there is any panacea. One thing is certain, that we have to educate and reach out. And here, as the Rav used to say, "Lubavitch and I have one agenda in common. We don't give up on any child." In one sense, it is easier in America because if they want to be Jewish, they seek religious identification. If their need is answered intelligently, there is some hope of success. But in Israel, the religious problem is that you are Jewish simply by living here, speaking Hebrew. You do not need religious identification. Too, religion here often represents to the public mind the religious parties and their extortion. Religion should be taken out of politics and made a great educational venture. Rav Schach said a few years ago, "You Zionists have built a wonderful state, turned a desert wasteland into a fertile state. But what is your connection with the Jews of the past, with your spiritual heritage? What kind of Jewish life can be had without *Shabbat?* family purity? So, we must raise the banner and reach out. Obviously, I'd rather have assimilated Jews in

Israel rather than outside. Nonetheless, the problems are great. There's no panacea. Raise the banner of Torah in dignity.

S. F: But isn't this possible only when there is some real connection between the religious and political, the spiritual vision of the nation? Many who dislike the present government in Israel nonetheless do not look forward that eagerly to the alternative because it, too, is a secular party devoid of spiritual vision?

Rabbi Rakeffet: I would like to see a situation similar to the one that pertains in America in which religious Jews are vital to the large parties but the parties themselves are not religious. No serious politician in New York City can disregard the vote of religious Jews. We need religious Jews in Israel in the Likud. When politicians know a large percentage of votes is coming from religious Jews, they will respond appropriately. Religious Jews like Rav Amital and Rav Lichtenstein can vote for the *Maarach*.

S. F: Many of those who see the Redemption of the people and Land of Israel as the divine action in history see our present government's actions as a real setback. How do you understand the situation of Israel now?

Rabbi Rakeffet: Rabbi Motti Elon, who speaks on *Parashat Hashavua* each Wednesday night at Yeshurun Synagogue, gave this past week an amazing talk on the Prophet Jeremiah and his purchase and redemption of the field of Hanamael in Anatot. The Prophet's act of faith, his belief in the future Redemption at a time of disaster, was perhaps meant to be a consolation to us. Many people left the *shiur* feeling comforted. I heard the talk, and I thought about how tragic the situation is. In 1967, our thought was on return and rebuilding, and now we find comfort in the prophet of Hurban. Look how much we have gone downhill in twenty-seven years. It's very depressing. There is no question but that this government has created a setback in Zionist and Jewish feeling. If this continues, a lot more religious

Jews are going to become *Haredim*. The *Haredim* don't admit that they helped create this government. It's a tragic event. The Aguda has erred in every major historical situation of the Jewish people in this century. *Shas* is a direct result of the Aguda. Who would ever believe that these people would put in power people who are so antireligious? One should say these words and sit down covered with ashes.

If there is a choice between "*Haredi*" and "secular," there is no choice: I am *Haredi* a million times over. I have nothing in common with secular Jews in any way. Our Sages knew what they were doing when they made being an observer of *Shabbat* the criterion for being a believing Jew. The minute a person makes the *kiddush* for *Shabbat*, he acknowledges that there is a Creator above us all. When you don't make *kiddush*, then the only basis for morality is what is inside the human and the human becomes the creator of morality and ethics. We know human spiritual development cannot go very far when it is based on a worship of humanity alone.

The situation now, in which such people are in power, is frightening. But who said the process of Redemption would be easy? We know there must be ups and downs. I was here during the Yom Kippur War when Israel was nearly wiped off the map. The saving hand of God helped us then. So we must not lose faith, but instead must be solid and firm, with our feet on the ground. We must educate and argue, do our best to convince the people to bring this present government down.

The whole world has to be made to understand what Jews have gone through in these past years. No one justifies the action of Dr. Baruch Goldstein, but one must understand what he went through, the situation where his best friends were murdered near him, where Jews were subject to violence and threat, day after day. The humiliation and loss of Jewish self-respect is great when we cannot reply to those who rise up to kill us. They are not only throwing rocks but they are shooting at us, and we cannot answer. I went to Beit El on the very bus that last night was shot up. Automatically, a bus with Jews is stoned. This is a desecration, and we have to yell and shout out our protest.

Now the *Haredim* are laughing at the Zionist dream. But I would like to believe that it will not go that much further. Everyone knows there has to be a compromise, but it has to be a compromise we can live with as Jews and Israelis. I told Rabbi Daniel Tropper, "You can't shout compromise at the beginning, or you have nothing left to compromise with at the end." I want to believe that if the government goes too far, some of the Labor Party's own members will not abandon their principles but rather will pull out and so make it impossible for the government to abandon Judaea and Samaria or the Golan.

S. F.:　The central concept of this work is the concept of *Avodat Hashem*. Do you see your life and work in terms of this concept?

Rabbi Rakeffet:　My whole life is *Avodat Hashem*. Here I invoke the teaching of the Rav. The Rav taught that everyone has to do in life what they have a special calling for. The Rav used to say that the greatest expression of *Tzelem Elokim* (Divine Image) is the uniqueness of every individual. The concept is that we all have different abilities and inclinations. And no matter what the calling is, the Jew must do this for the sake of God. Our life's ultimate goal should be for us to be great Jews who "serve God." In this there must be the surrender of the individual will to God's will and Torah. The Rav used to say that the community of Israel has no time limit. Abraham Avinu is a member with us, and Mosheach is a member with us.

　　Those of us who feel a calling like the tribe of Levi to teach Torah have the greatest calling in life. I am very fortunate. From the age of twelve I had only one dream: to be a rebbe. This was my goal. And I was given to fulfill the dream beyond my greatest expectations. I started teaching kids of high-school age. I have taught college and now postgraduate. In teaching, I feel my whole life is one song of *Avodat Hashem*.

　　I often think of Reb Isar Zelman Meltzer, who when he started his first *shiurim* at Slobodka was overwhelmed, wondering where he would get all the Chiddushim to teach such bright students. I started my first *shiurim* over thirty-five years ago and, *Baruch Hashem,* I am still going strong. I have taught tens of thousands of students, but it has always been one times ten thousand, not ten thousand times one. Each one is precious. When I walk in the class, I have the sense that the *Melamed's* task is the most sacred. The Jewish people will survive, whether or not there are doctors and warlords. They will not survive without a *melamed,* without the person passing it on to the next generation. And to me, this being a *melamed* is a sacred profession.

I am very grateful I was able to come on *aliyah.* Many people said to me back then, you have to be an Israeli in education. But I said, "No, I have to remain an American in my teaching approach." Today everyone is knocking on the doors of Americans because they have turned out to be great teachers in Torah. We were among those who brought *teshuvah* to Israel. And this is in accordance with the Gemara at the end of *Megillah* that in the future, Houses of Prayer and Study of Babylon will be established in the Land of Israel. When the Ingathering comes, we will need the traits of every Diaspora community. The American Jew learned how to teach Torah in dignity. The profession of teaching, as I understand, is a holy profession, upon which rests the future of the Jewish people in the world, the future of God's blueprint. God cannot be in the world without Torah and the Jews to study it. The *Zohar* puts it succinctly: "Israel, the Torah, and God are one."

Rabbi Ze'ev Chaim Lifshitz

Rabbi Ze'ev Chaim Lifshitz has been, for over thirty years, one of the important teachers of Torah and community counselors in Israel. He is the founder of the Enosh Seminar, which provides a variety of family-counseling services, including a comprehensive marriage-counseling program. Rabbi Lifshitz was the personal secretary of the great European Posek Rabbi Yechiel Yaakov Weinberg (the Seredei Esh), and studied developmental psychology with Jean Piaget in Geneva. Rabbi Lifshitz is an original thinker who has developed a system of Jewish psychology based on traditional Jewish content and modern psychological technique.

As a frequent attender of Rabbi Lifshitz's Friday lectures, which were given in his Beit Midrash in the French Hill district of Jerusalem, I had before our interview a fair acquaintance with the character of this thought. In our interview, Rabbi Lifshitz talked about one of the major problems of modern man, the "too much, too soon" appetite, which leads the individual to become a slave to his own *yetzer hara*. Rabbi Lifshitz also reveals his own unique way of helping others find the way to help themselves and bring out their own creative spark. For Rabbi Lifshitz, each and every human being has their own special God-given gift, through which they can sanctify life in the world.

S. F.:   Rabbi, could you describe your present activities in teaching and counseling, and your other work?

Rabbi Lifshitz: I have for forty years been involved in the guidance of Jewish youth, those who are looking for some sense of purpose and meaning in their lives. The range of people I deal with go from the extreme ultra-Orthodox, such as Satmar and Belz *chasidim,* through the Lithuanian *yeshivot,* to the modern Orthodox, and then to the *Baalei teshuvah.* The common denominator of these young people is that they are intellectuals, people who think and want to understand, though they may not, at times, know this. I consider this my most important activity. We have a *yeshivah* for these youngsters, which is based upon the principle of developing their own opinion and thought. In many other *yeshivot* they are encouraged to accumulate knowledge and know the opinions of various teachers in the Gemorah. But our emphasis is on encouraging them to think and encouraging them to seek to understand the essence of various concepts. We encourage them to create within the mode of talmudic thought.

There is a daily course that is given by my son. It is totally free. There is a short class to guide them in the *suggiah* each day. And at the end of the week, I give a more global and comprehensive picture to help them put the thought together. In the afternoons my son teaches them a class in *Halachah,* its foundation and development. We want them to know the problematic side of *Halachah* and to show how *posekim* made their decisions.

The guidance that is given is based, too, on my own life research in human behavior. I have, through years of work, developed my own theory on the cause and dynamics of human needs, from within and without. This has brought me to—I would not say psychological treatment, for I do not believe in what is called "psychology," but rather in "guidance." I give guidance to those who have problems in behavior. And a side activity is the research I have done in order to discover the dynamics of "coupling" in human relationships.

S. F.:   You have developed an overall theory of human relationships?

Rabbi Lifshitz: I would not say I am looking for an overall theory but rather placing special emphasis on the study of one-to-one relationships. Friends, husband and wife, partners in business. I ask questions such as: "What makes people love, or hate, each other? What is needed for there to be a good couple?" These kinds of questions touch upon another major activity of mine. I have for years been involved in the task of making "peace" (*shalom bayit*) within the family. I am working with twenty assistants. During the past twenty years, I have been working with Sadnat Enosh, which I founded in Jerusalem. We are, I believe, the largest center in the Jewish world for "peacemaking" within the family. We have on file close to twenty-five thousand cases. We have an excellent success record, and for every ten couples who wish to divorce, we send nine home together. The tenth case is the one in which we encourage the divorce because without divorce the couple would bring serious damage to each other. They have what is called "*din rodef.*" In this case, it is necessary to separate them. But for the great majority of the rest, we found out they often do not know how to read the map of their relationship and can, when corrected, learn to live in harmony. I use my theory of "one-to-one relations" to help the couple reestablish the positive relationship they started with, begin to appreciate each other and cooperate with each other again, even in happiness. And all these activities are based on my research as to what the human being is from the Jewish point of view.

S. F.:   Rabbi, what is your educational background?

Rabbi Lifshitz: It is problematic, as I am problematic. I am the enfant terrible of the society of rabbis, and in another way, of the society of psychologists. I am trained in the Israeli black *yeshivot,* and my *rebbe* is Rebbe Shlomo Zalman Auerbach. Although all my youth was spent learning Torah in *yeshivot,* the main source of education and inspiration for me came from my home. I was blessed and come from one of the most distinguished rabbinical families of the Jewish world. I am cousin to the greatest, such as Reb Moshe Feinstein and Rav Soloveitchik. My late father was an absolute "*talmid chacham*" who I do not remember not learning. He slept a little, ate a little and learned: a real *Litvak*. In his "*hesped*" I said that he learned "Torah for its own sake." He did not get either riches or honor from this. He was a pupil of the Chafetz Chaim. He was my source of inspiration and teacher. My mother was the daughter of the rabbinical giants of the previous generation. So I was literally taking in Torah with my mother's milk.

I also consider myself a religious animal, someone religious by nature. I am sure that had I not learned in *yeshivot,* I still would be very religious. I have a religious personality – one that does not look for the here and now but for the beyond and the above. If I were to describe my nature, I would say that I am a religious creature.

After the *yeshivot* here, my family sent me to Switzerland. There, I was the right hand of one of the greatest "*poseks*" of our time. Reb Yehiel Yaakov Weinberg. I was his right hand in writing his "questions and responses." He was a very clever man: worldly, educated, a professor of old Semitic languages in universities in Germany. And this was after he was a *Gadol* in Torah. He advised me to go to Geneva and study with Piaget. I did this and was Piaget's assistant for six years. This was in the tradition of my family, which, though extremely religious, were not closed into a sect but open to learning and to the development of all our talents, whether in painting, in literature, in philosophy, or in science.

S. F.:   What did you learn in the six years with Piaget?

Rabbi Lifshitz: My purpose when in university in Switzerland was to learn everything Western culture could teach about human behavior. I began with French and French literature, then went on to study education, sociology, anthropology. I then, with Piaget, learned what I considered the most valuable research being done in genetic epistemology, the stages of human mental development. I then studied clinical psychology and worked in it in Geneva.

When I came back to Israel after ten years in Switzerland, I was appointed the spiritual director of one of the biggest *yeshivot* in Israel, Kerem B' Yavneh. This was the period when they were just starting the *Hesder* stream of *yeshivot*, and this *yeshivah* became a center for youth both from abroad and from Israel. Many of these were the best of Jewish youth intellectually and were caught between two cultures. These were very brilliant, curious, intellectual youngsters who wanted everything from both the Western and the Torah worlds. And they pushed me to confront this problem of how to bridge and coordinate two seemingly contradictory approaches to human life. And thanks to them, thanks to these youngsters, I developed my own thought and Jewish philosophy. I developed a Jewish philosophy that is, I believe, wholly within Orthodoxy and yet no less creative in including Western culture.

I myself am an artist, trained in the Academy of Music in Geneva, which is the best school for tenors in the world. I was offered a place in the Metropolitan and LaScala. I refused, for I felt God gave me a voice for the synagogue and not for selling tickets to entertain people.

When people ask me why I, after receiving such high degrees in music and sculpture, do not use them, I reply that I do my real artistic work with human beings. Michelangelo, when he was given a piece of marble, said he saw the masterpiece already there and had only to remove the excess stone. I, too, when I see a human being, understand I only have to take the *klippot* away to show the beautiful human being God created. And that's what I feel like—a sculptor—when I am trying to help someone. Ordinarily, my fingers do not tickle me when I do it. But during vacation when I am not doing it, my fingers start to tickle me.

S. F.:   When you are doing this shaping of the human character, do you have one ideal goal in mind for everyone?

Rabbi Lifshitz: Never. There is not just one goal for so many different human beings. If I think of how to describe my personal attitude to God, then I would say that I am allergic to categorizations, classifications. When God created humanity, He did not start with many, but with one, because He is One. Our being reflects the quality of the divine, and this quality is not to be measured. So each human being is, as our Sages say, "a whole world." The individual human being has the right to be his own unique self, without categorization.

My greatest effort is dedicated to find the uniqueness of the person. I believe in the uniqueness of each and every one, and I am never looking for some common denominator. Often the human being needs a second, nonbiological birth through which he gives birth to his own real, adult self and personality. By learning of his own real self, he knows his own place in life and how to act on it. I concern myself with the micro, the individual, not the macro. And I am against trying to deal with human beings by stuffing them into artificial categories.

S. F.: You deal primarily with the talented people of higher abilities. But what of those who have no special talents or abilities? Where is their place?

Rabbi Lifshitz: That's a very good question. Every human being has his own uniqueness. This need not be academic or intellectual. This uniqueness exists whether the person is important or not.

S. F.: Rabbi, the concept that is at the center of this group of interviews is that of *Avodat Hashem*. How do you relate this conception of the uniqueness of each human being, of your own life and work, to *Avodat Hashem?*

Rabbi Lifshitz: As I said in the beginning, I am a religious creature. Everything I am looking for is related, both directly and indirectly, to *Avodat Hashem*. But what do we mean by *Avodat Hashem?* The ritual or technical *Avodat Hashem?* I don't believe that this is the most important *Avodat Hashem*. I am a halachic Jew, a very strict halachic Jew. But I don't believe the exterior aspect of behavior in relation to *Halachah* determines what you are. What determines what you are is bringing out the unique element in yourself that God has given you, making your unique contribution. We are all a part of the divine throne. Each one has his own uniqueness of soul, the spark of divine in him. If he does not use it, he misses himself. If God gives us any talent, any uniqueness, we have to serve God with it, certainly within the framework of *Halachah*.

And it is our task to make *chiddushim*, to contribute something new. And each individual Jew has to contribute to the wholeness of the Crown. This is why God gave us our uniqueness. If we use this for His goal, we exist, and there is meaning to our existence. Without it, we do not have any meaning, and our existence is a waste. This is my approach: to have a broad definition of *Avodat Hashem* to accommodate the variety of ways to God within the *Halachah*.

S. F.: Rabbi, from all parts of the Jewish world people come to seek your help. You have done this for years and so have a knowledge of the Jewish situation. How would you describe the situation of our people today?

Rabbi Lifshitz: I don't believe the Jews have problems that are different from those of other human beings. I believe, as the Sages say, that the world is organized around a center and the center is God. The Jews are the people of God, so what happens to them happens to the world. So, as Rebbe Israel Salanter said, if a Jew in Kovno is talking while reading the Torah is going on, a Jew in Paris violates *Shabbat* because of this. The mistakes and errors of a Jew have greater weight in humanity than do the mistakes of others. So I feel there is today the same problem for Jew and non-Jew. And the sickness of our world today is "too big, too much, too quickly."

S. F.: What does this mean?

Rabbi Lifshitz: Everything happens today in such a way that the individual cannot adjust. The relationship between the world and the human, the object and the subject, is greatly disturbed. And the human being, human uniqueness, is lost. Everything is categorized through science and statistics and through the nonpersonal approach rules. This works through all the main institutions and structures of humanity.

Consider the structure that is the foundation of society, the family. A society is sick when the family is sick. The world is lost when the traditional family is lost. As for the Jewish world, we have three sicknesses that make one big cancer: mixed marriages, divorce, and singles. In the Western societies, we too have the problem that those who are married do not, when they leave the world, leave after them on average even two Jews. This is one central problem of the Jewish future today.

S. F.:   That's the situation in the Western world, not in the Third and Fourth Worlds, where population is still increasing rapidly.

Rabbi Lifshitz: It's only a question of time before the Western world's attitudes prevail everywhere.

S. F.:   There are signs in Israel of what you might call these "negative demographic trends" increasing in recent years.

Rabbi Lifshitz: Now this is true even in the religious world. The rate of divorce is escalating. In the Western World, it is every third couple, and now among our religious, it is one out of ten. I have studied for years to learn the cause of this. The sickness of the world as I understand it is the outlawing of the individual's right to be himself.

S. F.:   But many social critics blame the family problems in the Jewish and Westerns worlds on the exaggerated place given individual rights. Narcissism and selfishness mean loss of communal and collective responsibility.

Rabbi Lifshitz: The more my individuality is endangered, the more I become selfish. The more my sense of self-preservation is augmented, the more I become a taker, not a giver. My right to become myself is threatened, so in order to preserve my individuality, I become more egotistical.

Here it is necessary to understand the distinction I make in my thought between the self and the ego. The self is the qualitative, the creative element. The ego concerns itself with self-preservation. Fighting for my rights, I am using my ego. I am a taker. I hate, am jealous, am afraid of others.

Now the ground and conditions that encourage us to be ourselves are given in the family. Within the family is the harmony that enables me to be myself. You can grow, cooperate within the family. Your uniqueness has a natural growth within the family. If you want to achieve something outside the family, you will expose the fragile individual to the larger group, where he must fight for his own preservation. If you bring him up in a normal, healthy cell of a family, he will achieve his belonging without giving up his right to be himself.

S. F.:   So is there a way to strengthen the traditional family?

Rabbi Lifshitz: Just to look at this from another point of view: this question of the family is what led me to study the *kibbutz*. I lived for many years at Kibbutz Yavne. I also have family in *kibbutz*. The *kibbutz* came to the idea that in order to fight egoism, you have to bring the larger world in. Yet, paradoxically, no one is a greater egotist than a child in the *kibbutz*. Because he has been deprived of parental love and closeness due to him, he is always fighting to replace it. The *kibbutz* experiment with raising children outside the family failed. We cannot fight God and nature, and the family is the most beautiful natural framework.

S. F.:   So how do you work against those trends that might cause further disintegration within the Jewish world?

Rabbi Lifshitz: I am against the categorizing and the rule by externals. The color and shape of your *kippah* tells how you got up in the morning. The way to fight it is through the renaissance of individual humanness, the building of the uniqueness of the individual.

S. F.: Do you then try to help individuals largely through your own one-to-one, individual relationship with them?

Rabbi Lifshitz: My approach is to make use of a one-to-one relationship. But I do not do this to impose my theories. And if the person is not religious, I will not be a missionary. My concern is with his needs, not mine. I am antidogmatic, as I believe Judaism fundamentally is. I want him to find the unique element of creativity through which he can contribute to the world.

S. F.: And you do this through your own theory? Could you say a bit more about this new kind of Jewish psychology?

Rabbi Lifshitz: Jewish psychology means providing a new picture of what the human being is. The sources are the Bible, Talmud, and all Jewish philosophy, chasidic, Maharal, and some kabbalistic. The method, however, that I use comes from Western psychology. The meaning and content: 90 percent is from traditional Jewish sources.

S. F.: How do you measure success and failure in what you do?

Rabbi Lifshitz: In one sense, if the person's nervous symptoms go away, it can be said to work. But most important, if a person becomes selective, comes to know himself, make use of his own freedom to achieve, he then becomes a creative human being, which means a healthy human being. The more we create, the healthier we are. And this creativity means bringing out the uniqueness of the individual, any talents that God gave him. It is the qualitative potential as expressed toward a goal defined by values. This is what is meant by bringing the divine into the world and making a contribution. And this life of creation for the individual is what I try to guide all my students to.

Dr. Yaakov Fogelman

Dr. Yaakov Fogelman is a teacher of Torah who runs the Torah Outreach Center in the Jewish Quarter of the Old City in Jerusalem. A graduate of Yeshiva University and Harvard Law School, he has devoted the years since his *aliyah* to bringing the Torah's message to Jews and non-Jews. His most effective instrument for doing this has been the weekly *parsha* sheets, in which he uses traditional sources to provide a Religious Zionist critique of modernity. He has also done the important work of putting on film and tape a good share of the important public *shiurim* given in Jerusalem in the past ten years. More than any other person, he helped me become acquainted with the work of a number of the teachers interviewed in this book.

In his interview, Fogelman provides a detailed record of his own life story, which is rich in his appreciation of many of the good people he has known. The interview reveals his generosity of spirit, his great eagerness to help others, his willingness to go out of his own way to make the connection that will be useful to others. The interview gives the example of the Jew who greets every human being with a gracious countenance and meets the world with intelligence, humor, and an eagerness to teach Torah to the world.

S. F.: Could you please describe your present work?

Rabbi Fogelman: I study and teach Jewish Tradition and its interface with the contemporary thought, feelings, and knowledge of the universe; I share my own ongoing, lifetime exploration with others who are trying "to figure the whole thing out," and refer them to interesting and relevant material. I direct the Torah Outreach Program and its Jerusalem Jewish Information Center in Jerusalem's Jewish Quarter.

S. F.: One of the things I believe you are most known for is the weekly Torah commentary sheet you distribute throughout Yerushalayim and, through visitors, all over the world. Could you say something about the way you prepare the sheet and about the thought behind it?

Rabbi Fogelman: The sheets attempt to give a broad overview of the weekly Torah reading, to explore its issues, and to provide comprehensive commentary, squeezing about 34 K bytes onto a two-sided piece of tersely written paper. I'm now doing a final revision after ten years of developing them, to give greater clarity and more sources. Though I may add a point or contemporary application occasionally, they don't change much, as they are a complete synopsis of the weekly readings. But my monthly studies, on broad Jewish topics not limited by the *parshah,* are completely new and take much time to prepare. Some recent topics are "Who's a Jew," "Chasidism and Zionism," "*Ashet Chayil,*" and "Conversion." All my writings now appear on the Internet Network, often within hours of their completion. Readers then print them out for friends and fellow congregants. On Internet, I include revised short summaries of the *parshot* that I wrote from 1989 to 1991 in *Your Jerusalem* and our *Jerusalem Jewish Voice.*

S. F.: Could you tell me something about your family and educational background?

Rabbi Fogelman: My father's family, of chasidic, probably Habad, origin, came to America from a tiny settlement near Vilna. The older siblings came before World War I the younger (including my father, who had *payot* as a child), after several had died in Europe came with my grandfather Yaakov. My grandmother Riva, a quiet, saintly woman, led her children, often without food, across Europe to America. My father and his siblings, though naturally bright, had very little formal education and had to work hard to survive. They all came to speak English but spoke Yiddish amongst themselves. Their children generally attended Hebrew school until *bar mitzvah,* and many received academic educations. But religiously, many fell by the wayside in a primarily Gentile environment. I am the only one, so far, to return to traditional observance and Israel.

My mother was born in America to European-Russian parents whose families settled in the Philadelphia–Camden area. Her paternal grandmother was a Yiddish poetess who lived into her late nineties. My mother's mother, Cecelia Weiner, was strong and pious; her father, Chayim Zubrow, was a more gentle, biblical humanist. Both violently opposed discrimination against any human being. My grandfather recalled the beautiful radiance of Rav Yitzchak Elchanan, whom he once saw passing through the streets. They kept a warm mom-and-pop grocery store in Woodlyne, New Jersey, with my Uncle Sam, and were beloved by their neighbors.

Relatives brought my father's family to Reading, Pennsylvania, where I grew up. I attended its public schools through tenth grade. The moral and religious values that the public schools imparted were basically good and wholesome, though from a Christian perspective. The reading society was basically nonintellectual and nonsophisticated. I joined Jewish Cub Scout groups and won a medal in cycling, becoming a lifetime enthusiast. I was in business from about age eight (dealing in stamps) and was quite independent and individualistic as a child. Though I performed poorly in first grade, I was a topflight student from second grade on. (This had its social disadvantages vis-á-vis the tough lower-class kids, and in the end, I formed my own gang in defense). I received a bit of Jewish education in Kesher Zion (Conservative) Hebrew school until *bar mitzvah.* We'd go to children's services on *Shabbat* and then to the movie double feature. The teachers gave us a good feeling about

Judaism but, as with most American children, my *bar mitzvah* was the end of my Jewish education.

But then something happened that changed the whole course of my life. Chaim Seiger (now of Denver), a young and dynamic rabbi, brought all the Jewish children he could find to his old, dying Orthodox *shul* for really stimulating teaching. When I saw him sitting on my porch in his suit and panama hat, I was convinced he was a postal inspector coming after me for some stamps on approval that I had not returned! So I avoided him. But my mother insisted that I attend in light of my close friendship with a charming lady of another faith. He later took myself and a friend, the late Dr. Mordechai Botvin *z"l*, to his *musar yeshivah*, Chafetz Chaim, which was in the heart of *Haredi* Williamsburg. We both took to it like ducks to water. I left my secular school and studied Talmud and *Musar* for about five years under the kind and saintly Rav A. H. Leibowitz. At night I completed high school and began my higher secular studies at Brooklyn College. Uri Katz, a Harvard returnee and my mentor at the *yeshivah*, discovered that a child below age eighteen could become an "emancipated minor" to avoid going to high school during the day.

Chofetz Chaim was then a small, rather disorganized *yeshivah* of very kind and fine folks, who were nonetheless rather narrow and self-centered in scope and vision. Months were spent on a few comments of *Tosafot*, attempting to recreate the elaborate structures of abstract conceptualization upon which they were supposedly based; yet many so engaged had not even read the whole *Tanach*, let alone Talmud and *midrashim*. The net result of this was to develop supercritical minds who restricted their critical faculty to analysis of the *Tosafot*. As an outsider, I did not so restrict my developing mind and used these tools to critically evalute the *yeshivah* itself, and its life-style, which went so much against my free and open grain. They simply did not know how to cope with this, and had no program such as those in *baalei teshuvah yeshivot* today. In 1960 I left Chofetz Chayim before it developed into today's fine and well-organized network of Torah institutions. I was unaware then of how atypical it was in the *yeshivah* world, which disdained its preoccupation with *Musar* and *pilpul*. I particularly recall there Chayim Blumberg *z"l*, a seeming *miskane* whose entire life was prayer and study, yielding to his "evil inclination" to listen to a bit of classical music. I later learned he had cancer and wanted to get as close to God as he could during his few remaining years. My *chavrutot* were Sheldon Farber, who was later active in New York State politics, and Israel Chait, who became *Rosh Yeshiva* of Bnei Torah and whose teachings I value and spread. Both of us now work with United States *Bnei Noach*. The religious secretary, Mrs. Fuchs, was a lovely mother figure to all the boys; she and her daughter Naomi, who is now in Israel, enjoyed my fledgling *divrei Torah*. I often felt that many people in the *yeshivah*, while fine, were too gentle, too soft and feminine in their demeanor. If someone were suddenly hurt, the street-corner bum in a motorcycle jacket might have acted more quickly and efficiently to save him. Rav Soloveitchik later told me that many *Musarniks*, while meaning well, had little sense of the psychological needs of a human being. They might have turned me off from Torah had not my intellect so attached me to it. In retrospect, my life might have been different had I been in a less-insular *yeshivah*, for example, Ner Yisroel. I might have remained in the *yeshivah* world to this day. I might also have married the lovely young Satmar girl in the office, Sara Feder, with whom I exchanged books under the old hebbetzin's benevolent eye. I also remember from that time John, a Polish drunk redeemed by the old *rebbetzin,* who served the *yeshivah* as general handyman ever after. He left his estate to Chofetz Chayim, and the whole *yeshivah* turned out for his non-Jewish funeral. The old *rebbetzin's* sister, Menucha, was widowed young and childless, and though she spoke little English, she somehow appreciated my religious soul. I lived in the generous *rosh yeshivah's* house for some time.

After leaving Chofetz Chaim, I taught first-grade secular studies to chasidic children for about half a year in the S'chuster Rav's *yeshivah*. At this time, I discovered the world of Modern Orthodoxy in Rav Shor's Temple Bethel of Borough Park, and I was impressed by these people, who seemed to be both fully in Torah and part of the vital, upbeat, creative modern world.

I then transferred to Yeshiva University (YU) and graduated in 1961, concentrating on Math and Psychology. People in the "*yeshivah* world" had told me the college was a den of iniquity, but I thought I'd help improve it with my *Musar* background. Of course, I soon realized their words were slander and nonsense, and I was most impressed by YU's many quietly pious *talmidei chachamim,* then including Shimon Eider and Hershel Schacter. Still one didn't feel God in the air at YU as at Chofetz Chayim, especially in the secular departments. I found the cafeteria food fabulous after our government surplus meals at Chafetz Chaim, but somehow the *Shabbat cholent* of YU lacked the special flavor of that at Chafetz Chayim, which was cooked by a sweet old widow.

I studied Torah at YU's RIETS Yeshiva under Rav Dovid Lifschitz *z"l,* and others. I entered the world of the prophets, which was not taught in Haredi *yeshivot,* through the teaching of Dean Sar. I then studied law at Harvard. I found Western legal thought much simpler than Talmud, though much more focused on the aims and purposes of its laws. Jewish Law had not been the law of a nation on its land for almost two thousand years. I also attended Rav J. B. Soloveitchik's public lectures and classes in Boston and taught Hebrew school for Rabbi Korff. Later, especially after his wife died, I used to walk Rav Soloveitchik home from *shul* on *Shabbat* and drive him about when his son-in-law was in Israel. I value those hours as my prime Torah learning experience and try to incorporate what I recall into my study sheets. The Rav was a dynamic model for a nonceasing search for truth and integrity in every realm until one's day of death. A different profound educational experience, though not "intellectual" was imbibing the chasidic faith, joy, and common sense of the Bostoner Rebbe, Levi Horowitz, and his family. Brookline in the 1960s and 1970s was a wonderful place for a young Jew like me to be.

S. F.:   You, despite your continuous involvement in learning Torah, never received formal ordination, or *smichah.* Can you explain why?

Rabbi Fogelman: Rav Soloveitchik noted that true and valid ordination consists of permission of your main teacher of Torah to
continue the chain of *mesorah* by teaching others. Without it, one
may not do so. There once was a formal *halachic smichah*, with
anointing by oil, which was similar to inauguration of the high priest.
But it ceased after Yavneh, though it was briefly revived in Safad,
where Yosef Caro was among those anointed. Such ordination was
then banned by the rabbis of Jerusalem. What we call *smichah* today
is simply a certificate attesting that one has studied Jewish Law,
usually stressing possible bodily defects of *kosher* animals, and so can
give rulings in ritual matters. I don't feel it's very relevant to my own
particular Torah mission. In fact, few who hold such *smichah* are
asked about questionable meat today, and they call expert rabbis if
and when such questions do arise. Some rabbis grant *smichah* on laws
of *Shabbat* and other realms more relevant today, as did Rav Moshe
Feinstein *z"l*. He ordained one of my favorite teachers, Rav Dr. Leon
Ehrenpreis, who integrated Torah and math in his classes on mathe-
matical thinking at Yeshiva College.

S. F.:   Rav Soloveitchik urged you to teach. What did he see in you?

Rabbi Fogelman: According to what he told me to encourage me
to teach Torah—God's gift of a good and open mind, coupled with
an ability to communicate and teach and a strong sense of contemporary relevance. Once we were stuck in a traffic jam between New
York City and Boston, and I went about talking to other drivers
about ideas and religion, as was, and is, my wont. His response was
that I was an admixture of a modern Conservative rabbi and an old-
time *chassidisha rebbe!* I recall arguing against his Lithuanian belief
in not expressing emotion—his father never hugged him (as mine),
though they were very close. He turned and embraced me, exclaim-
ing, "You think I can't do it?—I just don't believe in it."

S. F.:   I know that during those Boston area years you learned and
were also in business. When did you decide to come to Israel?

Rabbi Fogelman: In 1974. I first had visited in 1968 but, to my regret, I put off settling here in order to build up my business. While in Boston, I was active in religious causes and often wrote in the *Jewish Advocate* and other newspapers. But, as I view Torah's teachings, we must always strive to come here, to be in the pure and purifying Holy Land. God himself dwells in Jerusalem and is a very good neighbor (Psalm 135). He's more distant, harder to get close to, elsewhere. One can meet a multinational executive in any of his many offices around the globe, but if he invites you to his home, you experience him differently. If God and Zionism have now made it possible, there's no reason for Jews to live elsewhere, a sentiment that was echoed recently by the Belzer Rebbe to Belgian Jews. I also felt that the chances of my descendants being Jewish are better here, "that your days and your children's days be multiplied on the land which God swore to give your ancestors, as days of heaven upon earth" (Deuteronomy 11:21). This is the only country where Jews can easily be both fully Jewish and fully part of their nation. Everyone should contribute his utmost to speedily develop Israel's messianic rebirth. Many of my religious friends from Chofetz Chaim, YU, and Boston, including Rabbi and Mrs. Mordechai Goldstein of the counterculture Mt. Zion Diaspora Yeshiva, have settled here though they, like myself, have no formal Zionist education or affiliation.

S. F.:   And you have been a student and teacher of Torah all your time here?

Rabbi Fogelman: Yes. At first, I mostly attended classes, and then I gradually began teaching others. I was one of the early teachers at Israel Center in a program originally organized by Dr. Reuven Ben Dov at Machon Meir. For several years I ran programs at Beit Meir, Beit Alon, and my own center. My study sheets grew out of my weekly talks at Israel Center so that students would have something to take home and share. In time, I realized they were far more important than the talks themselves in terms of the number of people I could reach.

S. F.:   I believe you do a lot to reach out and help many people, though you seldom talk about it. You must have one of the largest personal acquaintance networks of anyone in Jerusalem.

Rabbi Fogelman: Every decent human being tries to help others in whatever way he can. We must especially do so when they benefit and we lose nothing. Jews, who have suffered so much, are especially sensitive to others' pain. One should be friendly and helpful to every human being, though you should distance yourself from those likely to be a bad influence on you and your family. Having been actively involved here for twenty years, I often can very quickly and easily connect with people for their mutual benefit. At one time, I was inclined also to try and help those with very deep problems, but after a while I felt I was not qualified to do so. I sensed I could accomplish more working with those needing a bit of information, insight, or encouragement. Often that which is crooked cannot be made straight.

Just as a businessman looks for the right location to maximize sales and profits, so one "selling" Torah should seek the most receptive and productive audience. Nevertheless, I admire those who try to deal with the most difficult people, though they often fail. I too try to give such people a bit of time, if this can make their existence more tolerable. Sometimes, just steering someone to the right address, for example, Israelight, or Discovery, can make a profound impact on their lives. It's especially important to approach visiting strangers in Jerusalem, as they are often unaware of what is available here in such things as *Shabbat* hospitality and "lectures" in Torah. There are many examples where such initiative has helped. One renowed teacher recently married a woman who had become enthused after seeing his video lecture at our center. Years ago, I approached a young Jew and his non-Jewish girlfriend on Habad Street in front of our center. They were traveling around the world. I got both to attend Aish HaTorah's Discovery program. She returned to marry within her faith, and he became a Torah scholar, happily married to a fine Jewish woman. I recently approached a couple on the street, gave them *parshah* sheets, and arranged for their Friday night dinner at the fabulous family of Mordechai and Henny Machlis, who often host sixty to seventy guests (religious and secular, Jewish and non-Jewish) besides their ten children. The young man, a doctor with a strong *Haredi yeshivah* background, came here with his fiancée, who had little religious background—but a great Jewish soul—and their dream and plan was to get married in Israel with a *Klezmer* band. It turned out that Mordechai had been his enthusiastic and inspiring counselor years before. At the Machlises, this couple met Avi, who was helping Israel TV find a couple to get married at the *Klezmer* festival in Safad. Sure enough, a few days later, all was arranged for their publicly televised wedding as highlight of the festival.

As do many families in the Jewish Quarter, we host guests on *Shabbat,* though not on the grand scale of some remarkable Jerusalem families for example, the Kaufmans, Machlises, and Sheinbergers. God rewarded our hospitality, and one young Israelight student guest's return to her roots led to her marriage with my son and the birth of their baby, Maytal, my honorable tenth grandchild.

Unfortunately, many bourgeois Orthodox Jews do not realize the importance of hosting non-Jewish visitors too, to honor both God's good Name and our mission as a "Kingdom of Priests" to all mankind. (A Jew's ultimate messianic goal should be to teach every human being, whomever you happen to meet and wherever this may be, to share your Torah and life experience.) So the rabbis labeled those who eat together without exchanging words of Torah as "diners on sacrifices of the dead." Rav Shlomo Carlebach *z"l* noted the need today for "street rabbis" more than *shul* rabbis.

However since time, energy, and resources are limited, each has to judge where his efforts are likely to give the greatest Torah dividends, for example, with youth or mature adults, with people of logic or of emotion, Jews or Gentiles, by teaching and preaching

Torah or by helping to develop the world in its light. "Which is the right way a man should choose for himself? Any that is glorious to him and society? "This is both criterion and consequence—if a certain life-style fits you and you really thrive on it, others are likely to truly appreciate you and benefit from you. So Rav Kook noted that Aryeh Levin's stress on kindness was appropriate for him, though others might thrive better on science, agriculture, or talmudics. Levin suffered much and found his comfort in relieving the suffering of others. I, too, have seen and experienced much sadness and feel that each gesture to improve and brighten the world is a return to its Edenic essence and origins and its messianic future. While mourning is a basic part of a sensitive Jew's experience, he must never enter existential despair or feel cut off from the eventual joy resulting from even the worst sadness, though it not occur in this world (Rav Nachman). Males usually find themselves in conquest, especially in the detached, emotion-free, abstract seeking, learning, and teaching of truth. The primal and ultimate conquest is knowledge of God Himself through His revelations in Torah and nature. The feminine mystique lies in nurturing and empathy, bonding rather than detachment.

S. F.:   Isn't the kind of clear, traditional distinction you make between the roles of man and woman contradicted by the fact that today's world is filled with women of intellectual distinction?

Rabbi Fogelman: I don't question female ability in traditionally male realms, and I don't oppose its development, per se. Both biology and Torah indeed point to the bisexual nature of man and woman—each possesses a bit of the other's leitmotif, but only as a submotif. Biologically, a male has nonfunctioning breasts, a reminder by God that there's a bit of a nurturer in him; similarly, the clitoris is a vestige of the penis, the symbol of male aggression and conquest. One who really works to develop his or her submotif may develop it even better than one who ignores it. But most people are not superpeople who can and will do both; therefore, one must educate the vast majority according to their sexual leitmotif, training most women to be fulfilled, happy, capable mothers and most men to be engineers, talmudists, and so on. You also want to *somewhat* develop their submotifs—male nurturing and female aggression. But provision must also be made for those who do not fit the general or desirable model—for the masculine woman and the feminine male.

I think Judaism assumes that woman, who is a step removed from the dust of the earth, is innately closer to God, Who made her like His own Will or Personality (K'Ratzono). It is only the mother who determines if the person is Jewish. Her deep intuition and empathy can atrophy or be destroyed by over involvement or abstract learning, which entails the repression and suppression of feelings. The most important person in one's primal consciousness is his mother, who gives birth to him and nurses him. For males to feel similar importance in the familial and social structure, they need their own unique, vital contribution: the defense and support of their families. If women have an equal role in these realms, men tend to drop out of family and society and use their aggressive, conquering nature for war and crime rather than the conquest of ignorance and poverty.

S. F.:   Another important element in your way of thinking is the redemptive role you give the State of Israel.

Rabbi Fogelman: I very much believe this. God's clear biblical goal for mankind, at least from the days of Avraham, is to come back to Eden via the State of Israel. Its existence today, a confirmation of the fantastic prophecies of Redemption of the land and people made thousands of years ago, is perhaps best evidence of the Divine Origin of the Only Testament. Those things called "holy," or "*Kadosh*," transcend natural laws and defy natural explanations. The holy Jewish people survives thousands of years of dispersed exile and returns to its ancient land, just as the Bible predicts, and this when other exiled people disappeared after a few generations. The

Holy Land remains basically desolate, while its chosen folk are in exile for almost two thousand years, though quite capable people have captured it from time to time. The Bible predicts this and the universal Edenic rebirth with Israel's return to Israel. Once gone, normal languages don't return, but the Holy Tongue is suddenly back as a spoken language after almost two thousand years of use only in prayer and scholarship. On the other hand, we're just as clearly warned of the disasters that will overtake us if the Jews don't stay close to God. Then others may rule us, and we may even lose parts of our land.

S. F.:   So you believe that eventually, every Jew will observe Torah in the ideal State of Israel.

Rabbi Fogelman: Of course. Otherwise there's no purpose in our being here, or even remaining distinctively Jewish. But Torah observance doesn't just mean conformity to laws, customs, and rituals but also the integration of their messages into one's soul, mind, and heart, applying them to every moment of life. So Rav Dovid Hoffman explains Israel's mission in his interpretation of the verse from Exodus, "You shall be for Me a kingdom of priests and a holy people." The first stage is that every Jew imbibe God's many messages by studying and observing the Torah. But they then must use their insights and holiness to build a model nation to bring all mankind back to Eden—a holy nation. Every realm of human endeavor is to be fully developed in Israel, but with a unique Torah perspective. So Yaakov begins as a wholesome man who dwells in the tents of Torah and family. But Rivka knows he'll have little impact on the world if he remains there, leaving the world to his adventuresome, wild, and earthy brother Esav. Rivka shows Yitzchak that Yaakov can also deal in the world if necessary, and she sends him to Uncle Lavan to learn the ropes. When he comes back with wives, children, servants, and property, Esav is impressed and leaves the Holy Land to his gentle brother. Torah is the only way for a truly Jewish State—but it must sanctify all life, not replace it.

S. F.:   In the twenty years you have been here, do you see movement toward or away from this goal?

Rabbi Fogelman: I see both; overall tendencies are hard to find, as there is constant movement in and out of both religious and secular societies. I don't travel about the country much, and I tend to see those who are interested and involved in Torah here in Jerusalem's Jewish Quarter. Progress in physical development clearly has been tremendous. Jerusalem is a well-run modern city, planned with taste and beauty. Israeli clothing has advanced from "country bumpkin" to international leadership–unfortunately much of it is immodest. In focusing on international beauty and sports competitions, Israel automatically loses–adopting trivial non-Jewish values rather than teaching our own. Our advertising is now as sophisticated as any but equally profane and silly. Our profane television uses continually refined techniques but contains very little Torah content. Many Jews have returned to Torah in Israel, and increasingly, new, technical methods are used. But little reaches the largely ignorant secular community. Israel's politicians are often a disgrace. On the plus side, religious music has entered the mainstream culture and religious spokemen skillfully defend Torah on talk shows. Religious retreats, such as Arachim, reach many of those bereft of Torah, and we have an effective, inspiring Ashkenazic chief rabbi–Lau's my favorite candidate for *Moshiach.* Open Torah institutions, such as Machon Hartman, Pardes, and Yakar, attract secularists into Jewish Tradition. But Torah insiders must clean up and inspire their own society. Orthodox self-righteousness and attempts to control others drive away many Jews. It may be that those entering the Tradition are more inspired than those raised as observant. I personally think one goal is to vastly increase the quantity and quality of religious television, as television, for better or for worse, is today's main educator. Torah must also be taught in secular schools by those who believe in it, even if it's debated and questioned.

A major problem is that much of Israeli Orthodoxy has not completely emerged from the Middle Ages, the era of belief in magic and superstition. Sensitive Torah scholars abroad tried to interface Torah with modernity, such as Rav S. R. Hirsch in Germany and Rav Y. Kapach in Yemen. Rav Kook, who was so open, loving, and in tune with life, was unfortunately unable to reach most of his "spiritually constipated" brethren.

S. F.:   From reading your sheets, I know you often cite Rav Soloveitchik and Rav S. R. Hirsch. Who else serve as important sources in your thought?

Rabbi Fogelman: I also hold A. Y. Kook in very high esteem though I am not comfortable with his mystical, poetic style, which is so often hard to decipher, so I cite him less. I stress his universal love and tolerance while also noting his limits, for example, opposition to women's right to vote and unreasoned castigation of Rav Yichya Kapach's attacks on the *Zohar*. Rav Dovid Hoffman strikes me as one of the greatest, but little of his work's available in English, my main reading language. Abarbanel is similar, though his Hebrew, as his thinking, is quite clear and modern. He's much closer to today's mind-set than many rabbis of the last hundred years. I try to quote as many different sources as possible, both secular and Jewish, in order to give my readers a broad perspective. I feel close to and quote many sensitive, open, Modern Centrist Orthodox rabbis, such as Norman Lamm, Shlomo Riskin, Shalom Gold, Aharon Adler, Shubert Spero, and so forth. I feel Lamm might accomplish more for Torah as a teacher of the intelligent masses rather than as president of YU. I also relate to many points of more universal, bright left-wing Orthodox teachers such as David Hartman, Yitz Greenberg, and Aviezer Ravitsky.

I often cite experts in so-called secular realms who are also Torah scholars and attempt to integrate the two worlds, such as biologist Baruch Sterman, physicists Natan Aviezer and Gerald Schroeder, and psychologists Moshe Halevi Spero and Miriam Adahan. Gedaliah Fleer, Shlomo Carlebach, Yaakov Tauber (whose weekly studies I distribute), and Lopes Cardozo are among my sources for *chasidic* and *kabbalistic* thought. I also quote, and often argue with, traditionally heretical scholars who advocate the documentary hypothesis, if they are learned, honest, and intelligent, for example, Moshe Greenberg and Louis Jacobs.

S. F.:   I know you have a wide acquaintance with rabbis and scholars and seem ready to follow the talmudic dictate of learning from each one you meet.

Rabbi Fogelman: We are taught, "Who's wise? Who learns from everyone. "I try to experience as much as possible – every good thinker, scholar, and personality whom God decided to place on earth during my brief stay – and to pass on a bit of them to my readers. I've met very many. I often introduce one to another. This is a form of *chesed* that appeals to me as it's both quick and clearly valuable. Others who are more slow paced and patient may be better at helping the handicapped, and so forth. We are supposed to spend minimal time at our livelihoods and spend the rest in study and good deeds.

S. F.:   In your sheets you often refer to the evils of Western Civilization. Does that mean for you that we should strive for *aliyah* of all Diaspora Jews?

Rabbi Fogelman: Yes. But just being here doesn't bring automatic salvation. Western decadence is highlighted by violence and sex-as-snack on television, by the decline of traditional family life. Perversions are called alternative life-styles. Unfortunately, Israel has adopted Western television as prime molder of its youth's souls. Nevertheless, Israel is called the pure land, that which brings out the purity still latent in man's soul. Many immigrants find it here, if they're not broken financially. While I'd be much happier to have my children grow up in the beautiful Torah and Derech Eretz communities of Baltimore and Monsey rather than in Eilat and Haifa, you cannot compare such communities to Jerusalem or Efrat. Israel's probably also the land where your great-grandchildren have the best chance of staying Jewish, "that your days *And your children's days* be great upon the land which God promised your fathers as days of heaven upon earth." While the moral atmosphere's far from ideal, especially in secular circles, the benefits of democracy compel us to teach and preach rather than force or legislate Torah values.

S. F.: So you follow the injunction of the Sages not to rebuke anyone who you know for certain will not be helped by your rebuke?

Rabbi Fogelman: Absolutely. Rebuke, a *mitzvah,* is to prevent wrongdoing, not to vent our own wrath. Better that people sin carelessly than willfully, after being warned and thus becoming more culpable. We are concerned with the sinner's welfare, too! So while we condemn any wrong act, we don't condemn and abandon he who does it. Rambam tells us, only God can judge the totality of a human being. Rav Soloveitchik deplored religious coercion in any form—it makes twentieth-century man your enemy. We want religious Jews to be viewed as friends, not foes, by others. Many Israelis work very hard, often at several jobs, so there's not much energy left for higher realms, especially admidst basic concerns of survival. Yet it's important for observant Jews to be in touch with them, set examples to emulate, and teach them in a noncoercive manner. Rebuke is relatively easy when one just hopes to improve another's behavior within a shared value system. Today, however, the vast majority of Jews do not share the basic Jewish Tradition, that the God who created the universe has given a plan of life to mankind via Israel. It's not just that some secular Jews admire Torah, but they find it too hard. There are many who view the Torah way as antiquated and morally inferior to their own. The presentation and explanation of a radically different worldview must precede any "rebuke" or behavior modification.

Rav Soloveitchik once said his function was not to make Jews observant; he was working on the first step, a sine qua non—to convince intelligent modern man that the Torah was at least a worthy object of their serious intellectual consideration, that it had something to say to modern man. I was somewhat disappointed when he said that, but I now understand it. It's easy to bring lost, disturbed souls into a warm, stable community, but it's much harder to attract those whose lives are in order and who are creative, prosperous, and flourishing in their present state. They may welcome a bit of nostalgia and tradition in their lives, but only Reform Zalmanian style, where it fits their existing feelings and outlook, with little personal sacrifice. To deal with them one must be able to bridge the huge chasm between secular and religious outlooks, to project himself into questioning, nonbelieving minds and hearts, while retaining his own attachment to Torah. This was the emotional intuitive genius of great chasidic *rebbes* or the intellectual genius of Rambam, Hirsch, and the Rav.

S. F.:   A religious way of life is the way of a community, not just an individual. How does this relate to your own view?

Rabbi Fogelman: A major factor in "selling Torah" is indeed the potential buyer's impression of the Torah community, for himself and his family. If he senses true love, kindness, faith, and joy, he may overcome or overlook a lot of his cognitive dissonance. Especially in *Haredi* communities, one cannot but be impressed by the sense of responsibility for others in need, be it in the various *gemachim,* visiting the sick, helping new mothers and so forth. While by no means perfect, it's way above the secular standard. The beautiful scene of families walking home from Orthodox *shuls* on *Shabbos* with friends and neighbors has high impact. But a religious community that is petty, narrow-minded, and dull can turn off prospective returnees. If even riding a bicycle (as with other signs of life and vitality!) is viewed as "immodest" for women, if magic red strings replace science, if listening to one's own thoughts and feelings is viewed as the devil's work, even those raised in such communities may leave. Naomi Regan explores such worlds in *Sotah: The Wayward Wife.*

S. F.:   Could you say something about your plans and future projects?

Rabbi Fogelman: My creative desire is to constantly learn more and deeper, to initiate new projects, to make new contacts. But I also need to order and structure that which I have already done. Thus, I am in a quandary as to which direction to focus my limited time and energy. Ideally, I hope to find others to do all the backup work, while I continue to forge ahead. Life is short and we have so much work to do. We need pleasure and relaxation, too, otherwise we can break; but we must be on constant guard not to slip into self-indulgence and laziness. I found myself overweight whenever I primarily used a car rather than a bike.

I hope to publish my writings in a more attractive format, nicely designed and printed books. But that requires money and lots of time and energy for revision of the present study sheets. I envision two books – one on the Torah readings and another on Judaism and basic life issues. I'm working on an English translation of Yaakov Emden's frank and open diary, *Megillat Sefer,* which we published in Hebrew. I also hope to expand everything else I am doing now. It's not for us to complete the work; neither are we free to exempt ourselves from it.

S. F.:   Thank you very, very much.

Rabbi Fogelman: Thank you for this opportunity to take a self-overview – past, present, and future. Such reflection may indeed help guide the rest of my life.

Rabbi Gedaliah Fleer

Rabbi Gedaliah Fleer has for many years been a teacher and lecturer on Jewish thought. A pioneer in spreading the teachings of R. Nahman of Breslov to the English-speaking world, he is the author of *Rabbi Nahman's Fire* and *Rabbi Nahman's Foundation* (an edition of the *Tikkun Klali*). He is one of the important religious guides whom Herbert Weiner met in his exploration of Jewish mystical thought, *Nine and One-half Mystics*.

I spoke with Gedaliah Fleer in his home in the Jewish Quarter overlooking the Western Wall. I had thought the conversation would center on those "mystical subjects" he is known to have expertise in, but a good part focused on his conception of what might be called *"menschlicheit"* the "basic human goodness" required of every Jew. This ethical concern also was evident in his discussion of the problems in outreach teaching today and in his discussion of teaching non-Orthodox Jews. Fleer's popularity as a teacher comes from his ability to combine a depth of Jewish thought with a down-to-earth, often humorous, colloquial language and the chasidic gift of the storyteller.

S. F.:   Could you describe your present teaching activities?

Rabbi Fleer: Presently, I travel three months a year to the United States and Britain, and I give lectures wherever they let me in, in synagogues, in private homes, in Hillel, in institutions as, for instance, the Jungian Institute in San Francisco. I speak on a variety of topics, mostly connected with mysticism and the philosophy of chasidic thought. I just a short time ago finished an all-day seminar on messianism at the Jungian Institute. Here in Israel, I teach privately. And presently, I am working on something that has to do with understanding the nature of "will" in Judaism. I also, at present, am teaching "Prayer" at Machon Ora to young women who are just recently involved with Judaism.

S. F.:   What is your background in learning?

Rabbi Fleer: I spent many many years in *yeshivot*. I began at Torah V'Daat, went on from there to Navardik, and from there to Breslov. Navardik is considered the most extreme *Musar yeshivah,* while many might say that Breslov is extreme in the Chasidic world in that they have had only one *rebbe,* never taken another *rebbe* after Rav Nachman. I have *smichah* from Breslav, have taught Breslav Chasidism for many years. Even now I give classes at least once a week on the teachings of Rebbe Nachman.

S. F.:   As I understand it, you were involved in the first real upsurge of interest in Jewish mysticism in the United States.

Rabbi Fleer: In 1973–1974, Shlomo Carlebach *z″* asked me to go and teach at what was then the "House of Love and Prayer" in San Francisco. I taught at that time, in New York, Breslov Chasidism to many Orthodox people of *yeshivah* background. Many of them were seekers of truth. And this was a time of a great deal of searching in new directions.

S. F.:   How would you describe your own *hashkafah,* your own particular way of seeing Judaism?

Rabbi Fleer: I was recently asked by a wealthy community in Carmel, California, to give a seminar on "Mysticism and Chasidic

Thought." The synagogue, which was Reform, was in transition, and so I spoke in a kind of dining room, which they had converted to a lecture hall. There was a large crowd, and I had the opportunity to speak with a large number of Reformed Jews. And I like Reform Jews because they are Jews. In any case, I spoke at length about Jewish mysticism, and they were all very interested, so long as I kept things on a theoretical level. When, in the last hour and a half or so, I tried to bring things down to the level of everyday life, to talk about *mitzvot* and covenantal relationship, I saw they were not with me. So when someone asked me what I thought about the Reform movement, I said, "There was once a painter and he threw five cans of paint on the wall and said, 'You see, that's Jewish art, and if you ask me why, it's because I am Jewish.' " In my opinion, this is something like the position the Reform movement takes, that is, one can be a good Jew simply because he is born or identified as a Jew, one can be perfectly all right with their own Jewishness without having to take any obligation or any responsibility. But if you believe, as I do, that true Judaism means involvement with Jewish history, culture, authority, and practice, then Reform Judaism does not have a leg to stand on. I can think of no precept, that the Reform movement insists on its members adhering to, and here I mean Jewish religious precepts, not broad, humanistic, moral ones. It's fine to be humane, but it's possible to be humane without necessarily being Jewish.

And so what I am saying is that I believe that a Jew, to be a true Jew, has to live by the Jewish Tradition and accept its authority. The *mitzvot* are essential to a Jewish life, both because we are commanded by God to obey them and because they instill in us a very special kind of consciousness. The Jews have no more monopoly on mystical or spiritual experience than they do on moral experience. What defines us and makes us specifically Jewish is our adherence to a Torah way of life, our dedication and responsibility to the commandments. The living by the *mitzvot* creates that kind of consciousness that molds and shapes spiritual experience in a way that is particularly Jewish.

S. F.:   As one who is frequently in the United States, do you have a sense of rampant assimilation, Jewish self-destruction?

Rabbi Fleer: In the major cities with large Jewish populations, the assimilation is less than in the small areas. But it is a mistake to think that because Jews are assimilating, they have lost a sense of spirituality or religious quest. The fact that they have not found the answers that are provided in the traditional Jewish frameworks does not mean they are not seeking. The psychological need to relate to God, to transcend the mundane, is as real as the need to sleep, to eat, to have sex. It is impossible to completely deny these primary needs of our being. Unfortunately, it seems to me that the religious community, the people who have safeguarded Torah, have become in the last twenty-five years more strict and exclusive. There even seems to be an animosity and infighting between various religious subgroupings. The religious community has, in some cases, moved out of the major cities and cut itself off from the majority of Jews by establishing enclaves like Monsey or Lakewood. More and more people who have the Torah to teach are insulating themselves and leaving the outreach job to professionals. The problem is that most of these "professionals" are *baalei teshuvah* who do not have a deep background, a consistent religious education. These people are sincere, passionate, and believe strongly in what they are doing, but they have limited experience and often relate only to the particular aspect of Judaism that has touched them personally. What you find, however, is that whatever does not fit into their own framework they are incapable of understanding. Often, a person in charge of an outreach program will take a question and, instead of responding to it directly, turn it toward a fixed answer, the formula answer that was prepared before. He actually does not understand what is being asked or how to respond to it. Many of these programs do things like saying, "We are now going to give you such an overwhelming amount of evidence of the truth of the Torah that you have to be a fool to reject it." I don't believe most "seekers" are interested in approaching Torah in that way. Second, I doubt that we could influence highly intelligent people in this way. I have noticed that most who go to this kind of outreach program are from relatively poor educational backgrounds. Very few have an M.A. and fewer, a Ph.D. I think the major problem is that people running these programs know how to teach Jewish religious and ethical values but have no idea of how to convey a sense of Jewish spirituality.

S. F.:   Are you saying that these people attempt a too exclusively "rational approach"?

Rabbi Fleer: Often I hear from students something like this: "I have been to this or that program but I did not see any 'holy men,' any '*tzaddikim*,' there. When I was in India I saw people who were less articulate, but there was no question that they were devout holy men. Where are the holy men in the *yeshivot*?" So what I am saying is that we have to teach people to do *mitzvot* in such a way that they become better, more sensitive human beings, more capable of relating to God in a transcendent way. The doing of the *mitzvot* must be as the ladder that Jacob saw in his dreams. It must be firmly planted in the ground, its head extended to the heavens, with angels going up and down. In other words, Judaism, if it is to be worthwhile, has to be both physical and spiritual. The angels go up in order to tell us to take the physical and elevate it to the spiritual. They come down in order to tell us that we must make the transcendental part of our everyday life. And if the movement is not in both directions, there is something basically wrong.

S. F.:   How would you describe your own particular approach to teaching Judaism?

Rabbi Fleer: I am a synthesizer. I was born with a capacity for synthesis and a sense that without synthesis there can be no complete truth. I deal with, and live in, the realm of paradox. I understand from modern physics that though we can know the laws of physics, there will always be a random factor, which makes choice possible. I know, too, that certain questions cannot be answered by us and that this, too, allows the choices we make to be real. God created the world as potential. And it is for us through our freedom to actualize that potential. To say we have an answer for every problem is to say that we have no purpose in life. And this is because in life, we grapple continually with the unknown and strive to prevail.

S. F.: Do you understand your own life and work, your own personal striving as *Avodat Hashem?* How do you understand the concept *Avodat Hashem?*

Rabbi Fleer: To the extent that I am able to, I would like to be a vessel for bringing God's awareness to the world. The most precious of God's Creation is mankind, and therefore, to be of service to mankind is perhaps the most worthwhile thing a person can do in life. For me to be of service to mankind means to bring people back to a sense of their origin in God. I try in doing this to create not simply a bridge for the person but a kind of synthesis in thought that can be meaningful for him. I think we are all created in the image of the immanent and transcendent God. Prayer, Torah, and *mitzvot* put us in touch with that God who ultimately allows us to appreciate our own "Undifferentiated Transcendent Consciousness." This is a concept beyond our comprehension, and we cannot really say anything about it. Still, if I can give a person a sense of God, then I can give the person a sense of how to value the essence of his own transcendent being. As for the "I" of my own inner world, this is totally subjective. The "I" facilitates everything, but it's not part of what it facilitates. I take this to mean that this provides a possibility for repentance and forgiveness. That is to say, there is a distinction between the things I do and the "I" that constitutes the essence of my being. If I do something wrong, I am obligated to make amends. Still, I have to have a profound respect for the essence of my own being, which cannot be exhausted in anything it generates in the world. And if I can learn not to associate the wholeness of my essence with any manifestation of itself, there will always remain some aspect of myself that is pure and holy – no matter what I might have done wrong. And that is the source for new inspiration and continuance and further hope. This doesn't mean the person is not responsible, or should not be responsible, for his own actions. As I said, when we do wrong, we should always be striving to make amends, trying to generate the goodness of His essence through actions and speech. But on the other hand, we are all fallible beings. And to allow a mistake I have made to destroy me is to violate my own divine essence. Again, as I have said, when a person has a sense of God, he has a sense of both immanence and transcendence. This is not to say that there are two gods. I am trying to say that God's reality is known to me through my experience and being in the world, and is, on the other hand, transcendent. And I, within myself, contain the desire to interact with both these aspects of God. And that for the Jew, the path to knowledge of God comes through prayer and through study of God. The Torah life should be the refining of the human character, through which the human being knows to respect God, in every aspect of life in which God is revealed to him.

S. F.:   Are you referring here to the idea that in Judaism, *teshuvah* (return) to God is not a process only for, or even primarily for, the nonreligious but is, normatively, the daily spiritual activity of even the most religious Jews? In other words, that even the most religious Jew must continually reasses his own actions and strive to come closer to God?

Rabbi Fleer: It's important to know that the word *teshuvah* does not primarily mean "Repentance" but rather "Return." There are too many people out there who are worried about all the things they did wrong. Not enough people are worried about things they could have done right. Too many classes are being taught in the religious community today that deal with the negative – for instance, how not to speak Leshon Hara, or what not to do on *Shabbos*. All these things are important, but there should be more emphasis on *gemilut* *chasadim,* even on simple, small kindnesses like standing for the elderly on the bus or donating time to do volunteer work in a hospital. It's nice to have guests for *Shabbat* from one's own circle, but what about the traditional custom of inviting the indigent, those who really need a *Shabbos* meal? The commandments are essential, not only as precepts but for their effect on our character, in making us more human. Living by the Torah should mean coming to a higher level of goodness. Because there is not this emphasis, I think we have all kinds of sincerely motivated people in the religious community – who are dedicated to *mitzvot* but not sufficiently spiritual beings.

S. F.:   Are there any people you have known in your life who represent for you models of this higher kind of spirituality?

Rabbi Fleer: Certainly. Unfortunately, generations come and go, and many have passed from the world. One I think of is Aryeh Levin, who many know of from Simcha Raz's book about him, *A Tzaddik in Our Time.* He was a great scholar, a learned man whose whole life was doing goodness for others. Secular Israelis are notorious for their lack of sensitivity to Orthodoxy, but when he passed away, practically the whole Knesset came to his funeral. He was a saint and holy man, a higher being in a way that people could see and recognize. There's a story about a condolence visit he made to General Ariel Sharon, who had just lost a son in an automobile accident. Aryeh Levin went to the *shivah* house and noticed there was no *mezzuzah* on the doorpost. Reb Aryeh came into the house and silent, began to think about the meaning of the loss of this young man in his prime until he began to weep. After a while he got up without uttering a word. When the *shivah* was finished, he returned to the house to visit Ariel Sharon and this was the beginning of a lifelong friendship. This kind of openness to the Jew, whether secular or religious, this sensitivity to the needs of our fellow human being, is what we need more of today. I think the right attitude is given by a *Mishnah* in *Sheviit.* What happens in the

Sabbatical Year, when you are not allowed to plow your field, and your neighbor, who is a sinner, knocks on the door, and says, "I would like to buy your plow"? Are you allowed to sell it to him? The answer is, "Absolutely not." You cannot help him sin. But what happens if he wants to buy your plowing ox? A plowing ox is worth five or six times a regular ox. It's all muscle, and the only thing you can use it for is pulling the plow. In this case, however, the Mishnah permits selling the ox, because there is the slightest possible chance that the neighbor wants to slaughter the ox and have meat that night. Now we know it's not very probable, because no one is going to pay five times the cost of an ordinary ox to get some meat. However, the *Mishnah* allows the sale because it does not want to set up a barrier that would cut us off completely from our fellow Jews even though they are sinners and will in all probability remain that way. Where today is this willingness on the part of the religious community to find a bridge to those Jews who are not religious?

S. F.:   You have been known for your connection to the Breslav community. Yet you are also known as a strong individualist who often teaches those without any communal connection. What is your own idea of, and relation to, community?

Rabbi Fleer: I believe that everybody needs a community, especially as we get on in life and have our own children. But what I mean by this is belonging to a synagogue, having connection with a learned and honest rabbi. You have to find a rabbi who has a good sense of who you are as a human being. It's like trying to find a psychologist—you go from one to another until something clicks. There's a *midrash* that says that when God gave the Torah on Sinai, separate and individual angels carried each word to the ears of each person. And the question is, why do you need different angels to carry the same words to each person's ears? And the answer is, because to "each one it was said in a different tone of voice." So you need a rabbi and community that shape a common tone of voice: a common sensitivity that allows them to face challenge while growing together. But today there is a big problem with communities closing up within themselves. Somebody goes to someone else's house and questions ten times about where the meat came from. This is from one Orthodox Jew to another. I don't think the function of the community is to set up standards of exclusion of this kind. The function of a community should be to exemplify the teachings of Torah through acts of love. In my opinion, it should be the obligation of leaders to encourage the creation of communities that are halachic but tolerant and open.

S. F.:   You have lived for a number of years in Israel. What is your relation to the Land of Israel?

Rabbi Fleer: I love the Land of Israel. I visited Israel thirty times before I settled here nearly thirteen years ago. The Land of Israel has a special *kedushah,* a holiness. It is the place where Judaism was meant to be lived and can be truly lived in the fullest way. On the other hand, I do not have a strong political involvement. I can understand the need for the religious to be politically involved in order to protect their own interest. But to utilize political power as means of coercion does more harm than good. There was always antagonism between the nonreligious and the religious, but up until about twenty years ago, there was a certain respect. Many thought, "The religious are honest people who spend their lives trying to serve God." Today, to my regret, the picture has changed. The nonreligious believe that the religious are selfish. So personally I would like to see less political involvement on the part of Orthodox Jews.

S. F.:   Rabbi, you are known as a serious Jewish mystical thinker, yet only a small amount of work of yours has appeared in print. Why?

Rabbi Fleer: I am much more a speaker than a writer. I have an innate sense of an audience and become inspired when I speak to others.

Rabbi Abraham Ezra Millgram

Rabbi Abraham Ezra Millgram was for many years a Jewish educator in the United States before making *aliyah* to Israel, where he, by and large, devoted himself to literary endeavors. He is most well known for three anthologies, one on the Sabbath, another on the *siddur*, and the third on his beloved city of Jerusalem.

It was the poet and writer Howard Schwartz who suggested that I speak with his mentor and friend of many years. To do so, I met with him at the home of his son and daughter-in-law in the Tsamert Habira district of Jerusalem. The interview, in light of Rabbi Millgram's ninety-three years, was the briefest of this series. Spry and lucid, he gave a classically spare and lively summary of his career.

S. F.: Rabbi, you have had a long and distinguished career in Jewish education and literary work. Could you tell me how your literary work had its beginning?

Rabbi Millgram: I was teaching in Graetz College in Philadelphia on the subject of Jewish literature. I had some very fine students, Junior Hadassah girls and others like that. My late wife suggested to me that I should publish my notes from the course. I wrote up my notes and went to see the late Cyrus Adler, who was chairman of the Publications Committee of the Jewish Publication Society (JPS). It was *An Anthology of Medieval Hebrew Literature,* and he suggested to

179

me some additions, which I later included. He also told me that Maurice Samuel and Ludwig Lewisohn were about to publish anthologies with JPS. And I said, "Who am I to be included with these giants?" He told me that JPS, if it accepted my work, would not publish it for three years, because in those days they only published three books a year, and they already had accepted manuscripts for the next three years. At the same time, a friend of mine who was head of the Talmud Torahs, which they now call "Bureau of Jewish Education," said to me, "Give me your manuscript and I will publish it." So I said, "Go ahead." And I gave it to him. He had various chapters read by individuals considered experts in each field, and he told me their opinions. It was very nice. And he published it. That was my first book.

S. F.:   That was in 1935?

Rabbi Millgram: Approximately. I received letters from a lot of people: Dr. Solomon Solis Cohen, Dr. Louis Finklestein, a lot of prominent people. I had a friend by the name of Solomon Grayzel who became the editor of the Jewish Publication Society. He came to me one day and said: "Why not do a book on the Sabbath? It's an important institution in Jewish life, has been honored by Jews for thousand of years. We ought to have a book on the Sabbath."

I had plenty of time, and I undertook it. And it was published. Then he came to me and asked me to do one on the Passover. I said it would be so similar to this work it would just be hack work. So I refused it. And a friend I knew got the job and did a whole series of books, which he told me were modeled on that first Sabbath anthology.

This started my work. And the books I did were all done on spare time. In the night when I did not sleep, I puttered around with them, and they were done.

S. F.:   So at the same time you were doing your literary work, you were working in Jewish education?

Rabbi Millgram: For the first ten years, I was a rabbi in Congregation Beit Israel in Philadelphia. Then, at a convention of the Rabbinical Assembly in Detroit, Sachar came to me and said I should take a
job with him in Minneapolis. I said I wanted to talk it over with my
wife. To move from Philadelphia to Minneapolis was, I thought, like
going to Siberia. I spoke to my wife, and she said, "Where you go, I
go." So we went and were settled there, and I thought it would be my
life job. Then, five years later, I received a letter from the United
Synagogue of America. They asked me if I'd be interested to head the
Bureau of Jewish Education. Although we liked Minneapolis very
much, a fine community and a wonderful campus, and although we
had many friends there, I knew my wife was homesick. So I took the
job and had it for sixteen years, which I think were the most
productive years of my life.

S. F.:   What was so special about those years?

Rabbi Millgram: The very first day there, I decided I would have
peace in the field. The head of the Jewish Education Committee was
Azriel Eisenberg, a very good friend of mine since the days we had
been students together at the Teachers Institute. These were years of
productive work, when Jewish education was at its peak in America. I was there for sixteen years, and after sixteen years I left
for Israel.

S. F.:   You had been thinking of *aliyah* for a long time?

Rabbi Millgram: I was what was called a *verbrente* (impassioned)
Zionist all my life. I had been chairman of the Histradrut campaign,
chairman for the New York area of the Poalei Zion. So I resigned to
come to Israel and look for another job. I was still young enough and
was at the top of my career. When I came here, the kind of jobs
offered were the kind I did not care about. So I decided to do what
my friend Grayzel had been begging me to do all along, a book on
Jewish worship, or as he called it, on the *siddur*. I had told him in

America, "What do I know about liturgy, except that a Jew knows how to *davven?*" But I began daily to go to the library, and I read many articles on liturgy. I had no idea so many existed. And I wrote my most important book.

I remember the editor of the JPS, Potok, was here in Jerusalem for the summer. I called him up and went to see him on Aza Street. I told him Grayzel had suggested this book, but Potok did not know about it. Still, he was interested in the subject. I told him we had spoken about three hundred pages, but the book was nearly seven hundred, and I was worried that some of it might be dull. He said, "First of all, seven hundred pages do not frighten me." And then he said: "A book of seven hundred pages? Have you ever seen a book of seven hundred pages that does not have some parts that are not dull?" So I promised to send it to him, and he was happy. Within a year, he had it.

After that, I said to myself: "Jerusalem is a wonderful city, a historical city, with so much Jewishness in it. I'll putter around with that." And I wrote a book, *Jerusalem Curiosities.* The editor of the JPS then was Sheila Seigel, and she liked it and pushed it through. And it was published recently. And that's all.

S. F.:   Thank you, Rabbi. The main subject of this work of interviews is *Avodat Hashem,* the worship and service of God. Do you understand your life as *Avodat Hashem?* How do you understand this concept?

Rabbi Millgram: It's a big question. You can write many books on it and not exhaust it. Could you ask me the question again?

S. F.:   I agree, it's a very big question. When you were working through these years on your books, did you feel you were trying to serve God?

Rabbi Millgram: Definitely. This is seen by the subjects of my work. The Sabbath has been the greatest institution the Jews have produced. The *siddur* is the classic of Jewish theological thought, and it is spiritually incomparable. *The English Common Book of Prayer* does not approach the *siddur*. And Jerusalem, the city: there's no other city like Jerusalem. I think of it as the greatest city. Where does New York compare? It's bigger, but not greater. Jerusalem is greater. So these are my ideas, the subjects of my work: the Sabbath, the *siddur*, and Jerusalem.

S. F.:   Rabbi, I would like to ask you one more general question. You have witnessed in your own lifetime various stages of Jewish history. How do you see the situation of the Jewish people now?

Rabbi Millgram: In what has been my profession, Jewish education, I know that in New York anyway there has been a decline. I think that in the United States as a whole, Jewish education is in a very sad condition. I don't want to think of it. I was fortunate in being in the field when Jewish education was reaching its peak. So I enjoyed.

S. F.:   How about the situation in Israel?

Rabbi Millgram: I don't really know, though my son and daughter-in-law are in education. When I first came to Israel, they welcomed me in Mea Shearim. Now, they keep me out.

S. F.:   You mean there has been greater polarization between religious groups in the time that you have been here?

Rabbi Millgram: This does not bother me. Let Mea Shearim be Mea Shearim. I was always on good terms with the Orthodox. I knew Williamsburg would survive. I wasn't sure about the rest of the Jews. I'm sorry to say I am pessimistic about the situation in America.

S. F.:   And about Israel?

Rabbi Millgram: I am more optimistic about Israel.

S. F.:   Well, Rabbi, I know your books have made a significant contribution to Jewish education. I remember the joy your *Sabbath Anthology* gave me when I discovered it in America. Is there some other achievement in your life, outside books and family, about which you are especially happy?

Rabbi Millgram: There are people who have been my students, whom I value and who still value me. Though they are, by this time, middle-aged men, fathers, and grandfathers, they are, to me, still my "boys" from Philadelphia. They honor me and regard me as a kind of father. Their humor and their loyalty to me are something I have valued greatly. They are all members of synagogues and contribute to the Jewish community.

Professor Emil L. Fackenheim

Professor Emil Fackenheim is one of the most important Jewish thinkers of the twentieth century. He has published a number of original philosophical works, in which he often uses a mixture of *midrash* and essay to illimunate a basic position. Among these works are *The Jewish Return into History: Reflections on the Age of Auschwitz and a New Jerusalem* and *To Mend the World*. For many years a member of the Philosophy Department of Toronto University, after moving to Israel, he became a Fellow of the Institute of Contemporary Jewry of Hebrew University. A former intern of the Sachenshausen concentration camp, his thought centers on the experience of the Jewish people in the modern world and how they are to continue to live after the Holocaust.

I met with Professor Fackenheim with the sense that somehow, the key question of this work, the question of service of God, is not the one he would want to address directly. And in truth, at the heart of our conversation was the conflict with which he lives all the time: the desire, on the one hand, to be true to God, and on the other, to be true to the victims of the *Shoah*.

Though Professor Fackenheim's views are articulately expressed in his many books and articles, I do believe there emerge, in the course of the interview, some insights that may be of use to serious students of his work. I felt it a great honor and privilege to meet with him. And if I find myself at the end of each of these interviews deeply grateful to the learned person for speaking with me, I felt doubly so in Professor Fackenheim's case. The basic integrity and decency of the man shone through every word he spoke.

S. F.:   One central element of your thought is your concern for the survival of the Jewish people after the Holocaust. This is embodied in what is perhaps your most well known idea, your postulation of a 614th commandment, by which you indicate that the true moral obligation of every Jew is to work for the survival of the Jewish people. How did you come to the idea of adding this commandment?

Emil L. Fackenheim: I come from a liberal, but really quite devout, household. My father was an extremely busy lawyer, but he laid *tefillin* every day. He did not understand very much about Judaism, because the Jewish education in Germany was not very good. And I think his faith was basically a simple, traditional faith. My mother was much more broad-minded, and she read philosophy and so on. She had her own piety. The main thing I remember of her piety was expressed when we would come home from *Erev Shabbat*. She would often say that the "*Hashkivenu*" prayer is the greatest prayer: "Spread over us the Tabernacle of Your Peace." This had a very powerful appeal to her. So a certain devoutness was in the home.

   Now one thing I remember distinctly was my reaction to the coming to power of Hitler. I was sixteen years old, and thought, "There has to be a Jewish answer to this." I was very dissatisfied that I knew so little Judaism. That's why I went to Berlin to study; I did not go to become a rabbi. Actually, I was a congregational rabbi for five years and was never very comfortable with it. This was, in the first place, because preaching means that the congregation cannot talk back. You are the great authority. And I never want to be a great authority! I do, however, remember fondly many of the duties of being a rabbi because *amcha* (the common people) are more important to me than the professors.

   But again, the interesting thing was that even before I got to Berlin, I was sure that Judaism had the answer. And I never lost that. The reason I came to disagree with people like Richard Rubenstein, whose "God is dead" theology gave a powerful challenge, is that he should have said, "Now I will study the Jewish sources and see what is found in there," even if you could not hope to say that you found anything adequate to the catastrophe. I found nothing that was adequate, certainly not Haman, although Haman comes closest. Amalek is harmless in comparison to Hitler, for Amalek never wanted to murder the whole people but rather just wanted to rob them. But then, too, no matter how deeply one studies the resources of the Tradition, the Holocaust is an unprecedented challenge. One who did understand this need to look to the Tradition was my late close friend, Pinchas Peli, whose masterful work has not been truly appreciated.

Until 1967, I wrote quite a bit about evil. But I did not write about the Holocaust. I stayed away from it, as so many other people did. But in 1967, I was morally forced by the threat to Israel: *Ein Breira*. Steven Schwartzschild, who was then the editor of *Judaism* magazine, arranged for a symposium on Jewish Values after the Holocaust, to which he invited Elie Wiesel, Richard Popkin, and myself. I didn't want to, but he said, "You have no choice," and then I went through one of the biggest crises I had ever had. In fact, I was made very sick by it and remember flying with my wife to New York and being sick all the time. But once I had finished what I had to say, the sickness was gone. What I had to say was the 614th commandment.

And what was the sickness? The sickness is the dilemma I still have. If you want to be faithful to the *Ribbono shel Olam*, but to do it at the price of ignoring the victims, that's a betrayal of the victims. But if you are faithful to the cries of the victims, you have, as a result, to abandon the *Ribbono shel Olam*. Now that's the dilemma. And the only solution I could find to it is the 614th commandment. And that, I wanted to make clear to my Orthodox friends, does not abrogate any other *mitzvah*. But I do disagree with them when they say, "One cannot add." You have to add one *mitzvah* that, like the majority of *mitzvot*, is negative. "The authentic Jew of today is forbidden to hand Hitler yet another posthumous victory." The positive aspect of this *mitzvah*, which is the one thing that is radically new, is the imperative to "survival," survival even if there was nothing else. Many people have misunderstood this, and once I was at a conference where a theologian asked, "What's the point of mere Jewish survival?" Milton Himmelfarb exploded and said, "After the Holocaust, don't you dare call Jewish survival *mere!*"

I also spoke about the difficulty of remembering and surviving without giving up all ethical obligations to the *goyim*. There is, after all, every reason for the Jews to despair of mankind, but we are forbidden to do it. I then spoke at the end about the *Ribbono shel Olam*. "If you say you believe in God and nothing else counts, then you have betrayed the victims all over again." But if you say, "You can't believe in God," this is also a posthumous victory to Hitler. So what remains is a new struggle. I thought at the time that the one I knew who was doing this struggle was Elie Wiesel, though others were doing it also. I think this struggle underlies almost everything that I am doing.

S. F.:   When you write about the survival of the Jewish people, do you do it in relation to the idea of our return to history? Can you elaborate on the meaning of this?

Emiel L. Fackenheim: In Germany, almost every Jew was an anti-Zionist, and we certainly were brought up as anti-Zionists. And this was not only because of the political fear of being accused of dual loyalty by the Germans. That was at the low level. At the highest level, we sincerely believed "*Lo b'chayil v'lo b'koach*" (Neither by power nor by might). It went so far that the great philosopher who represented German Jewry, Herman Cohen, said that the destruction of the Jewish State was a good thing, since it means that the Jewish people now are universal. But from 1933 on, in Germany you could no longer be an anti-Zionist, for that would be to be divided by your persecutors. This, by the way, is one of the most shocking things Rabin has done, equating the Jewish opposition in Israel with the Hamas terrorists. No Jewish leader has the right to undermine Jewish unity, especially under the impact of persecution. After this came the terrible years of the Holocaust. And then came, in

1947, the United Nations proclamation. I was pro-Zionist in Canada at that time, but I was naive, as Diaspora Jews today still tend to be. I thought, "Isn't that fine?" The ensuing war almost passed me by. The fundamental betrayal of the Jewish people by the liberals is something I had to learn after this, through long weary years.

It was as a result of the War of 1967 that I became involved in politics. You know, I am a harmless man. I have enough to do writing books. Before the war, the largest Protestant weekly in Canada, the *United Church Observer,* did not mention the threat to Israel. After the war, they began to viciously attack Israel, and this went on for months. Then I received an invitation to receive an honorary doctorate at a United Church College in Saskatoon. The speech I gave there defending Israel, attacking those who had attacked it (including this newspaper and its editor), resulted in my real involvement starting.

But that's the smallest part of the story. When we, my wife and I, felt before the Six Day War that Israel might suffer a second Holocaust, the idea came that we must move to Israel. It took us a long time, but gradually, through the years, I had been coming to this conclusion: for better or for worse the future of the Jewish people and the Jewish religion depends on what is going to happen in Israel. It is the true center of the Jewish people.

S. F.:   There are Jews who, while conceding that Israel is the center, argue for maintaining large Diaspora populations on the grounds that this, in a nuclear age, is a prerequisite for preventing our enemies from being tempted by one single target.

Emil L. Fackenheim: Charles Krauthammer made that point in a wonderful article, which I have on my wall, and I believe he understood me better than most theologians. I think if one wanted to say, "We need that there be a strong Jewish community to help us in our battle for survival until the day peace comes," then I can understand that. And in fact, I have never been the kind of Zionist who believes all Jews must live in Israel. A Zionist means someone who knows the forefront of the Jewish people, and its future is in Israel.

So now we come back to the main thing. If you ask me, "Why is it possible for the Jewish people, after the greatest catastrophe we have known, to go on believing in God?" The answer is, "It is because after the greatest manifestation of Exile, the worst Catastrophe, we have returned to Jerusalem."

S. F.:   If I understand some of your recent writing, you are not happy with the way the present Israeli government is conducting the struggle for Jerusalem.

Emil L. Fackenheim: Why does our foreign minister believe that just because he says, "Jerusalem will not be divided again," people will automatically accept this? We have been saying the same thing for thirty years, during which time nobody has listened. I think it's futile to begin saying: "Jerusalem is three thousand years old. It was never the capital of anyone but the Jews." This is true, but it's not what anyone listens to.

I think you have to explain by beginning differently. Who was the worst enemy who wanted to take Jerusalem from the Jews? Titus occupied Jerusalem, destroyed the Jewish State, but for Hadrian, that was not enough. Hadrian wanted to finish the Jewish people, and he knew that if you take away Jerusalem, the Jewish people are, in some sense, finished. Now what does the Palestine Liberation Organization (PLO) want? They do not just want some representation in East Jerusalem, or access to the holy places. The Muslims already have this. They want political domination of the holy places, ours included. And why? Because they want to finish us off, because they want to finish off Zion.

Now, if Jerusalem were taken away from us either by force or, by worse, our own cowardice, then I think the effect would be demoralizing everywhere. American Jews would be turning away. And after this, the hypocrisy of the world will be even worse.

S. F.:   Do you believe one way of preventing such a disaster is through a Jewish return to religion? Many of the present government's critics say its errors are in great part the result of its lack of deep connection with the Jewish Tradition.

Emil L. Fackenheim: There is only one congregation I was the rabbi of, and it belonged to the Reform movement. Of course, there are good people there, but the movement still suffers from an original error of progressive thought, the notion that if the right-wingers are our enemies, the left-wingers must be our friends. This blind and mindless belief in the modern world, and in progress, had its most disastrous refutation by the Nazis. And now Peres has this kind of view, and when he looks at the twenty-first century, he finds the religious Jews to be the bad guys, and the ones he trusts are Jewish enemies of the left. This is just not real.

S. F.:   I believe you have written about secular Jews' positive contribution to the Jewish people at a different phase of Israeli history.

Emil L. Fackenheim: I have just written something where I say, if you want to single out one monumental act by a Jew of this century, it was when Ben-Gurion declared the State of Israel. Ben-Gurion was a secularist, but he had a very fundamental Jewish loyalty and also had his own life with the Bible. At that point, had it not been for secularists like him, we would not have had a state.

The first time we came here, we had a taxi driver named Eliahu. And I started talking about miracles, and he said, "I don't like miracles." And I answered, "There are no miracles without human action." At that time, this human action was done by Ben-Gurion. And I would never want to slander the many secular Israelis who were prepared to give their lives for their mission. But now I, too, try to understand this in another way. What Ben-Gurion did could not have been done without faith because the cards were so greatly stacked against him. When the generals said, "You should give up the state for the time being," they had realism on their side. So Ben-Gurion acted as though he believed in miracles. I think there is a bridge between the secular and the religious in those who serve in the Israeli army.

Now I have been quite hostile against those ultrareligious who refuse to serve in the army, such as the Satmar. The Satmar Rebbe of the time told his *chasidim* in Poland that they must not go to Palestine, and they were murdered because they listened to his advice. And he was saved by the Zionists. It's a morally untenable position. And yet, the more rabid these leftists become, the more I understand the ultrareligious who do not want to serve in the army. And I think it's a very unhappy development.

S. F.:   In talking about Ben-Gurion's courageous decision, you hint at your own way of thinking about historical development and free action. Now recently, there has been much talk about an idea of history that I believe has much influenced Foreign Minister Peres and his idea of the New Middle East. Basically, the claim is that with the fall of the Soviet Union, liberal democracy has globally triumphed. Francis Fukuyama has written about this process as kind of inevitable, Hegelian end of history.

Emil L. Fackenheim: That book was supposedly written in the spirit of Hegel, but he got Hegel completely wrong. I spent ten years writing a book on Hegel and reached the conclusion that Hegel was a realist who affirmed "progress" only because he was a Christian before he was a philosopher. And the transformation of Christianity into the modern world was the basis of his thesis. But then, toward the end of his life, he became skeptical even of that, as he found both Christianity and secular confidence very weak.

But Hegel never predicted the future; he believed it possible to understand only the past. He made some guesses such as that the world spirit will emigrate to America. But the foolish notion of predicting history was left to Marx. Hegel said that history is an owl that takes flight only as night comes, but Marx thought history a cock, announcing the coming of a new day.

I don't see how anyone can be, in this century, so foolish as to maintain the possibility of predicting the future. There have been two major cataclysmic events in the century, one Nazism, the second the collapse of communism, which none of the experts rightly foresaw.

In history, we live in the realm of the uncertain. Another point was made by my major mentor, the great Jewish philosopher Leo Strauss. He radically disagrees with the claim that all problems can be solved. The solution to communism has dropped into our hands, but no one knows the outcome. There's a fellow now rising in Russia who could become a great threat, though he does not have one thing Hitler had – a private army.

But no one can say, "This cataclysmic event has happened and I know the inevitable outcome." One change has, however, taken place since the fall of the Soviet Union that should be noted. Our strategic importance is not as it was before. But whatever the political consequence of that event, I again believe the last thing we should do here is fight among ourselves. I think there should be a fundamental Jewish unity and that we have to learn to put first things first. And the first thing is security and the need to remember that we have been under siege for many decades. For the Israeli government to do as it did recently, to tell the Americans not to veto an anti-Israeli proposal on Jerusalem at the United Nations, seems to me the epitome of foolishness.

All this brings me back to an earlier thing. Ben-Gurion was not all that religious, but he knew what was sacred to him: the Jewish State, the Law of Return, and the End of Exile. And the present leaders don't.

S. F.:   Again, if the secular leadership of Israel seems to have lost its connection with fundamental values, don't you think the way to strengthen the Jewish people in its struggle for survival is through return to the religious Tradition?

Emil L. Fackenheim: I would not say this, because it can easily lead to the old-fashioned argument we had between the religious and nonreligious fifty years ago. Now if we say "return," it can be asked, "return to what?" Now what we have already done is make a good return to Jerusalem. To me, this is the most thought-provoking thing, because I find in the return, it's not thinkers and rabbis and philosophers but the people as a whole that is important. Ben-Gurion may have been alone when he made that decision, but he brought the whole people with him. If that decision had not been made, Jewish life would be in terrible shape. We would have had a UN trusteeship here, Jews would not have come, and it would have been an endangered ghetto.

Now you can imagine what would happen, God forbid, if Jerusalem were taken away again? The demoralization would spread all over. But as I have said in a piece I wrote, "Maybe sooner or later we will run out of excuses for the Holocaust."

S. F.:   I don't understand.

Emil L. Fackenheim: For a long while, the traditional explanation was that we were punished because we sinned. But it's not the only traditional answer. There are various *midrashim* with other answers, including the one that says that when Israel went into exile, God went with them.

But then, what happened when Israel went to the gas chambers? You are not going to become a Christian at this point and say, "God was murdered with them." You have to say either, "God was murdered à la Neitzche, "or that there was, as in Christianity, "Resurrection."

But this whole approach is now not only lost but deliberately destroyed. If Hadrian wanted to destroy Jews by paganizing Jerusalem, the Nazis wanted to destroy Jews by the gas chambers. But the gas chambers go beyond Hadrian, for thus you rob the Jews even of their martyrdom, which came of their having a choice.

I remember that once there was a liberal rabbi from Germany who, immediately after the Holocaust, wrote something that could not have been written ten years later. He wrote that the Holocaust was a purge of the last medieval element of Jewish superstition! This is ridiculous and disgusting. When I said, "You run out of excuses," I meant that the Tradition does not always supply answers, that there are mysteries that are not fast found out.

The latest thing I have come to is the "suffering vicariously" idea, as in Isaiah 57. The Jews did suffer vicariously, not for the sins of others but for the virtues of others. Because their grandparents decided to bring them up as Jews, which was a virtue, they suffered as Jews. Now what are we going to make of that? I am still trying to cope with that.

The serious thought of the Holocaust has hardly begun. I know I am now thinking about things that did not occur to me twenty years ago. It is not because you are stupid but rather because it is so painful and shocking. Still, so long as we have returned to Jerusalem and stay there, my faith that we can come out on the other side is unshaken.

S. F.:   I would like to finish our talk as our Tradition commends, on a positive note. I know you are impressed by the development of Yerushalayim through the years. Could you say a word about this?

Emil L. Fackenheim: I am glad you end with this. In the first place, if I want to have a mystical experience I read the papers, then I go out and walk in the city. The mystical experience is given by the sharp contrast. I read the papers and then I walk, and here is a new building or restaurant or a nice *shul*. And Jews show no signs of leaving, and there is development in so many ways.

I will say another positive thing. In my view, the greatest man of the century was Winston Churchill. Had he not defied the Nazis, we would not be here. But he not only defied the Nazis, he led his nation in defiance. I am not sure he could have done it for forty years, as we have. The task we have is to last through the siege until we can get rid of it.

Rabbi Shubert Spero

Rabbi Dr. Shubert Spero is Irving Stone Professor of Jewish Thought at Bar-Ilan University. Rabbi emeritus of the Young Israel of Cleveland, Ohio, he is the author of *Morality, Halakha, and Jewish Tradition* (Ktav). One of the most important Jewish thinkers working today in the philosophy of history, he also writes on public issues in the press in Israel. A longtime contributor to *Tradition* and other Jewish journals, his work has done much to illuminate the moral and existential situation of the Jew in the modern world.

I met with Rabbi Spero in his home in the Talbieh district of Jerusalem. Reluctant to speak about details of his own life, which he believed would be of little importance to others, he was much more at home considering the general implications and meanings of his story. Essentially, he reads the story in terms of two critical decisions he made in service of God: the first, the decision to go into the rabbinate, and the second, to make *aliyah* in Israel. Rabbi Spero connects the conception of service of God with the feeling of gratitude that comes to the human being at the sense of goodness in his own life. Though the interview with Rabbi Spero is one of the longest in the book, I felt it was too short, for there was much I wanted to hear, especially in regard to his conception of the overall historical process as understood by him through traditional Jewish religious terms.

S. F.:   Rabbi, when and why did you come on *aliyah?*

Rabbi Spero: I came on *aliyah* in 1983, after having been the rabbi of Young Israel of Cleveland for thirty-three years. That had been a dream we had entertained ever since the Six Day War. Naturally, like most Jews, we had always been interested in *Eretz Yisrael.* Our first trip to Israel as a family was in 1966. I had been here in 1950 with my father and uncle. What galvanized us was the Six Day War, which gave us the feeling that the time whose religious significance had not been clear could now be seen as the "beginning of the Redemption." It seemed now that with all the holy places, such as the Old City of Jerusalem, Har HaBayit, Hebron, and Shechem, in our possession, that somehow God was talking to the Jewish people through history, telling us that He wanted us to come back to our land. From that point on, we began to make plans. It took a number of years until they reached fruition.

S. F.:   Could you say a few words about your educational and teaching background?

Rabbi Spero: My parents were both born in the United States; my father was born in Cleveland, Ohio, in one of the few observant families in the city at that time, and my mother was from a large New York East Side traditional family. Americanism was paramount in my upbringing; nevertheless, I knew my Yiddish-speaking grandparents, and there was always that continuity with European *shtetl* life. When my parents married, my father moved to New York and I was born and brought up in New York. I remember that the question of whether I should be sent to a *yeshivah* day school or not was discussed. Many relatives of my mother warned her that if I went to a *yeshivah,* I would come out speaking with an accent and would not be fully Americanized. But my parents decided nonetheless to take the chance, and I was sent to a day school, which was the traditional Yiddish-speaking *yeshivah,* Torah VeDaas, in Brooklyn. Actually, I was one of the few who entered the *yeshivah* at the age of six and did not emerge until the age of twenty-four. I went through all of the divisions of the school and came out with *smichah*.

S. F.: And then you immediately began your work as rabbi in Cleveland?

Rabbi Spero: Well, no. But first, let me just say this. Torah VeDaas had only an elementary and high school division in general studies. After high school, I went to City College of New York (CCNY) in the evenings, which the *yeshivah* permitted at the time. That's where I got my bachelor's degree. At that time, I was interested mainly in history; I majored in it and minored in philosophy.

S. F.: And the historical element is still prominent in your work, though you are thought of academically primarily as a philosopher?

Rabbi Spero: Ironically, it was precisely history, the history of my time, that persuaded me to enter the active rabbinate rather than follow an academic career. This was during the Second World War, when the draft was on. I was approved as physically fit but, as a divinity student, I was exempted. I decided then that having accepted an exemption, I was morally obligated to apply the education I had received, enter the rabbinate in a serious way, and give my services to the Jewish people. So at that point, I decided to stay on at the *yeshivah* for *smichah* and enter the rabbinate.

S. F.: As one who has for many years been both congregational rabbi and university teacher, could you say which you prefer? And what do you feel are the relative advantages of each profession?

Rabbi Spero: That is an interesting question, because I was never quite sure that I was cut out to be a congregational rabbi. In fact, I was never quite sure what was required of an American Orthodox Rabbi. I was never very interested in the administrative, fundraising, or social aspects of congregational life. I entered the rabbinate in 1947 and took my first position in Brookline, Massachusetts,

where, with the help of a few devoted families, we founded the
Young Israel of Brookline. I saw the rabbinate basically as a teaching
position. The opportunities were many. First of all, there were the
adult education classes, Second was the *drashah* (sermon), in which
I developed a keen interest. I saw it, not only as a powerful vehicle
for education, but as a kind of art form as well that was able to reach
the people. I felt that the talmudic rabbis had in this form of the
drashah already been working on the making of this, an entirely
new literary form, for the Jewish people. I tried to develop a sermon
that would be based on a very substantive element of the *parashat
hashavuah*. The idea would be to teach *Chumash* while having it
philosophically grounded, and at the same time, give it some application to current events.

S. F.:   When you moved to Cleveland, you started a new phase in
your work?

Rabbi Spero: When I got to Cleveland, there was a change in my
attitude. I began to feel that I needed to go further in my studies, so I
enrolled at Western Reserve University for a master's degree. I see all
of this now as providential. When I started at Western Reserve, I did
so in the Religion Department. But after taking one or two courses, I
realized it was all heavily based on Christian theology. When I
switched to Philosophy, I was told, "You are wasting your time
because Western Reserve University does not give a master's degree
in philosophy." But I decided to start any way and to study philosophy *"leshem shemayim."* Soon afterward they began to expand the
department, and I was the first student to get a master's degree in
philosophy at Western Reserve University.

S. F.:   At this same time, had you already begun your literary work,
the articles that have been featured for many years in *Tradition?*

Rabbi Spero: Yes, that began in the early 1960s. My first article
was in the *Jewish Spectator,* on a question of Zionism. It was a

response to somebody who had written that, "today no one can realistically expect American Jews to go to Israel." I felt such a claim required an answer. When *Tradition* started to be published, I thought it was so great that I became a member of the Rabbinical Council of America (RCA), which sponsored the journal, though as a graduate of Torah VeDaas. I had been a member of a different rabbinical association called the Rabbinical Alliance of America. I recall that in the very first issue of *Tradition*, there was an article by a rabbi who compared William James's *Varieties of Religious Experience* to Rambam's *Hilchot Teshuvah*, As James was one of my favorites, I felt the comparison was wrong and wrote a letter to the editor saying that *teshuvah* is a process of return, whereas James talks about a different religious experience called "conversion."

S. F.:   James distinguishes between the firstborn and the secondborn type of religious experience, the second being the deeper experience and a kind of conversion.

Rabbi Spero: Yes, anyway, that was my start.

S. F.:   I was just reading an article you wrote about the same time on the *menorah*.

Rabbi Spero: That was also in response to the stimulus that came from my philosophic readings. For a while, I taught aesthetics at the Cleveland Institute of Art.

S. F.:   I do sense that along with moral philosophy, aesthetics is central to your thought. I was going to ask you the topic of your doctoral dissertation.

Rabbi Spero: It was *The Justification and Significance of Religious Belief.* There's a story behind that, too. Western Reserve did not have a master's program in philosophy, but then a merger took place between Western Reserve and Case Institute of Technology, and they initiated a Ph.D. program in philosophy. That was good news. In Western Reserve I had done a lot of my work with a Jewish professor, Mortimer Kadish. He was a fine person with broad philosophical interests. However, the expanded philosophy department of the merged Case Western Reserve University was top-heavy with logicians and mathematicians who were interested primarily in philosophy of science, whereas my own interest was more toward metaphysics, morality, and philosophy of religion.

From the work of Rabbi J. B. Soloveitchik, I began to see the Jewish elements contained in existentialism. In fact, I wrote an article for *Perspective* magazine on the positive connection between Judaism and existentialism, which was subsequently quoted in *Time* magazine. I knew Rabbi Soloveitchik from the time I had been in the Boston area. Now one problem I faced was that the Philosophy Department of the new Case Western Reserve had little sympathy with existentialism. Luckily, there was a Korean named Kim who was persuaded to join my doctoral committee. Perhaps as an Asian, he had a somewhat broader perspective.

At that time, the main philosophic threat to religious faith was coming from logical positivism, which argued that statements referring to God, Soul, or Spirit could not even be judged "true" or "false," since they lacked all cognitive meaning. So that before I could even attempt to justify religious beliefs, I had to establish that they had meaning or significance. Hence the title of my dissertation, "The Justification and Significance of Religious Belief." I had to demonstrate both points using the accepted methodology of philosophic analysis.

S. F.:   And after this you immediately began writing *Morality, Halakha and the Jewish Tradition?*

Rabbi Spero: I finished my doctorate in 1971. I began the book in 1975.

S. F.:   As I understand it, in this work you make an argument for deriving all morality from a single principle, "walking in the way of God."

Rabbi Spero: Well yes, but that is already found in *Chazal*. Julius
Guttmann makes the point that there were already two aspects of
Judaism that *Chazal* had begun to develop philosophically. One of
them is the attempt to reduce the morality of Judaism to a single
principle that assumes an inner logic. If *mitzvot* are just a collection
of commandments, then this cannot be done. There are 613 *mitzvot*,
but no one ever asked how they are related to each other. But when it
comes to moral commands and principles, you are dealing with
concepts that are tied together by logic. Thus, Chazal says in Sifri,
Ahavta Leraachah Kamochah, "Love your neighbor as yourself," *Zeh
Klal Gadol B'Torah*. This is a great principle in Torah? What do you
mean by "principle"? They use *Klal* in a very technical sense. It's a
general principle. So the implication is that from a general principle
like "Love your neighbor as yourself," you can deduce any number of
particular rules.

S. F.:   You can subsume whole worlds under one principle?

Rabbi Spero: Exactly. In *Hilchos Avelot,* Rambam says that the
rabbinical *mitzvot* like *Bikkur Cholim* and *Haknassat Kallah* are
deducible from "Loving your neighbor as yourself." So in a sense,
they are even biblical.

S. F.:   The principle of walking in the way of God is, I believe,
equivalent in a sense to what is the central idea of all these
interviews: the concept of service of God. Do you see your life and
work as in some way subsumed under that fundamental principle?
Is that principle, *Avodat Hashem,* the same principle as walking in
the way of God? Or do you see *Avodat Hashem* as more technical,
confined to *Kohanim* and their service in the Temple?

Rabbi Spero: No. Quite the contrary, *Lalechet b'derech Hashem,*
"to walk in the way of God," is first of all a very daring principle. I
do not know of any other religion that makes such a statement. I
think Buber talks about Imitatio Dei as a very unique concept in

Judaism because in the pagan concept, the gods were no models to emulate. They were jealous and violent. So no one wanted to emulate those gods. On the other hand, if you have a very meta-physical religion that speaks of the Absolute, then there is no way in which the deity can be a model for man. If you take Christianity, then there it is no big deal to speak about walking in the ways of God, since its central conception is that God appeared on earth and lived as one specific person.

S. F.:   I think also in Christianity the emphasis would be on suffering and dying for the world to come, while in Judaism the emphasis is on life in this world.

Rabbi Spero: Right, that's as far as the content is concerned. But the very idea that you can emulate a God in Christianity is not interesting. However, in Judaism we are talking about the unique and unseen, about whom we say, *Kadosh Kadosh Kadosh,* transcen-dent and beyond everything, even beyond man's concepts. If so, then in what sense can man follow in the footsteps of God? And the answer is that because Judaism has this concept of a moral God we can imitate the ways of; we can follow in God's footsteps, "As He is merciful so shall you be merciful, as He is gracious so shall you be gracious."

S. F.:   I know you have also written about man walking in God's footsteps through cultural creation.

Rabbi Spero: I am glad you noticed that. But this is already an extension of the concept. The basic attribute for imitation is moral, but then our attention is brought to bear on God's attribute of creativity. I think Rav Soloveitchik points this out, that man is supposed to be creative, just as God has created and continues to create. But the ultimate creative task of man is to recreate himself as a moral personality. That's really the main point. God created a world that is essentially incomplete as far as man is concerned. Man has to mine the metals, grow the bread, has to work to make it more usable. Each person is given the ingredients for personality, which is initially raw and unfinished. Each person has the task to forge for himself a moral personality.

S. F.:   This completion is, I know, in your thought also connected with the whole historical dimension in relation to the Jewish people. Could you perhaps elaborate on this collective side of it? I think it is easier for people today to understand the notion of individual perfection, but they have trouble understanding this conception in terms of community, in terms of the special role of Israel. In this regard, the point you made in an article a short time ago about the present government of Israel doing something the Jewish people did not do for two thousand years, give up "rights of ownership" in *Eretz Yisrael,* struck me as painfully true.

Rabbi Spero: Unfortunately, that is correct. In the past, the enemy was always outside. Now, within our own people, we have this threat and strife.

S. F.:   Is your idea of the process of perfection and Redemption in Jewish history close to that of Rav Kook?

Rabbi Spero: There is no question that Rav Kook had this view of history as developing and progressing in a real, detectable way. Rav Kook started to write about the importance of historical development before any religious person could really see any possibility of progress coming via a Zionist organization. Already after World War I, Rav Kook saw that the developments of rising and liberating nationalisms, scientific developments, and the reshuffling of the international balance of power were part of the messianic process. People tend to oversimplify the views of Rav Kook. They saw Rav Kook was the one who saw Zionism and settlement in *Eretz Yisrael* as the sole element in messianic fulfillment, but in fact, his view was much broader.

S. F.:   Clearly, he was influenced by the central place of the idea of evolution in nineteenth-century intellectual history.

Rabbi Spero: I find that anyone who looks at our own Tradition, *Tanach* and *Chazal*, will see suggestions of evolution and progress. It's all there. I am trying to clarify this in the book I am presently working on. Of course, Mosheach can come at any time, even today, "if you but hearken to His voice." But what is often ignored is that there are many teachings of our Sages that point to a gradual process of Redemption with recognizable patterns and stages. They have said that even if we do not have a national *teshuvah* movement wherein all the Jewish people in some sudden, dramatic way, turn to God, the Redemption will come anyway but will arrive through the historical process. This is a worldwide process that involves Jewish history as well as world history, technological and scientific development, the growth of medical knowledge, the spread of democracy. All of this is necessary in order to bring about what we might call a "Messianic Man."

S. F.:   How do you see this Messianic Man in social and communal terms? What confuses many of us is, on the one hand, all these technological developments with their not necessarily beneficial consequences, and then the moral situation of mankind, in which there does not seem to be progress at all.

Rabbi Spero: It is difficult for me to reply to all of this orally because there are many different strands that are involved here. But to give it some perspective, I feel there are a number of different conditions that have to be brought into existence in order for us to be able to talk about Redemption. And these conditions have been evolving and developing. Some of these conditions reside in the Jewish people themselves, while some of them are on a global basis, in terms of mankind as a whole. This is occurring in various fields at once. Take the political field, for example, the book by Francis Fukuyama, which attempts to demonstrate that there is a direction in history toward liberal democracy and a market economy. I believe this is one of the necessary conditions for worldwide Redemption as seen by Judaism. I maintain that Judaism does believe in a progress theory of history.

S. F.:   Again, you indicate in your book that there is scientific and technological progress but not real, moral progress.

Rabbi Spero: True. But in some sense, technical progress serves moral progress. Material conditions have an instrumental role to play in moral development. I am not sure that there can be radical moral change without fundamental improvement in the quality of life of most people on this planet. Besides, I am not sure that morality works in this sense. How do you become a moral person? Is it a developmental thing at all? Let's put that aside. That's the toughest question of all. I find it easier to trace, at first, certain empirical lines of development necessary for Redemption, a gradual recognition on the part of man that the only decent and feasible method of people governing themselves is liberal democracy.

S. F.:   I know Fukuyama's theory. It was timed beautifully with the collapse of the Soviet Union. There have been many developments since then that testify against the validity of his thesis.

Rabbi Spero: I raised it as a kind of example. Take something closer to home. There is the development of Torah itself. Now Torah is surely a necessary condition for the Redemption. But the Torah was, like most other things, given as incomplete. First, all the Written Torah is dependent upon the Oral Torah. What can you do with the Written Law if you do not have the Oral Law? What can you do with the Written Law if you do not have the Oral Law to explain what it all means? Then it has to be made accessible to the people. It has to be put in a form that can be studied by any literate person. As the Rabbis put it, "Place it before them as a 'set table.' " (*Shulchan Aruch*). It has to be in a form ready for immediate consumption. First, in 200 C.E. you had a Mishnah, and in the year

500 c.e., you had the *Talmud Bavli*! What would Judaism be without any of this? Surely, it must have been extremely difficult for the average person in the early generations to attain spiritual growth without the help of a fully developed Oral Law literature. By 500 c.e., you have *Talmud Bavli*, but you still don't have Rashi, and you don't have Maimonides. Time was needed for the Jewish people to elaborate generation by generation the meaning of the Torah. This is only one line of development in the Torah. But then there is the problem of applying the Torah to new situations, which begins to develop in the responsa literature. But all this refers to the *Halachah*. What about *Aggadah*? What about philosophy and moral theory? All that had to be developed, had to be drawn out of the principles of the Torah. People ask us why we have experienced such a long *Galut*. The answer is that it was necessary because there are many necessary conditions for Redemption that had to develop as historical process, and this takes time. One reason for the length of the Egyptian servitude was the need of the children of Israel to grow from seventy souls to six hundred thousand adult males. One of the schema given by Chazal states that the world's history will last six thousand years. Two thousand will be *tohu* (chaos); two thousand, "Torah"; and two thousand, "the days of the Messiah." In what sense do we need two thousand years for Torah, and what does it mean to say that the last two thousand years are the days of the Messiah? I take it to mean that the Messiah is a possibility only during the last two thousand years. For if you have not developed Torah to a certain minimal degree, then you cannot even begin to think of Mosheach. Chazal perceived that human history has to develop in time, even as Creation and nature itself have to develop over time. This is the Divine Will.

S. F.:   Do you feel this process of Redemption is going on in Israel now, when on the one hand, many are involved with Torah learning, but many more are not involved in this at all?

Rabbi Spero: I think one of the short answers to that difficult question is places like the institution at which I teach, Bar-Ilan

University. I see that as an example of nonpolarization in a country where so much is polarized. There are *baalei teshuvah yeshivot*, but you do not enter one of them unless you have already developed some kind of interest. At Bar-Ilan, you have eleven thousand students, half of whom are nonobservant. What are they doing there? They are there because it is also a good general university to get one kind of degree or another. But once they are there, they must take courses in Judaica. That's where I meet them. True, many of them are very far from Judaism. But it is an opportunity to present Judaism in a nonpressured way to all of these young Jews. It gives hope of getting people here to where we are supposed to go. There's no doubt that the question of the kind of culture we are developing here is a crucial one. In what sense are we a Jewish State?

S. F.:   Could you say a bit more about the courses you teach here and the character of your students?

Rabbi Spero: Many of my students are serious. Many are in the army and open to existential problems of life. In my classes, we have furious discussions on civil disobedience and a Jew's moral responsibility for his fellow Jews. My course is built around my book, *Morality, Halakhah and the Jewish Tradition*. The course is called *Daat v'Musar*, the role and place of morality within Judaism. But the first third of the term is spent talking about morality in general before coming more specifically to Judaism.

S. F.:   As I understand it, you believe there to be universal moral principles that can be understood without necessarily making any specific reference to Judaism.

Rabbi Spero: Exactly. And what I try to do is to begin in a very objective, nonideological approach. I tell them, "Look, I want to talk to you first about moral problems without any relation to any philosophical or religious commitment as to what morality is." But is that possible? Is it possible for us to discuss morality as such before getting into the substantive question as to what is morally "good" or "evil" or whether there is an objective morality? I suggest that there is an objective institution in constant practical use that embodies morality and that there is a moral language that is part of every natural language. There is a sublanguage of moral terms, as there is a language of science and a language of aesthetics. This moral language has its own logic and its own function. You can do things with moral language that you cannot do with any other parts of the language. My point is that by analyzing the structures and uses of moral language, we can arrive at some important insights as to the nature of morality.

S. F.:   So your basic position is in contradiction to Dostoevsky's and Neitzsche's that without God, it is impossible to know right and wrong?

Rabbi Spero: Not exactly. According to Judaism, God is indeed the source of all morality, but not in the simple, direct sense in which it is usually understood. There is much in the Torah and *Chazal* to suggest that the basic principles of morality were known to man from the very beginning.

S. F.:   So your position is that the principles of morality are intuitive?

Rabbi Spero: Yes. Because they are intuitive, every developed society has evolved a moral language because people sense a difference between customs, laws, and what they call morality.

S. F.:   The next step is to go beyond the general morality and ask if you believe in a uniquely Jewish morality.

Rabbi Spero: My conclusion is that in terms of basic concepts like justice, righteousness, and fairness, Judaism has nothing new to say. But where Judaism does have something new and important to say is on aspects of morality dimensions that I call height, depth, and intensitivity. One of these dimensions is what I call the sense of urgency. Morality must be implemented and not merely ordained. Aristotle and Plato had deep insights into the nature of morality, but to them it was more an aesthetic matter. If there were widows and orphans starving, no one got too excited. If there was slavery, no one was too concerned. But because of the Torah's belief in a moral God, there is an urgency to have such concern. The Torah tells us that the Creator of the world knows the pain of these miserable slaves. Heschel had an important insight, that the hysterical tone of the prophets reflects their understanding that from the divine perspective, injustice is intolerable. This is one of the unique contributions of Judaism to morality.

S. F.: Again, Rabbi, the main concept of this work is *Avodat Hashem*. How do you understand this concept? And do you see your own life and work in terms of this concept?

Rabbi Spero: The concept of *Avodat Hashem*, service to God, actually emanates from two different sources. One source is from the side of theology, that is to say, if the person has a belief in God, then it is natural to ask, "What does this obligate me to?" or "What are my duties?" One of the important characteristics of any living religion is to ask, "What difference does it make?" Belief in God, in and of itself, is not the important difference between religious and nonreligious people. So that, assuming one believes in God, the question is, "What difference does this make in your life?" More specifically, in terms of a revealed religion such as Judaism, the question would be, "What is it that God demands?" In answer to this particular question we should remind ourselves of the verse in Micah where the Prophet proclaims, "It has already been told to you, Oh Man, what God requires of you." In other words, what is the discussion all about? He *already* told us what He wants from us. The Prophet then focuses on three specific terms God wants from you: to do righteousness, to show steadfast loving-kindness, and to walk humbly with your God. The service of God has to be understood not in terms of specific acts or rituals but in living one's life totally with a certain attitude. In other words, if you think of "walking humbly with your God," that is something that you do all the time. Throughout your life you are "walking," existing. So before we talk in terms of specifics, we should realize that what God really wants from you is some general attitude or approach to all of your activities, so that all your life becomes a service to God. Now here I would point to a statement by *Chazal* that Maimonides singles out as being of exceeding importance: "And all your actions should be for the sake of heaven." So that the Jew has to see the service of God, not as focusing on any particular activity but rather, *everything* you do has to be devoted to God. Whatever I do as a rational human being should be done for the sake of heaven.

Here I would add another source from which springs the notion of "service to God," that is, from the particular existential situation of the human being himself. And by this I mean that if the human being sees his life as good, and I think most people see it that way, and they have as a result some sense of gratitude for having been given this gift of life – if one has good intelligence and is reasonably healthy and is developing himself in a satisfactory way – he has to ask himself, "To whom do I really owe any thanks for having been given this life?" A person seeks out the answer to the questions of, "Why am I here? To whom am I responsible?" And, "Okay, I know why I have been doing the thing that I like to do. But is there anything I ought to do as response to the good that has been given me in life? Maybe I have been put here for some special purpose, and while I enjoy being a good lawyer or a good mechanic or raising a family, and all this gives me a tremendous amount of pride and happiness, am I missing something? Is there something else I *ought* to be doing?" And think, this leads the person to question, or to examine more carefully, what it is that he is doing. You have two things: first is a *generalized* sense of what God requires of me as a Jew and as a human being. The answer to that might be in general terms: "Every Jew is supposed to serve God. Every Jew is supposed to be good to his neighbor. "But then there comes a time when one has to ask about the "I,"—the "I" in my existential and historical situation. The Prophet has spoken in terms of "man": what God expects of man. I want to know what God asks of Shubert Spero. And here, I think, one has to examine one's own life in a more personal way.

I would add one thing, and I alluded to this earlier in the interview: looking back, it seems to me I made two crucial decisions in my life that were of major importance. First was the decision to enter the rabbinate, which I saw then as my response to my historic situation. I saw myself in the *yeshivah* studying at a time when, had I not been there, I would have been drafted into the army to serve my country in World War II, I decided that that situation obligated me to spend part of my life utilizing my Torah learning by serving my people as a rabbi. The second major decision was when, after the Six Day War, I decided that Providence was calling me to come back and live in *Eretz Yisrael*. God was calling us home. I think that through those two major choices, I have tried to respond, not only as a Jew who sees his total life as service to God, but in more concrete terms, as part of my own existential situation.

David Herzberg

David Herzberg is a private teacher of Judaism who also works as a tour guide in Israel. His main area of specialty in learning is Chasidism, which he has studied for many years and which he seems to effortlessly live. Our interview includes a brief historical summary of the chasidic teachers he has learned from, but more important, it gives insight into a unique character and approach in serving God. Herzberg is the kind of "*chasid*" who seems to bring and spread "goodwill" into the world, wherever he goes. He always seems to find a way to lift the human spirit and provide help for others. He also, in his interview, raises an idea about the meaning of *Avodat Hashem* (that it is really the "*Avodah*" of *Hashem*, the work of God, and that our task is to participate in it) that I believe points to another central concept of Judaism, "Covenant." What I felt throughout the interview is that kind of human relation for which the dignity and well-being of the other is not an abstract idea but living reality. Much of his *varmkeit*, which Herzberg says the Baal Shem Tov saw as the highest quality, is revealed in the small deeds of kindness I have witnessed Herzberg doing in the *shul* at the foot of the hill in Jerusalem's French Hill district. The unique quality of his character and spirit inform this interview and make it, I believe, one of the most inspiring in the book.

S. F.: Could you tell me something about your background in "learning"? Where did you "learn" to learn?

David Herzberg: I grew up in a modern Orthodox family in New Jersey. I went to day school for twelve years at what was called the Yeshiva Day School. For these twelve years there was always approximately three hours of *Limudei Kodesh*.

S. F.: I know you as a teacher of *Chasidut*. How did you come to this?

David Herzberg: One of the things that brought me to *Chasidut* was my own searching. I generally felt that there was something missing in the Judaism I received. Through all the years of learning, I did not really feel I was getting the essence of Judaism. I just did it, and there was something missing. I never really knew or had contact with anyone who was learning *Chasidut*. But I would say that one of the very strong influences in my life was Reb Shlomo Carlebach *z″l*. When I was freaking out in my young hippie days I ended up in San Francisco, and I stayed at the House of Love and Prayer, where Shlomo would come a few times of the year and teach during the summer. And then, after all, the really straight learning that I went through which wasn't that much, just twelve years and just a few hours a day, so it was nothing you would call intense, like a Slobodka atmosphere or *Musar* movement, I was able to read Hebrew and understand it somewhat. But Shlomo opened me up to that type of learning. And even from the time I met Shlomo, it took many years before I was actually able to open up a *sefer* in *Chasidut* and feel it was my particular Torah, my particular piece that I could live in and give over.

S. F.: How did you really begin and develop in this study?

David Herzberg: I guess where it really started was usually around midnight in San Francisco in the House of Love and Prayer. I still have very clear visions of the eternal light, the *ner tamid* over the Ark. And there was a wonderful library there that was filled with almost every book you could ask for in the world of *Chasidut*, which Shlomo himself put together. Obviously, it was mostly for him. But as with many things that we do in life that we think are for ourselves, actually it turned out it was for somebody else as well. So I would spend many, many nights, whole nights, just delving into everything I could possibly find. And I basically could not understand 90 percent of the stuff I was reading. It was probably a good couple of years, and then, one night, I actually began to understand a little bit of what I was reading. And I got worried because I wondered if this is really what it meant. But it did come together a little bit. I never worked with a dictionary, believe it or not. I depended on hoping the words would come together. I guess the background I got was more than I thought I was getting. And that was where it started a little bit.

S. F.:   How did you come to *aliyah*, and *Eretz Yisrael*?

David Herzberg: I belonged to B'nei Akiva in my last years of high school. In these B'nei Akiva meetings they got me into this very Zionistic mood. And it got to the point where I went to a Zionist camp in Wild Rose, Wisconsin, Camp Moshava, and from there I went into a Hachsharah work-study program, in the year 1969. There, there was a lot more work than study. As far as *Chasidut*, there was none. The first time I came to Israel was in 1969. I went back when the program was up. I then came right back and joined the army for a year. I served in the army for a year on the volunteer program. Then I went back to the States. And that was really where my spiritual journey began. Basically, everything I had done to that point was preparation. And that was where I ended up going to San Francisco, actually hitching a good part of the way. The car that we were driving turned over and, six people, each wound up going on his own way. Some of us ended up meeting in California. That was where the adventure started, and I ended up going to the only address I had, the House of Love and Prayer, and I ended up settling there for a couple of years. And at that point, at the tender age of twenty-four, I met someone who I thought at the time was my true soul mate, a lovely convert from Indiana. And I was blessed with two beautiful girls. And I stayed, and we lived in San Francisco almost ten years. And I was married for approximately five years before I actually came to Israel again. About the last four years, I was in San Francisco, from where I don't know, but something happened inside of me that I have never been able to understand or explain to anyone. But something happened. I knew I had to get back to Israel. And I knew that my whole life depended on it. And it got to the point where I was so obsessed with getting back to Israel that I literally made everybody that I met crazy. There was a period of almost a year when almost anything that anyone would ask me I would answer, "Jerusalem; Israel." I was so totally obsessed that even one time I hitched from California to New Jersey, the whole way – over three thousand miles. I held out a sign in Hebrew that said "Yerushalayim." And I got rides all the way. And actually, only one person was able to read the sign. Just to give you an idea of what was going on in America during the time, one guy who picked me up said, "Hey brother, going to Yerushalayim?" And I said: "If you can handle it. If you've got enough gas." So anyway, I was totally obsessed, I had to get back, especially the last three years that I was in California. I had a decent job. I was working for cable television. I was drilling up the streets with a jackhammer and cementing them back together, and I was having a great time. But at that point, my first daughter was born. And a year and one half later, when my second daughter was born, that was when I got to the point and realized that as much as I loved San Francisco, I didn't want to see my kids educated and brought up in this type of exile. I just felt the decadence was too strong. And I couldn't handle it. I had a flash. I see, now, interestingly enough, fifteen years later, seventeen years later even, I see now that my greatest fear of bringing up kids in "chutz laAretz," outside of Israel, is absolutely true. And that is, on a certain level, the worst that a kid can do in Israel is better than some

of the best things that can be done in *"Chutz LaAretz."* I don't mean
to be saying it as a put-down of living outside of Israel. I really feel
it strongly now. I see my children, and I see that, thank God, they
speak a perfect Hebrew and a perfect English. And not only do they
have the merit of walking just four cubits of Israel, but thousands
and thousands of cubits in Israel; thus they have had the great
privilege and merit of growing up with *"menschlichkeit."* They
have grown up like good people, good human beings, not just good
Jews. I don't believe they would have gotten that in America. Maybe I
am wrong. It's okay. If somebody wants to prove I am wrong, that's
their option.

S. F.:   Did you come with the intention of learning and teaching
Torah all the time? What intention did you have in coming as to
what you would do?

David Herzberg: I came with one single intention, and that was
to see my family living in Israel and being educated here, especially
the children. That was my main intention. And when I originally
came, I came to a *moshav* to work on the land, which I did do for the
first two and one-half years of settling here. And other than that, I
didn't come specifically with the intention of immersing myself in
the world of Torah or *Chasidut.*

S. F.:   How did you come nonetheless to find yourself more and
more in the world of Torah and *Chasidut?*

David Herzberg: I just found that living in Israel was such
a perfect harmony with the world of Torah and *Chasidut*, that it,
in a certain way, came very naturally. It's like when the Rebbe
of Slobodka was explaining the passage of "How to love your
neighbor as yourself." So he says, on the surface, it looks like
it's impossible. He says, "How can you possibly love other people
like yourself?" But, he says: "When you look at it in a different
light you realize that when you love yourself, you don't do it because

God commanded you. You do it because it's a very natural thing. The most natural thing in the world." This is basically, he says, the way the Torah commands us to love other people: in the most natural way, and not specifically because God commanded it. Because if you are doing it the latter way, it can become very perfunctory. You can even say: "Well I loved that person today. Now I have fulfilled my obligation." But if you are doing it because it's so natural, it is you, whereby, instead of just reading the Torah and learning the Torah and trying to fulfill it, you actually become the Torah and people can read you. They can do it just from seeing who you are. This is what I felt happening when I was living in Israel for a while: that the things I was struggling with became much more "natural." And the Torah, which I was perhaps fighting all the time, to sit and learn, here is such a natural thing because here everybody (perhaps not everybody, but the world we know) is involved in the world of Torah. So it was more of a natural metamorphosis than something I had to force.

S. F.:   When I think of you as teacher of *Chasidut* I not only see you learning with *seforim*, I rather think of how I see you act toward others in everyday life. You seem to have a good word, a word of encouragement and blessing, for everyone you meet. Where does this come from?

David Herzberg: I guess it's something I have always had a little bit of. As far back as I can remember, even in kindergarten, I can remember cheating on naps but doing it in such a way that the teacher would enjoy it. There was something that God gave me, even from a young age, that I always knew that, charismatically, I had an effect on people. Thank God we have our whole life to develop it. The Rabbis, when they saw that Rabbi Tarfon was sick, came to him and said: "Rabbi Tarfon. You are such a loser. You have not even begun to understand how to honor your parents." And it's known through so many stories in the Gemara that Rabbi Tarfon was the world's expert in honoring his mother. He got to the point where he would even put his hands under her feet so she shouldn't walk on the ground. He did everything he could possibly do. And yet, the Rabbis saw that he had perfected it to the point where he had nothing left to do with this particular *mitzvah*. So everybody has their own particular *mitzvah*. Hopefully, we are always in a state of evolving and growing in whatever we are doing. And I don't feel that I have come close to realizing how to fully love people and give them *koach* and strength.

Being short has always put me in a place where I felt I was an underdog. Here I was. I was always the first on line. I was always singled out for being the littlest. I saw, I thought, that maybe I could give a little bit of encouragement to the tall people; because you know it's not so easy to be tall. I felt that being short was hard, so maybe people were having a hard time with other things. You know, when Mosheh was not able to go to *Eretz Yisrael*, God said to Moshe Rabbenu, "You tell Yehoshua that you have to go. And it says *Chazkehu v'Amtzehu*, "You have to make him strong. And you have to give him courage." That means that a person who himself is lacking certain things is often the one who is given a gift to be able to help other people that lack the very same thing.

S. F.:   Maybe another way of describing the quality we spoke about is that you have the capacity to bring *simchah* to other people. Do you relate this to your learning in *Chasidut*?

David Herzberg: I would say it's a combination. Basically, it is the particular personality I was maybe born with or realized at a very young age. And it is also the most important gift that I was given by both my parents. My father who always, to this day, has a joke, and always no matter whom he meets, always has something to say to give them some *koach* and cheer them up. And there is my beloved mother, may her memory be a blessing, *aleyah ha-shalom*, who, till her dying day, had the wonderful gift that the Baal Shem Tov would bless his students with. He would say, "You should be blessed with *Varmkeit*." The biggest problem that we have always had is that there are so many cold people, so many cold Jews, that you can even know somebody for your whole life and when you meet them you always walk away cold. My mother had this wonderful gift of such warmth, such love of people. That whatever it is, the little bit I may have been given to this point, is all due to the combination of my mother and father. I'll give you an example. It was approximately a week before my mother left this world. And obviously she was very weak, dying of cancer. And she was in the hospice, and everybody knows when you are in the hospice, that's the end. And it was a struggle, a great struggle for her and for all of us. And yet, a week before she was leaving this world, and at that point, it was quite obvious also to her, there were two young girls who were working in the hospice and had just started that day. And they were working as volunteers, training to be social workers to help people deal with dying. And obviously, they knew nothing. They had no idea of what to do. And they came to my mother, and it was amazing to see this, they were so scared. They had no words inside them. What do you say to an old woman who is dying? And my beautiful mother, she looks at them and, first, she goes, "What's your name?" And they both said their names. It was hard to hear, so she asked again. And she asked them what they were doing, and they told her they were working as social workers to help people. And my mother says: "Oh, that's wonderful. That's such a good thing to do." And my mother says, "Do you know how good it is to help people? A wonderful thing." She continues, "I really really wish you so much luck." She said, "You should have an easy, easy job, and it should be so good to do this work." And I looked at these girls, and I knew that what my mother had said had changed their lives. This was their first day working. Instead of them giving my mother strength, she had given them strength. And that in a certain way sums up, a little, little bit, the strength I got from my mother. And I guess the main thing to finish the circle was, of course, the learning of *Chasidut*, which made it into the perfect triangle.

I guess one of the main influences I received from my mother is that I don't ever remember that she spoke "badly" about anyone.

Never do I remember her speaking *lashon hara*. In truth, I do not know any people I can say that about. Perhaps one other person, my aunt. But I don't know any other people. And the other amazing thing that I remember about my mother: I never could remember that she would see anything bad in anybody, which is obviously why she would never speak *lashon hara*. It wasn't just guarding her tongue because she had something bad to say. It was that she really did not have anything bad to say. She really never saw anything bad in anybody. Even me, with all the things I put her through, she always would give me so much love. But my mother never saw that I did anything bad, even when I was in a situation where the world condemned me, and in honesty, this is what gave me strength. And this is what maybe gave me that spark that I always tried to emulate. Maybe now it's more natural than it was years ago. In general, I feel pretty much the way my mother did, that people are really good.

S. F.: So for you, *Avodat Hashem* is not some ideal principle that you must follow but rather something that comes from within in the whole way you meet the world.

David Herzberg: I think on a simple level that *Avodat Hashem* is literally God's *avodah*. It is not just that we are doing service to God, but *Avodat Hashem* really means the work that God is doing—as much as we can understand, even though it's certainly unfathomable. We do get the little tiny hints as far as how to serve God. I think the main thing is that our understanding of how God loves us and how God loves all His creatures is the main *avodah* we have. As God is doing His *avodah*, so we, too, try to emulate this, that very same type of *avodah*. That means sustaining every single person that we meet, physically or spiritually, depending on what we are able to give them. And if the only *tzedakah* that we are able to give a poor person is a good word, often that's much better than the money we might have. And all that we can possibly do for every single human being ultimately also means taking care of ourselves and the true service of God. Because what does God do all day? He makes "matches." He brings people together. The greatest *Avodat Hashem* is that very greatest thing of bringing people together, not just making matches on a physical level, but really seeing that there is peace and harmony in all our relationships.

S. F.: I know all this has verification in your Chasidic learning. Who are the teachers who have most inspired you? What books do you most constantly refer to?

David Herzberg: As every human being has their own unique-ness, there are no two human beings who have the exact same quality, not even twins and triplets, and not even people who grew up together during their whole lives. As every person has his own uniqueness, so, too, every rebbe, every Chasidic master has, too, his own particular uniqueness. Aside from encompassing the whole Torah and encompassing all the *middot*, the qualities, there is always one particular quality that stands out in each and every rebbe. This is the reason I feel so connected to so many of the rebbes. I feel that it would not be fair in a way to start singling out, because once I start singling out, I am going to get myself in a lot of trouble. I am liable to forget one whom I really love so much. So what I can just say in a nutshell is that obviously, the greatest inspiration was the Baal Shem Tov, who was the Source for all this wealth that we have of *Chasidut*. This is the source from which I draw very, very, much, which means that we are talking about the *sefarim*, such as the *Keter Shem Tov*, the Baal Shem Tov's *perush* on the Torah. It also includes anything that can possibly be brought down in his name, and especially the stories that are told of the Baal Shem Tov, which number in the thousands. So the main place where I am drawing from is the place where, obviously, we are all drawing from: the Baal Shem Tov Hakadosh.

As far as other masters who give me the qualities I need to work on and fix, each inspires in his own light and each in his own specialty. And it goes from generation to generation. I love learning the Torahs from the *Kiddushat Levi*, Reb Levi Yitzhak of Berditchev, the great defender of Israel, who probably my mother was most rooted to, never saw anything bad in any Jew or any person, and was always praying for all of Israel. And there was the Apter Rebbe, the Ohev Yisrael, who had a tremendous love of Jews and who wanted only one thing written on his epitaph: "Here lies the love of Israel." And his *sefer*, the *sefer* that cannot be compared to any other *sefer*, the *Ohev Yisrael*. And as the generations continue, there is not enough paper, not enough ink, to go into all the Chasidic rebbes, each one with his special gift. There is the love of Israel. There is the truth we learn from the Kotzker Rebbe, and the holy anger that we learn from Reb Baruch of Medzibozh, the great-grandson of the Baal Shem Tov. There is the utmost humility that we learn from so many that it's not fair to single one out. Nevertheless, we have to single out Reb Menachem Mendel of Vitebsk, who was so humble that he would even sign his letters, "He who is truly humble." And he would not even consider this an act of pride. And on and on the Torah continues to be elaborated, through the fifth and sixth generations of *Chasidim*. We are already moving into Reb Tzadik Hakohen, and Reb Leibele Eiger, and the Ishbitz Rebbe, who has so much to give over for this generation as far as serving God on the absolute deepest level. That we reach into the deepest depths of our soul so that even when we are doing the opposite of God's will—you can still understand how in the core of this it's a true service of God. It doesn't give us a license to blow it. But it gives us the depth to understand even sometimes the most trivial of our actions and thoughts. Then, moving on to the next generation, we have the grandchild and the great-grandchildren of Reb Akiva Eiger, the great commentator on the Talmud; we have Reb Leibele Eiger, who has to do with Reb Tzadik Hakohen and was also his rebbe. And there is the son of Reb Leibele Eiger, Reb Abraham Eiger, who gave us the great gift of finding in every passage an illusion to healing. In every particular portion and passage of the Torah, he understands how it is talking about a particular kind of healing on a physical level. And it was this particular generation of *chasidim* that gave us the magnificent gift in which each and every rebbe found his own speciality and uniqueness in every passage of the Torah. They could read in any passage and find in that (whether it was *Shabbos,* humility, healing, or God's greatness) the Torah theme that is related to everything. All we must do is search within it and within our souls. *Hafoch Bah, v'Hafoch Bah, v'Kula Bah.* Turn it over again and again, and everything is inside of us, and everything is inside the Torah. We are the Torah, the Torah is us. And God, Israel, the Torah, and us, are all one. And the Land is what especially brings it together, because "There is no Torah like the Torah of *Eretz Yisrael.*" And that's where we find our true selves. Because that's what we are.

S. F.:   I just want to ask you one more question. I know you as a teacher of *Chasidut* and as *shaliach tzibbur.* And it seems to me that you, as *shaliach tzibbur,* have a unique ability to help move those praying with you to deeper worship of *Hashem.* Could you say a word about how you understand "prayer" in service of God?

David Herzberg: On a simple level, *tefillah* itself, which comes from the word "Pillalti," in *Sefer Bereshit,* has as one of its meanings, "imagination." When Jacob sees Joseph's children, he says, "*Lo Pillalti.*" (I never imagined that I would get to see you. Now I even get to see your children.) So the idea of prayer, I feel, comes from this place that is beyond ourselves. When we get to this place, we are not just opening up a *siddur* and reading the words but also tapping into a place that I cannot "even imagine." But I want to so much. So it's not just that I am doing the reading, but the words automatically come out and, perhaps, because the thought may be so powerful, it lifts up the thoughts and feelings. And this is very much rooted to the learning of *Chasidut* itself. Because in learning *Chasidut,* it's not just the learning of the words, it's the ability to nourish our imagination. It's giving to that place that perhaps gets very little nourishment. It's giving that place the ability to be itself. And when we allow our prayers to lift us up, thinking that we are actually lifting the prayers up, I think that in itself brings out a different quality. They are the same words. Ultimately, it all gets down to what we are thinking. And I am thinking that I just want to be able to pray. I just want to be able to stand before God. There's nothing better, especially when I am saying *kaddish*. My mother is truly receiving "*nachat*" from this. And this also enables the prayers to be lifted up. And obviously it's all connected to the mood we are in. And if we are in a mood of joy, and if we have been learning Torah for the sake of God, that very day our prayers take on a different tone. Because the Torah and the *mitzvot* are truly united. It says, "If you learn after you pray, you go from strength to strength." In the world of *Chasidut*, one of the main ingredients is to learn *Chasidut* before praying. This is the vehicle that enables the prayer to be lifted up.

S. F.:   Almost all the people I have talked with are people successful and known in the world. You are not known and successful in the world. Yet paradoxically, it seems to me you act as if you have "more" and more to give than almost any person I know. Does it bother you that you do not have a wider following, more students, and a large reputation? How do you feel about all of this?

David Herzberg: I don't feel it's such a problem. When the Maggid of Mezhirech became famous, thousands of people were coming to him for his blessing and to hear words of Torah from him. He said it was a curse, a punishment from heaven, because one time he had traveled on *Chol-HaMo'ed* and had taken lightly the holiness of the Moed. This was because even though it's permitted by the strict letter of the Law, in the spirit, *Chol-HaMo'ed* is also a holiday. It's like walking out of the *sukkah*.

I have never been so famous as to judge whether it's a punishment or not. I don't feel that I am missing anything. I feel that I already have so many blessings. If it happens that there should be more people to learn with, and in addition more, quote, material success, unquote, I welcome it with joy. But it's not one of my goals. It is not one of my desires in life. In general, I have found that what I need the most in life I do receive. And if there is a point in my life, whether it be today, tomorrow, in the near future, or in the far-off future, when I am supposed to have much more in the world of students, and money, that would be what I would need at that time. But I don't go searching for it because I don't feel that's what I am longing for. The thing that I am longing for the most is hopefully what all the Jews are longing for, and that's to have that peace inside to see that real peace in Eretz Yisrael, and to have that true *shalom bayit* in *artzenu hakedoshah*. It is not so much the idea of amassing students and amassing wealth, because that can also be a very big ego trip. If that is what I need, I believe God will give that to me. And if I am to have ten thousand students, hopefully I will receive it humbly. And if I am to have a million dollars, hopefully I will know what to do with it. Until that point, thank God, I have everything I need, perhaps much more than I need. And I hope I will be blessed with the knowledge to know what to do with what I have at the moment.

This interview was given by David Herzberg in memory of and for the uplifting of the soul of his mother, Rivka bat Zeev Wolf and Hinda.

Rabbi Dov Berkovits

Rabbi Dov Berkovits is a pioneer in the search for ways both of teaching Torah and of making Torah provide solutions to real-life questions in contemporary Israel. For fifteen years the Director of Pardes Institute, he is presently the chief rabbi of Shilo and co-director of Yakar Institute in Jerusalem. He also teaches and lectures at Midreshet Rachel.

I met Dov Berkovits in his home in Shilo. In our walk around the *yishuv,* he pointed to the site that was for the tribes of Israel for over three hundred years the center of worship, the place of the Tabernacle and the Holy Ark. In meeting with him, I had a strong sense of the Jew dedicated to returning and rebuilding the Land of Israel, physically and spiritually.

Our conversation centered upon the kind of spiritual renewal required in Israel today. He made it clear that for him, the old Diaspora formulas were not adequate to provide the kind of innovative Judaism required in Israel. As one involved in the day-by-day life of a community, raising a family in a situation and world quite different from those anticipated when he lived outside of Israel, he has a strong sense of the correctives required to make the dream of a holy life in the Holy Land come true.

S. F.:   Could you please describe your present work in teaching?

Rabbi Berkovits: I am connected to a number of different institutions, trying to find the right balance in order to do that which I believe needs to be done these days. I teach at the Hesder Yeshiva in Shilo. Along with another member of Shilo, I have set up a *midrashah* in the new settlement of Rachelim, which was established after the terrorist murder of Rachel Druck and Yitzhak Rofe. The settlement was established at the spot where the murders took place. We run a seminar for high school students, and we have special classes for *yeshivah* students from all the settlements of the surrounding area. The *midrashah* works on a part-time basis, and I am its educational director. Along with this, I became involved last year in setting up a new institution in Yerushalayim called Beit Yakar. This was at the initiation of Rabbi Mickey Rosen, who had set up and worked for fourteen years in a similar institution in London and who afterward came on *aliyah*. He bought the old Misgav Ladach hospital building, and there we have set up a center that works to make the connection between "creativity" and the traditional sources. We have a number of different departments. In one such department, we have artists sitting with *rabbanim* and trying to understand what it means to be a contemporary artist capable of true Jewish expression. We have a department that deals with Kabbalah and Chasidism in the context of a search for psychological insights. There is also another department, which works on ecological problems. We try to open Torah to varying contemporary needs. We have all kinds and levels of people, from beginners to lifelong learners, and the whole institution has been developing very rapidly.

S. F.:   I know you have taught in Israel for many years. When did you come on *Aliyah* and how has your working life developed here?

Rabbi Berkovits: I came on *aliyah* in 1970. I think I was part of a minor wave of *aliyah* from the United States, which was more or less inspired by the Six Day War in 1967. Since my B'nei Akiva days in

Chicago, and with the year I spent in Israel during college, I knew that I would come on *aliyah*. I had decided after I finished my academic study that I was going to come to Israel. I received my *semichah* from Yeshiva University and a master's degree in Jewish history. By that time, I had much forgotten my year in Israel, but *aliyah* remained a decision I had made. I had offers to work in Hillel on campuses in the United States, but I knew I had to give *aliyah* a chance. So I came back in 1970 by myself, as my parents were not at that time here yet. I came as a bachelor, twenty-five years old, and began studying philosophy at Hebrew University. I assumed that I would continue my. Torah learning at the same time. I went to Yeshivat Mir in the morning and in the afternoon studied for a master's at Hebrew University. Somewhere in the middle of the year, and this because of the many "*tiyulim*" (trips) I was taking, I became deeply connected to Eretz Yisrael, and the renewed experience of the Jewish people here had a great impact on me. I felt it was both revelation and revolution in the meaning of being connected to *Hashem* by being in *Eretz Yisrael*. Fascinatingly enough, it was through a friend of mine, Rabbi David Miller, who is now a *rosh yeshivah* at Beis Midrash l'Torah (BMT), that I had a turning-point experience. He took me down to Reb Areleh's *Chasidim* for a *seudah shilishi* in *Neturei Karta*. We sat there for four hours in the dark on *motzei shabbat* listening to amazing *niggunim* of which we had never heard the likes before. And there was something in the connection between those *niggunim* and the new *Eretz Yisrael* I was meeting every day that led me, by the end of the year, to leave the university and go to Yeshivat Mercaz Harav. I had learned for a year with Rav Soloveitchik, of blessed memory, in America. And thank God, my father, Eliezer Berkovits, of blessed memory, had taught me a great deal. But there was something of the renewed meeting with *Eretz Yisrael* that gave me the feeling that I did not yet really know anything. I had to begin from some kind of new beginning, and I went to Mercaz Harav and began a search that led to my *aliyah*.

S. F.:   What happened from there?

Rabbi Berkovits: I learned there for two years and left when I was offered a job at a new institution that was being founded, a place called Machon Pardes. At the time, I was convinced that Machon Pardes was going to introduce a new way of learning Torah within the Jewish community. The people who were teaching there seemed to me to be the most exciting young scholars and "*talmidei chachamim*" in Israel at the time. The initial faculty of Pardes included Harav Adin Steinsaltz, Michael Rosenak, Rabbi Dr. David Hartman, and Professor Eliezer Schweid. And a fifth person was a fellow who was killed on the Bar-Lev Line in 1973, a young, brilliant, and original scholar of *Tanach* named Dr. Aryeh Toeg. A fascinating book might be written about the original faculty, why they came to Pardes, what they were looking for, and what they found and didn't find (because they all left after a year). Each one went on to create his own Pardes. Steinsaltz created Shefa; Hartman, Machon Hartman; Schweid created Kerem; and Michael Rosenak became the head of the Melton School of Education at Hebrew University. When these senior figures left, I, who was a junior member of the faculty, pretty much took over Pardes, which was on the verge of collapse. During the second year, I became more or less the self-appointed director of Pardes, and I went on for the next four or five years trying to put it together. What we tried to build there was an institution that gave a traditional Torah education and at the same time allowed maturing young adults to ask their own questions. Our aim was to treat those questions with respect and depth, so that the students could create their own personal relationship with Torah. I think Pardes has followed that path to this day. At a certain point, I invited Levi Lauer to be the director and I became the chairman of the faculty. And in that capacity I taught there for an additional ten years.

S. F.:   And when did you come to Shilo?

Rabbi Berkovits: I was married in 1977, and we moved to Shilo in 1980. We came out really innocently, out of a deep desire to be part of some young, idealistic community in *Eretz Yisrael*. Politically we were at the center, perhaps even a little to the left. But we came and began to build a new life here, a family life at Shilo.

S. F: You showed me this morning something of the development of the *yishuv* through the years. Yet as we talk, it is a time of difficulty for those in *Eretz Yisrael*, in Judaea and Samaria. How do you see your decision now?

Rabbi Berkovits: This question alone is one that requires much longer than the time available to us. I can try to speak about it a little bit. Over the years, I have become much more deeply committed to the whole historic Jewish venture that is building the settlements in Judaea and Samaria. I deeply identify with this. I have some important questions about what might be called the path of both the spiritual and political leaders of the settlements. I think my background at Pardes and my commitment to broad Torah education do not fit in with the frame of mind of many in the settlements. They were not educated in this way. The *Yeshivot Hesder* and *Yeshivot Tichoniyot* in Israel create deep ideological commitment but do not provide the educational framework to communicate to others the understanding of what is being done here. The political crisis we have in Israel today is, in my opinion, a spiritual crisis related to two very different readings of the meaning of Jewish life and history. These two groups are not in real contact with each other. And I have very serious criticisms of the political leaders here who have not opened up and made their own ideological position accessible to a good share of those in the other group. Many responsible Jews see us here as strange, anachronistic, messianic. And this is not really true. In terms of the real security needs of the State of Israel, strategically and politically, and in terms of the spiritual need to create a new kind of Judaism, the settlements are of utmost importance. As with every new and positive component in the historical development of the Jewish people, there is controversy connected with it.

S. F.:   But how can the bridging possibly be done when it is clear that those who are committed to a Jewish religious life are also those who feel most deeply connected with the Land of Israel, and while those without deep connection to the land feel no connection to Jewish spiritual and religious life?

Rabbi Berkovits: I am deeply struggling with this question, and in a sense, it is central to my lifework. I come from Yeshiva University, where I learned the ideal of *"Torah v Mada,"* the synthesis between the Torah and the modern world. My father, *alav hashalom,* was certainly one of the great integrators of general knowledge and had a deep understanding of Torah. My background is similar to that of those like Rav Aharon Lichtenstein and Rabbi Danny Tropper, who have tried to deal with this problem in Israel. We are all part of the attempt that began over a hundred years ago in Germany and continued in the United States, to somehow create a bridge between the Western secular, humanistic disciplines in science, philosophy, and culture and the depths of Torah. On a certain level, in my path at Pardes and Shilo, I have been trying to understand whether the model that comes from Yeshiva University can accomplish this goal in Israeli society. I think that the clarification of this question is definitely one of the critical dimensions of *Avodat Hashem* in this generation. I worked for a number of years with Beit Midresh *Elul,* a group of graduates of Yeshivot Hesder, on the one hand, and a secular kibbutz movement, on the other. We attempted to see whether secular and religious Israelis could learn together. I had serious questions as to whether such a framework would compromise the way Torah should be studied. There's an important difference between the approach of Elul and that of Pardes. In Pardes, you allowed for all kinds of questions to be asked, but the teaching authority was primarily in the hands of Orthodox teachers. In Elul, there were no teachers, no authority figures. The educational principle was one of humanistic democracy, and this meant no authority figures, no teachers on principle. The Beit Hamidrash operates as a *kibbutz.* On the one hand, this allowed secular Israelis to come and learn seriously, and they were doing that. On the other hand, it would not be compromising Torah. I went to Harav Yehuda Amital, head of Yeshivat Har Etzion, to discuss the question. Rav Amital told me that in the 1960s, he had set up a discussion group with Eliezer Schweid and other secular Israelis. After speaking with him at length, I came away with the impression that he was saying he had made a serious effort at bridging the gap and did not really believe in it. So, too, it seems to me that a group like Gesher does not bridge the gap. It approaches secular Israelis with the assumption that it is basically a one-way bridge toward something that in and of itself, has an important place, learning Torah. But there's a difference between the way such an approach works in the Diaspora and the way it affects Israeli society. There is a difference between setting up a seminar institute in the United States, where it's clear that any Orthodox institution must be a one-way bridge to *teshuvah,* and doing it in a Jewish State. The real question here is, "Can you revolutionize Israeli society in such a way that it will have faith in Torah?" Can we answer that question so the great majority in Israel will say that Torah is something we need to make a dynamic, creative society? The approach of working exclusively within religious frameworks to bring us return to *mitzvot* can have effects on hundreds or thousands. But what if this is done in such a way that it alienates the great majority? So the question is really how you present Torah in Israel in such a way that both the intelligentsia and the average person can see Torah as having relevance for their day-to-day living in a creative and productive society. Now, through the years of teaching and learning in Israel, I have come to feel there is a fundamental flaw in the old-style approach to bridging the gap. In the United States, the synthesis between the secular Western culture and the religious culture could be made because even the modern Orthodox Jew was not deeply committed to the other culture. He knew it was Goyish and so could protect himself by staying in his own community. While intellectually and professionally he was modern, he still remained in the Beit Haknesset and was Beit HaMidrash in the world of *mitzvot.* But that position is untenable in Israel because here, the Goyim are other Jews. And the fact that there are other Jews means you cannot just relate to them with your mind. The world of Yeshiva University was a tremendous intellectual world, a synthesis of the Lithuanian *yeshivah* world with the best thinking in the modern world. But for my children, being brought up in Israel, it does not work. They do not live in the mind alone. They live in the physical world, in the culture around them, and they are absorbed into Israeli society. We educate our children to love the Land of Israel, the State of Israel. We educate our children to love and be connected with all the Jews of Israel. So the idea of purely intellectual synthesis cannot be good enough, cannot work in a society where our relations are on all other levels of life also.

S. F.:   I have heard a number of modern religious Jews, among them Rabbi Rakeffet, argue that the real bridge can be made only by young religious Jews entering worlds that are now completely dominated by the secular, such as the media and other cultural areas. By making their voice felt, by expressing their values through their work, they can have an influence on the society.

Rabbi Berkovits: It seems to be the natural next step for a lot of intelligent and committed Yeshiva and Ulpana graduates to begin working in those areas. And this not as in the United States, where to be a religious physicist or economist was a "schizophrenic condition." But in Israel, that's not enough, because what we want here is a form of communications, economics, and literature that will reflect our own authentic religious statement of what this country should be. One of the real challenges of *Avodat Hashem* is, then, in my humble opinion, to make the State of Israel the reflection of true Jewish independence. This does not mean independence politically only, but first, and above all, Jewish spiritual autonomy over life. That's ultimately what our goal is; that's ultimately the cry of God into history. The State of Israel is something that God created. Now what we have to do is understand how Torah, and the depths of the

Torah (what is called in the language of my father "prophetic historic Judaism"), can make an autonomous Jewish face on this planet. This is the great question for the Jewish people. It is not enough to be an economist or a poet, on one side, and a believing Jew on the other. What has to be done now is a new synthesis, so that a poet can, for instance, by drawing on contemporary Hebrew language, express the depths of Torah. And if you are an economist, the question is not to work in the Bank of Israel during the day and study Torah at night, it is to try to understand how a Jewish economy should be run on the basis of all the tractates of the Torah, which claim that "*Malkhut HaShem*," the Kingship of God, is created basically in the world of society. *Parashat Behar*, the twenty-fifth chapter of Leviticus (*Vayikra*) is a description of *Shemittah* and *Yovel* and of the laws of redeeming the land. It's a socioeconomic model for dealing with power relations in society in the real world. We know what Marx and Milton Friedman have to say about these things, but what does Torah have to say about these things today? Now in order for a young religious Jew to do what you have described in an authentic Torah way, they have to believe that the Torah has voice, has a unique perspective on these questions. As I remember, there was, in modern Orthodoxy in America, a fundamental disbelief that the *Beit Hamidrash* would create a total picture of society as a whole. One cannot continue in Israel using this concept of Torah, though some leading figures seem to think this may work out. What needs to be done in my opinion is to set up an alternative voice, a voice that comes from Torah, from the depths of *Halachah* and from the depths of Kabbalah. This must be set up in a way that the fullness of the Jewish mind and soul is expressed in the face of real life. In my opinion, this goes beyond the question of the religious and the secular because it's a creation to which both religious and secular Jews can contribute. And this must be done in order to create a picture of society that comes from the depth of Jewish experience on this planet.

S. F.:   And once we achieve this, or in the process of this, we will become a "light to the nations."

Rabbi Berkovits: I have a problem with, and don't really like, that term. I think that first of all we have to be a light to ourselves. I think we have big problems today as a people. Assimilation and intermarriage are only the outward signs of a great spiritual crisis we are living through in this generation. We do not have a language that comes from the depths of Torah with which to speak about the conditions in which we live. We have, *Baruch Hashem*, a tremendous amount of learning and a tremendous amount of people who are becoming interested in learning. This is a sign of the *"Netzach,"* the eternal quality of Torah. From Russia to Australia and to the furthest spiritual distances in the suburbs of the United States, there is learning today. Torah for its own sake is important, and basically that is always the first condition, because Torah must speak to each person. You learn Torah because you love Torah. That is the inner engine of the Jewish people and of our history. But on the other hand, it is clear that our problem is our inability to take that Torah and help build life in community. So that assimilation and intermarriage are, for me, the outer symptoms of a real inner problem, our inability to be a light unto ourselves.

I would just like to add an additional point. There is a great teacher of Judaism from Paris who moved to Israel a few years ago, whose name is Harav Yehuda Ashkenazi. One of the things he has said is that once upon a time, there was a Judaism in which the *Beit Haknesset* was the center of life and the community was built around it. Today, the center of Jewish life is the whole world, all of life, and the *Beit Hamikdash* has to be placed in it. This is the picture we must have today, no matter what one's picture of the day-to-day practice of the *Beit Hamikdash;* in other words, whether there will be *korbonot* (sacrifice) or not. According to one opinion in the Gemara, there will be only one specific sacrifice. I would say that *Avodat Hashem* in this generation should conceptually begin to be a passage from the *Beit Haknesset* to the *Beit Hamikdash*. And this passage is one in which we move, in effect, from the community as a miniature reflection of the *Avodat Hashem* of the Jewish people to a condition in which, in effect, we actually live today, in which the Jewish people has a place that they call home and in which they organize themselves as a people among the nations, yet distinct from them. And the ultimate *Avodat Hashem* is that of the people, as a whole, standing in front of *Hashem* (which is what the *Beit Hamikdash* was all about). The question is how God's gift of life as a whole ("In the beginning, God created heaven and earth") is connected with ("I am the Lord your God Who took you out of the land of Egypt") with the Ten Commandments. This is the picture of the *Beit Hamikdash* that we should be moving toward. In order to do this, we must democratize the learning of Torah, not compromise its seriousness and depth. But on the contrary, we must make its seriousness and depth accessible to the living sparks of the divine in every Jew. We need to facilitate the possibility that every individual created in the image of God will learn to create divine things in this world, within the boundaries, which also constitute the holy uniqueness, of his individual life.

Preliminary and Partial Conclusions

For many of these rabbis, the first service of God, the one they express deepest love and devotion for, is the teaching of Torah. As Rabbi Rakeffet put it, the great model of us all, Moshe, sees himself more as *melamed* than as *sofer*. Not writing, not producing publications, but transmitting the Torah face-to-face to their students is the first love and priority of most of these rabbis. Rabbis Riskin, Brovender, Berkovits, Rabinovitch, Lewittes (z"l), Quint, Schweiger, Lopes Cardozo, Rakeffet, and Fleer all seem to thrive on the personal relationship with students, with the idea that teaching Torah for its own sake is the true service of God.

A complementary approach is employed by those who place the emphasis on making "practical life changes," whose idea is in doing service to the Jewish people. Professor Fackenheim and Rabbis Greenberg, Tropper, and Golinkin, while all valuing learning in itself, seem to see their service more as a way of effecting changes and action in the world. Rabbis Fackenheim and Greenberg are especially concerned with the message for life, which they wish the Jewish people to learn, not simply in everyday life but in an overall historical approach and attitude.

Here it is not surprising that while very few of the rabbis are of the "denial of the Diaspora" school, there is close to unanimous feeling in the belief that the future service of the Jewish people will be done primarily, both in quantiative and qualitative terms, in the Land of Israel. Most assert the conviction that not only will Israel be in the future a much larger proportion numerically of the Jewish people than it is today, but that the truer, the fuller, Jewish life, both now and in the future, is in Israel. It is, perhaps, natural that this would be the consensus, as most of these rabbis have themselves moved from the Diaspora to Israel, having made *aliyah*. But these teachers of Judaism are people of experience and integrity who have lived in and known both worlds and whose judgment is based not only on the rabbis' private lives but on what they have seen in the communities they have served.

A more surprising conclusion, however, emerged in regard to another question that was frequently asked. Though most of the rabbis saw primarily positive developments in Israel through the roughly half-century of its statehood, few were willing to speak with enthusiasm about the Jews as "light to the nations." Rabbis Greenberg and Tropper are exceptions here. But the overwhelming feeling of most of these teachers is that the Jewish people, even in Israel, have to first get their own house in order before they can think to be models for others. Rabbi Brovender reflected this sentiment in speaking of how much is involved in educating even one Jew, stressing the enormous amount of resources required. Other rabbis pointed to the distance from perfection that exists in so many aspects of moral and spiritual life within the Jewish people and Israel.

This sense of distance from perfection was most strongly expressed when the rabbis responded to the question of assimilation, primarily in the Diaspora but also in Israel. While one response of Rabbis Pearl and Quint was to point to the strange unpredictability of Jewish history, noting the precedents for dramatic turnabouts from great low points to miraculous positive developments, the prevailing feeling was of troubledness over a declining Diaspora. Rabbi Lewittes and others noted the spiritual revival of Judaism among a minority in the Diaspora, involving a higher quality of Jewish learning than before, while pointing out that this does not affect the great majority. As for practical remedies, there was a clear preference for concentrating more resources in day school education, among those with higher potential for true commitment, and in strengthening the "youth relationship to Israel." Some rabbis felt the only answer for Jews who wish their families to be Jewish in the long-term future is through *aliyah* to Israel.

As to the other major "communal question," which related to what its proponents call the "Middle East Peace Process," there was considerable disagreement. Many who were interviewed in the early stages of the work did not have the opportunity to express their view. Most of those asked strongly opposed the agreement. There was criticism, such as that of Rabbi Spero, who saw the conceding of parts of the Land of Israel to a foreign power as the very opposite of service of God, a breaking of a covenant and an action no Jewish generation – even when the Jews were in Diaspora – had taken. There was opposition to the agreement on other grounds, such as those related by Professor Fackenheim, who spoke of the real danger of the process toward the integrity of Jerusalem. On the side of the proponents, Rabbi Brovender pointed out the moral burden of having to rule over another people. Rabbi Greenberg, also a cautious proponent of the process, spoke of the whole process itself as an achievement of Jewish power, of Israel's long struggle to receive recognition. While all the rabbis aim, as anyone within the Jewish Tradition naturally must, for "peace," none of them was what might be called a "nownik" who sees in the spectacular events of a moment the real test of long-term intention. As Rabbi Rabinovitch indicated in speaking about the present condition of Israel, the question of state building is not a matter of one generation alone but rather of generations. Here again, in speaking of Israel as a society, while all had criticisms of various kinds, there was a fundamentally positive evaluation of its achievements and prospects. This comes across especially in the words of those who place special emphasis in their thought on the awareness of other periods of Jewish history.

Another question on this sensitive relation between politics and religion yielded an almost unanimous agreement. Whether it was Rabbi Riskin dreaming of a day when there would be no religious parties or Rabbi Tropper arguing that the secular in Israel have a mistaken view of the religious, in part because of the work of religious parties, the rabbis seemed to advocate a clear seperation of religion and state. This, too, perhaps reflects the American background of many of these rabbis, but they, by and large, would like to separate the world of service of God in religion from the complications and compromises of political life.

Somewhat paradoxically, however, in regard to the major question of the work, the service of God, all agree that this is not the work of a special area of life, or group of people, but of every Jew. The most systematic analysis of this belief in psychological terms is given by Rabbi Ze'ev Chaim Lifshitz. His work is, in a sense, devoted to finding the creative spark through which each and every individual can best serve God. For Daniel Tropper, who also emphasizes that the task of serving God is everyone's, the most dramatic instances of service of God are in the individual's using his God-given freedom in making major life decisions. He relates this to an idea that is central for most of these rabbis, the idea of *tzelem Elokim,* that man is created in the image of God. As Rabbi Spero explains, the overwhelming emphasis by our Sages, *Chazal,* is in relating this to man's moral quality, his capacity for doing acts of mercy and justice. Rabbi Fleer directly relates this to another key concept in Jewish thought, that of *gemilut chasadim,* the doing of a whole group of *mitzvot* by which the human being serves his fellow in society. Thus, it is clear that in the definition of service of God given by the rabbis in this work, there is no room for a Protestantlike concentration on an isolated relationship between the individual servant of God and his Creator. For all of these rabbis, the service of God means service to family, community, and people. In this regard, almost all the rabbis spoken with here are dedicated family people whose large families express what Rabbi Rabinovitch sees as the first sign of faith in the Jewish future.

Another aspect of the service of God in doing for others is revealed in the special kind of communal work done by some of these rabbis. Rabbis Riskin and Rakeffet, in their special missions to the Soviet Union, engaged in work that involved considerable personal risk. Here, the key point is the one made by Rabbi Meir Schweiger, that the true service of God for the Jew is in being responsible for others, for family, for community, and for the Jewish people as a whole. Rabbi Schweiger's critique of the modern individual's selfish subservience to his own private desires is his call for a kind of service of God that leads the individual to be able to see beyond himself, to see the world with the understanding that comes through reading the Torah. And again, walking in the way of God, loving justice, doing mercy, and walking humbly through this world is the way of life made evident in example by many of these teachers of Torah in and through their relations with community and congregation.

Many of these rabbis are involved daily in one required traditional way of helping other Jews: leading them in prayer. And clearly, the "work and service of the heart" is one of the fundamental ways in which the Jew serves God. Here, the Jewish ideal is that the human being should have a continual sense of his own smallness and humility before the Creator of the Universe. This sense of a need for continual prayer and continual consciousness of God is especially emphasized by the teacher of Chasidism David Herzberg. For him, the worship of God in prayer is the worship of God in joy. And the spiritual uplift that comes through this should, in his words, help the worshipper radiate a warmth and kindness to each and every human being. The service of God in prayer is not in opposition to the service of human beings but rather helps lead to a closer kind of good and right relationship with others.

And so we come full circle. These good human beings, these teachers of Torah who serve God by so doing, also serve other human beings. These good Jews, who live in helping other Jews by doing this, serve God. And they, through this service, point a way for each and every Jew, each and every human being, to give meaning in his life. Not for oneself alone must one live but for God and for others. And in this way, we help bring Redemption into the world.

Afterword:
Interview with
the Hidden Rabbi

I met with him in his home in the large district on the outskirts of Jerusalem. His apartment crowded with *seforim*, holy books, is enlivened by the playing of small children. A large, strong person, his voice has a calming, authoritative quality. Though he works primarily as a teacher in a *kollel*, he gives large amounts of his time to privately helping those with psychological problems. He is one of the quiet *tzaddikim*, who has helped many people without receiving either credit or pay for it.

Though my talk with him centers on one question, the question of *Avodat Hashem*, it does so only on a certain level. His vast reading of the mystical literature of the world, his own unique synthesis of this thought, is, unfortunately, not reflected in our conversation. What is, however, reflected is his genuine concern for helping others and his conviction that the true help for every human being is in leading them to find their unique way of serving God.

S. F.:   Could you tell me, Rabbi, why you do not wish to make your name known? And why you would agree to give this interview only on the condition that your identity be kept secret?

Hidden Rabbi: Who seeks to build his name, loses his name. My name is not important. What is important is to help Jews in what they have been put in this world for, the service of *Hashem*. And the reason I agreed to speak with you is that you told me this subject, the worship of God, is at the center of the work. So I agree to say a few words here in the hope that it will have some influence, however small, on other Jews in bringing them closer to God.

S. F.:   I know you engage in a wide variety of counseling activities. Could you explain the principles upon which you work?

Hidden Rabbi: God has given us our abilities and talents. It is our task to use these as best we can in serving God. Mankind is created in the image of God. What greater service of God can there be then than in helping our fellow human beings? Whenever we talk about walking in God's ways, imitating God, we mean first, and above all, being merciful. This is the first premise of all service of God and, *Baruch Hashem,* the Jewish world is filled with people who think and act in this way.

S. F.:   But you have told me that very often, you do not succeed in helping.

Hidden Rabbi: I am grateful every time I manage to help in some way, however small. I know there are many times I do not succeed at all. I can, at times, be saddened by this. But ultimately, I know I am striving to do the work of God and that as a limited human being, I must understand I can and will fail. This means the mercy of *Hashem* will manifest itself in a way that is beyond me.

S. F.:   As I understand it, though, you do not confine yourself to the level of individual problems. You try to understand how to help the Jewish people, mankind as a whole.

Hidden Rabbi: Every human being is a part of larger worlds, in which he is only a small part. I too know how small I am in relation to the whole of Israel. Yet I know this does not dissolve me from my responsibility. And so I do try to understand the great problems of our people and how we should act in the world.

S. F.:   What do you see as our greatest problems now, and what should be our response to them?

Hidden Rabbi: Our greatest problem is that the great majority of the Jewish people do not live by Torah and *mitzvot*. I know it is fashionable to argue that there can be a plurality of Judaisms. And yet, I insist that the Jewish people now need a drastic change in character and outlook. I believe a great turning point for us will be when the majority of Jews have returned to Torah and *mitzvot*. This is the spiritual legacy of our people. Living without it is living as crippled, disabled, whether the disabled know this or not.

S. F.:   But we live in a world of free choice. the majority of the Jews, both within Israel and without, have as an option the life of Torah and *Mitzvot*. And they have not chosen that option. Many who were raised within the world of Torah and *mitzvot* have, in fact, chosen to leave it. Perhaps the truly religious way is only for a minority, a remnant of our people.

Hidden Rabbi: I believe many Jews have not been given any choice. They are born in ignorance, they live in ignorance, and they will die in ignorance unless they are helped. I believe the Torah community has to be more open to other Jews, has to strive to produce people who can speak their own language with them. And I believe this means being able to speak to them on the highest possible intellectual and spiritual level. I believe we need to produce leaders who are true people of the spirit in the highest sense. And this kind of leadership must set an example in teaching that the true way to meaning in life, to the highest possible life, is, for the Jew, through Torah and *mitzvot*, service of God.

S. F.:   Yet, as I understand it, you work with religious people who have very serious psychological and emotional problems. Living by Torah is no guarantee of a good and fulfilling life.

Hidden Rabbi: There is no guarantee for the individual. That is true. Yet on a broad, general level, it is clear that the Torah community way of life does lead to a greater degree of spiritual and emotional well-being. There is no certainty, however, that living by *mitzvot* will bring ecstasy. We know the spiritual problems and torments of many of our great *tzaddikim*. Only they know how to use these torments to bring themselves to greater devotion to God. And this must be what we try to teach everyone—not that their happiness is guaranteed but that their lives can be made great with meaning through living as *Hashem* has commanded.

S. F.:   In speaking with many rabbis, I have found that many concern themselves with individual and community in what might be called a "local way," while others are more concerned with "Klal Yisrael." I know you fit into the second category and are among those believe that the Jewish people, in their return to the Land of Israel, in building a Jewish State, have really initiated the process of Redemption. How do you justify this position against those rabbis who believe that we, for one hundred years, have been "forcing the end" and will be punished for this?

Hidden Rabbi: One of the central premises of our Torah is the *brit* between *Hashem* and the people of Israel. We are to be entrusted with the land on the condition that we build here a society that lives in justice, walks in the ways of God. No matter how long we lived in

Golah, outside Israel, no matter how great our achievements – and perhaps our greatest has been in enduring as Jews there – our life there was never to be our main purpose. All our history and all our religious heritage direct us to the Land of Israel. Only in Israel can a Jew perform a maximum of *mitzvot*. And if we are today still far from the state of moral and spiritual perfection that would bring about full restoration of Torah life, there is no question that in living here, we are doing what God has commanded. So I, of course, see the return of the Jewish people to the Land of Israel and the building of the Land of Israel as a society in justice – a Torah society – as part of the Redemption.

S. F.:   In this sense, you are, as I understand it, deeply troubled now by the process that is to take parts of the historical land of Israel from the people of Israel and transmit them to another sovereignty.

Hidden Rabbi: No Jewish generation has the right to forfeit the rights of other Jewish generations. No Jewish generation has the right to violate and break the Covenant that was made with *Hashem.* The Land of Israel is simply not ours to give or to trade. It is *Hashem's.* Any Jew who knows the very first word of commentary of Rashi knows that this process was anticipated by our Sages. They said that *Bereshit* begins with the Creation of the world, precisely to show that all the lands are *Hashem's.* And if Israel was given to the Jewish people, this is their perfect right. No one should ever be able to accuse them of being robbers. It is God's, and God has given it to Israel. That is one thing that concerns me, the arrogance, the sin of doing what we have no right to do: the breaking of our Covenant with God. Along with that are the possible practical consequences and implications. Those who surrender the land claim they do so for reasons of *pikuach nefesh.* But it seems to me much more likely that surrender will mean more loss of life, not less. And that it can even threaten the sovereignty of the Jewish people in parts of the Land of Israel. I am deeply concerned about this.

S. F.:   But as one who believes that the "process of Redemption" has begun, don't you have the confidence that these "ups and downs" are a necessary part of it? Don't you believe that these "pangs of Redemption" simply are necessary to deepen our appreciation of the process of Redemption? And that all will be "all right" in the end?

Hidden Rabbi: I, of course, believe that the Good will ultimately triumph. But when is that "ultimately"? I have no guarantee that it is in a year or five, or fifty, or one hundred, or ten thousand years from now. As I understand it, there are no "guarantees." How can any Jew who has mind and heart open, in this generation, after the destruction of one-third of our people in the most evil and terrible way, imagine he knows with certainty how history will turn? We cannot delude ourselves by believing in inevitabilities. Rather, it is our task to shape our history in accordance with the teachings God has given us.

S. F.:   So your own increased political activeness of late comes out of a religious conviction?

Hidden Rabbi: Of course. How dare we divide the political from the religious, as if we could give the responsibility for our lives to others? Our task is to work in the world to realize God's purpose.

S. F.:   But you are a minority. On the one side, many religious Jews believe their task is solely to be a separate and sacred Torah living community. And on the other side, secular Jews believe that our task is to be a normal nation. And that's all.

Hidden Rabbi: The Jewish people, both in Israel and even more so without, must be reeducated in Jewishness. We need teachers who can speak to the whole community, who can address the people in such a way as to move them.

S. F.:   Are there any leaders on the present scene who you believe can do the kind of work you outline here?

Hidden Rabbi: In a sense, perhaps, only the *Moshiach* can do what I expect of our leaders. And yet, even if it's not for them to finish the work, they are not free to desist from undertaking it.

S. F.:   I know that though you live in the Land of Israel, you are acutely aware of what is happening to the Jewish people throughout the world. Is there any way to resist the process of assimilation and breakdown that is occurring in Jewish communities throughout the world?

Hidden Rabbi: I do not, in a sense, believe it is wise when we talk about assimilation to speak of the Jewish people as if we were wholly isolated from the world. Assimilation comes in great part because of processes and trends that are affecting mankind as a whole. And so, just as we are not to look for our own salvation and Redemption without also working for the Redemption of others, so we cannot see our problems in isolation. The modern Western world suffers from a breakdown of the traditional family, suffers from higher rates of divorce and bachelorhood, and suffers from the idea that the individual owns his own life, with absolute freedom and autonomy and a primary responsibility to look out for himself and himself alone. The modern world suffers from a kind of narcissistic individualism. And this is connected with many other ills, some of which, such as alcoholism, crime, and drugs, affect the Jews somewhat less than the general population, and others, such as the "search for alternative spiritual frameworks," that affect Jews more. Our answer to these problems is, of course, in a Torah life. But the real challenge is to make that Torah life a meaningful option for the many who have no idea of what it is. I believe, by the way, that there are strides in this direction. The level of day school education, the level of Jewish learning among a certain group of Jews, is higher than it has been in the past. But this group is not large enough. And again, I must stress that our way of life and Torah values are not for ourselves alone but for mankind.

S. F.: I have heard many rabbis say that we Jews have so many problems with ourselves that we had better "clean our own house first" before we go about preaching to others.

Hidden Rabbi: There are certain basic concepts of Judaism that, for the good of mankind, all mankind must come to share. The idea of the One Caring Creator God, Who demands of mankind to walk in God's way in morality. The idea of a higher morality for mankind by which we sanctify life. The idea of moral purity. All these ideas must be the basis for reeducating mankind as a whole toward the time of the Messianic Era. This is the Jewish message to and meaning for the world. Of course, the best teaching is a good example. And it is our task to do this in Israel. But it is our task. We are meant to be a blessing to all peoples on earth and not to find our own private salvation in which we escape our historical responsibility.

S. F.: These are big words. How would you translate them into reality, even in an all-Jewish society, it seems impossible.

Hidden Rabbi: Again I have said the goal must be to bring the Jews back to Torah. I would say, "not also in the Land of Israel," but first, and above all, in the Land of Israel.

S. F.: But this is simply not practical. The society is in good part secular. The cultural and political elite are secular, no matter how traditional a good share of the population might be.

Hidden Rabbi: I believe there is a group in Israel, the religious Zionists, who can set the tone for the future. They are not perfect. But they do, in large part, have the love of Torah and love of the people of Israel that are necessary. They do have the communal dedication, which is so lacking in our more individualistically oriented time. They can set the pace. And we should help them, insofar as we can.

S. F.: I see no sign that the great majority of people in Israel are moving in this direction.

Hidden Rabbi: We must work, and pray, and with God's help, we will find the way. The mistake would simply be to expect it to come easily. We must fight to make this happen.

S. F.: Do you mean "fight," also, for Jews of the Diaspora to emigrate en masse to Israel?

Hidden Rabbi: I have heard many disclaimers. There are rabbis who say that the Land of Israel is too small for all the Jews. There are those who say Jews should live outside of Israel as an insurance policy. There are those who say "Diaspora life" gives our history a dimension it would not otherwise have. I say all these are simply rationalizations for staying put. I say God commanded the people to return, and now that we have the opportunity, all Jews should return to Israel, however difficult, however great the sacrifice in economic terms. This is the process of Redemption.

S. F.: It is a nice dream, perhaps. But as of now, it seems far more likely that many Arabs are about to take up your offer, and not Jews. I wonder if you feel threatened by this.

Hidden Rabbi: If they come in huge numbers, and we don't. If they want it more than we do, then we can lose it. There is no question about that. And in fact, this is what is alarming in the resignation of those post-Zionist Jews who claim that peace is the Jewish people's only strategic goal. These people endanger Israel, for they wish to deprive it of all its uniquely Jewish character.

S. F.:   What is to be done then, Rabbi? If you were prime minister of Israel and *lehavdil* head of the United Jewish appeal, what would you do?

Hidden Rabbi: I would, first of all, stop the process of retreat. Second, I would offer some kind of autonomy program to the Arabs. Third, I would begin devoting a much larger share of government resources to Torah education. I would work to create a Jewish people that knows its purpose is to serve God. For I believe that true Redemption can come to Israel only when our people have a harmony in purpose and understanding.

S. F.:   We seem so far from this today. It is as if you are dreaming only. Moreover, wouldn't you be alarmed by the uniformity in thought and belief? Isn't there something preferable, after all, in a variety of approaches? Aren't we a more interesting people as we are now?

Hidden Rabbi: I find nothing interesting or appealing in sin, in family breakdown, in crime, pornography, empty violence, empty souls who do not know their place in the world. I find nothing appealing in people hooked on the mass media as if it were drugs. I find nothing appealing in people who hate being Jewish and care only to be "normal." I find nothing appealing in discarding our own sacred role in order to walk in pagan ways. I find none of this especially illuminating or good. And I believe that returning to the Torah will open for those people a new way of life, a new way of creation in culture, a new way of being a blessing to others. God has given us the means, and we can realize this. It is our historical goal to be a sacred, moral people, living as God as commanded. And this is what we must, should, and will do.

S. F.:   Rabbi, as you know, the central concept of this work is *Avodat Hashem.* How do you understand this concept in relation to your own life and work—and as a goal for the Jewish people in general?

Hidden Rabbi: I believe that every Jew should bear with him in his heart and mind always the intention of serving God. That is, each and every Jew should hold out, as the first goal, the very premise for all he does, this idea of serving God. And that whenever there is some decision to be made, some action to be taken, the first question should be, "Does this serve God best? Is this what God demands of me?" In other words, I believe the Jew should be continually serving God with the whole of his being. And this extends to every aspect of life. That we must, and should, be totally God-conscious in this sense. This does not mean necessarily bringing a certain idea of God to mind at a certain moment. It is rather that this attitude should be so ingrained in us that is informs all we do, that we, in a sense, cannot do anything without it. And this when, of course, at times of great problems, and decisions, the question of what we must do to serve God is more conscious for us.

S. F.:   Are you saying that the Jew should do whatever he does with the sense, not that he is doing it for himself first, but that he is doing it for God first? And given human nature, isn't such a goal, such a demand, simply unrealistic?

Hidden Rabbi: Please do not misunderstand me. I am not arguing for some kind of mechanical adherence to a fixed formula. God gave us our freedom, and it is for us to decide. But our true freedom is in choosing to use this freedom to serve God. This means that we are always aware of doing for "another." And this, of course, is the very kind of mind-set we must have in our relation with human beings. We, too, must want to give to them, to help them. The service of God is, as I have said before, in doing goodness for other human beings.

S. F.:   In other words, you are denying the idea that mankind is the center of the world, that all should be done, first and above all, for the human. And you are at the same time saying that our service of, and doing for, others is part of our higher goal of serving God.

Hidden Rabbi: Yes, that is exactly my idea.

S. F.:   But isn't the human being, especially in the modern world, confused as to what God wants—as to what the service of God means?

Hidden Rabbi: The Jew who lives by Torah need not be confused. Most of the questions asked in our time have been asked and responded to throughout the Jewish generations in the "responsa literature." Moreover, every Jew should have a rebbe of his own who advises on certain problems. But again, there is also the realm of freedom and decisions. In any case, the Jew who would serve God knows very, very much of what God demands.

S. F.:   But what of the claim that this being bound to the teaching of God limits our freedom and deprives us of our own autonomy?

Hidden Rabbi: But isn't it clear that there is no one more limited and less free than those who would establish the total autonomy of mankind? Where were they when the foundation of the earth was laid? And how long will they live into eternity? And how much power do they have over their own lives, their own minds? It seems to me that any truly thinking person must be led by an understanding of his own limitation, and the meaninglessness that these limitations suggest, to an idea of what is Beyond and Enduring, to an idea of God. The paradox of freedom is, of course, that we only have our freedom when we have given ourselves to something "higher" than it, when we have, in effect, recognized the limitation of that freedom.

S. F.:   But how does that freedom express itself in the lives of those who would serve God? What is it they share with each other? Can you perhaps sketch a portrait of such a servant of God?

Hidden Rabbi: You have yourself known many of these people. First of all, they are family people. They strive to live in love with their families. They live in good relations with their wives. They have children, whom they educate to walk in the ways of God. They have certain qualities of character: humility, a great capacity of gratitude, a basic love of their fellow beings. They are people of justice and mercy. They are always looking to help the other person: to do good, *tzedekah*. They bring blessing wherever they go and with whomever they meet. They love learning and know much. They take responsibility for their world and work to build it.

S. F.:   So you don't see the ideal in total withdrawal, total devotion to Torah?

Hidden Rabbi: For a minority, this can be the ideal. But I do not believe that a Jew who cares more for learning than for putting bread on his family's table is a good Jew. I believe in Torah and *drech eretz*, to use Rabbi Hirsch's phrase. I believe we must also serve God by our work in the world. We Jews must be responsible for our own world; otherwise, we stand in danger of losing it.

S. F.:   And this means, as you understand it, a kind of universal Jewish process of *teshuva*, through which the whole people returns to service of God.

Hidden Rabbi: The Jewish people is at a stage of our own history where we must, in order to fulfill our purpose in the world, return to the service of *Hashem*. The people-centered age of Jewish history has lead to a breakdown in Jewish institutions and community. Part of the retreat of the individual into his own, private world has been this emphasis on the human and the human alone. We must restore our transcendent goal, the goal of serving God. By serving family and community, the individual transcends himself. When each Jewish individual and the Jewish people as a whole are united in their determination to serve God, the world will be moving toward the ideal situation. And this is occurring at a time when it is clear that the special task of the Jewish people is to help lead all mankind to finding its own way in service of God. Just as every individual has his own unique quality with which God can be served, so, too, each people.

The crisis of faith, the breakdown of "isms" and ideologies, has left the Western world, and mankind as a whole, searching for a new way to define its ideal spiritual future. This is through a return to the idea of service of God. The Jewish people, by building in Israel a society in justice and by seeking to live in mercy and walk humbly with God, should embody the example that all peoples will learn. As Rav Hirsch has said, only when all peoples are united in their faith and love of God will there come true peace and well-being to the world.

Notes for Future Thought

A Partial List of Meanings of the Concept *Avodat Hashem*, the Service of God

1. Doing the will of God.
2. Living in accordance with *Halachah*.
3. Loving justice, doing mercy, walking humbly with one's God.
4. Prayer, learning, *gemilut chasadim*.
5. Overcoming one's own *yetzer hara* (evil impulse).
6. Sacrificing one's own individual will, desire, and pleasure to do the will of God.
7. Having constant awareness and gratitude to God.
8. The doing of *mitzvot* with joy and *hitlahavut* (joyful enthusiasm).
9. Using one's God-given freedom to choose to walk in the ways of God.
10. Providing for one's family.
11. Teaching Torah to others.
12. Doing the work God has given one special power to do with all one's heart, soul, and might.
13. Imitating God in being kind and merciful to others.
14. Helping others understand the character of the good life.
15. Spreading the word of God to mankind so that all will recognize the One Ruler of all.

16. Specializing in some *mitzvah* especially suited to one's character.
17. *Tikkun Olam,* improving the world in accordance with God's plan for it.
18. Risking one's life and property in order to contribute to the Jewish people.
19. Rising higher and higher in moral and spiritual goodness toward greater closeness to God.
20. The service of the Priests (*Kohanim*) in *Beit Hamikdash.*
21. Loving and fearing God.
22. Putting one's responsibility to the Jewish people before one's own, individual comfort.
23. To occupy and fill our minds with the precepts of God so as to free us from worldly business.
24. Perfecting the imperfect world, completing the incomplete world in accordance with the Covenant.
25. In each major life decision, acting in accordance with what God demands.
26. Setting an example for others through our own righteous behavior.
27. Engaging in acts of creation in imitation of God.
28. The service of the heart in prayer that is done with true *kavvanah* (inner intention).
29. Serving one's community to make it a more holy community in worship of God.
30. Transforming one's evil impulse into creative and good action.
31. Helping the Jewish people in its historical struggle.
32. Living in the Land of Israel and contributing to Jewish society.
33. Helping Jews return to their Jewishness.
34. Doing *teshuvah,* returning to the Lord.
35. Transmitting the teachings of Torah from one generation to another.
36. Helping others to help themselves, helping others to become independent of the need for human help.
37. Bringing joy and blessing into the lives of others, being a blessing wherever one goes.

38. Enhancing the beauty and splendor of God's world.
39. Strengthening Jewish life, the Jewish people, and the Jewish community.

Themes for Thought-work Related to the Concept *Avodat Hashem*, the Service of God

1. The service of God as the meaning of life.
2. Ultimate limitations mankind cannot hope to overcome by serving itself alone.
3. Why so great a part of mankind does not care to serve God.
4. Ideas on traditional Jewish ways of serving God.
5. Future forms of *Avodat Hashem* in Yerushalayim.
6. How the Jewish people can best serve God now and in the future.
7. Ideas on how to return the Jewish people to their world historical role of serving God and bringing service of God to others.
8. The "service of God" as the basis for the new ideology of mankind, the new single "ism" that will dominate the human future.
9. The service of God as revealed and understood through different periods of human history.
10. A new age of the Jewish people in which the service of God is the first ideal.
11. Service of Jewish people as based on prior service of God.
12. Parallel foundation principles to service of God: walking in the way of God, loving justice, doing mercy, walking humbly with God, loving one's neighbor as oneself; you shall be a holy people.
13. Kinds of action that do not serve God; sin and evil.
14. Improving one's own service of God, improving *middot*.
15. Joy in the service of God.
16. The Covenant and the service of God.
17. The worldwide goals of God's plan for history and the service of God.

18. The process of historical Redemption and Return to the Land of Israel as service of God.
19. The use of mankind's God-given power to explore and create new worlds.
20. The special skill of each person and people in serving God.
21. Improving the material life of all of mankind to a milk-and-honey status.
22. An age of peace between peoples in which each recognizes the others' own special ways of serving God.
23. The improvement of the moral level of mankind as a whole through following the way of the Noahide Code.
24. The service of God as the ideal that is the center of a new Messianic Age of peace, mutual help, consideration, and cooperation.
25. The service of God as mankind cocreating with God to help bring the Divine plan into being.
26. The new religious age as distinguished from an earlier one—greater tolerance, recognition of the others' service of God, greater freedom in choice whether to serve God or not.
27. The creation of a world in which each individual lives a life of goodness and blessedness in serving God and doing good for others.
28. The service of God and the effort to transcend human finitude.
29. The definition of God's work and the active role of God in relation to humanity.
30. The service of God as it relates to story and the outcome of any individual life.
31. Ideas on how we can know for certain what we are doing is service of God.
32. The "hidden face" of God and the service of God.
33. Conscious and nonconscious service of God.
34. The idea that the service of God as key to meaning of life is both a principle of revelation and a "conclusion" drawn from life experience.

35. Ways in which we are demanded to use our freedom in service of God.
36. Writing and the service of God. Intellectual work and the service of God.
37. Playing the right role in the drama of our own life as service of God.
38. The generation-to-generation history of mankind's service of God.
39. The service of God and the helping of those we love.
40. Our love of God and God's love of us in service of God.

ABOUT THE AUTHOR

Shalom (Seymour) Freedman is a Jewish thinker and poet who has lived and worked in Israel for more than twenty years. He holds a doctorate in English and American literature from Cornell University and has, in the years of his *aliyah,* devoted himself to Jewish learning in the Holy City, Yerushalayim. A contributor to a variety of Jewish publications, he has published three other books, the most recent of which is *Life as Creation: A Jewish Way of Thinking about the World.*